D1741337

CIM

STUDY TEXT

PROFESSIONAL DIPLOMA IN MARKETING

PAPER 5

MARKETING RESEARCH AND INFORMATION

In this July 2007 edition

- A **user-friendly format** for easy navigation
- Regular **fast forward** summaries emphasising the key points in each chapter
- Recent examples of marketing practice
- Fully revised for recent exams and developments
- A full **index**

FOR EXAMS IN DECEMBER 2007 AND JUNE 2008

BPP LEARNING MEDIA

Fifth edition July 2007

ISBN 9780 7517 4171 1
(previous edition 0 7517 2700 8)

British Library Cataloguing-in-Publication Data
A catalogue record for this book
is available from the British Library

Published by

BPP Learning Media Ltd
BPP House, Aldine Place
London W12 8AA

www.bpp.com/learningmedia

Printed in Great Britain by
WM Print
45-47 Frederick Street
Walsall
WS2 9NE

All our rights reserved. No part of this publication may be reproduced, stored in a retrieval system or transmitted, in any form or by any means, electronic, mechanical, photocopying, recording or otherwise, without the prior written permission of BPP Learning Media Ltd.

We are grateful to the Chartered Institute of Marketing for permission to reproduce in this text the syllabus, tutor's guidance notes and past examination questions. We are also grateful to Karen Beamish of Stone Consulting for preparing the assignment based assessment learning material.

©
BPP Learning Media Ltd
2007

Contents

The BPP Study Text

Aims of this Study Text

To provide you with the knowledge and understanding, skills and application techniques that you need if you are to be successful in your exams

This Study Text has been written around the **Marketing Research and Information** syllabus.

- It is **comprehensive**. It covers the syllabus content. No more, no less.
- It is targeted to the **exam**. We have taken account of the pilot paper, guidance the examiner has given and the assessment methodology.

To allow you to study in the way that best suits your learning style and the time you have available, by following your personal Study Plan (see below)

You may be studying at home on your own until the date of the exam, or you may be attending a full-time course. You may like to (and have time to) read every word, or you may prefer to (or only have time to) skim-read and devote the remainder of your time to question practice. Wherever you fall in the spectrum, you will find the BPP Study Text meets your needs in designing and following your personal Study Plan.

To tie in with the other components of the BPP Effective Study Package to ensure you have the best possible chance of passing the exam

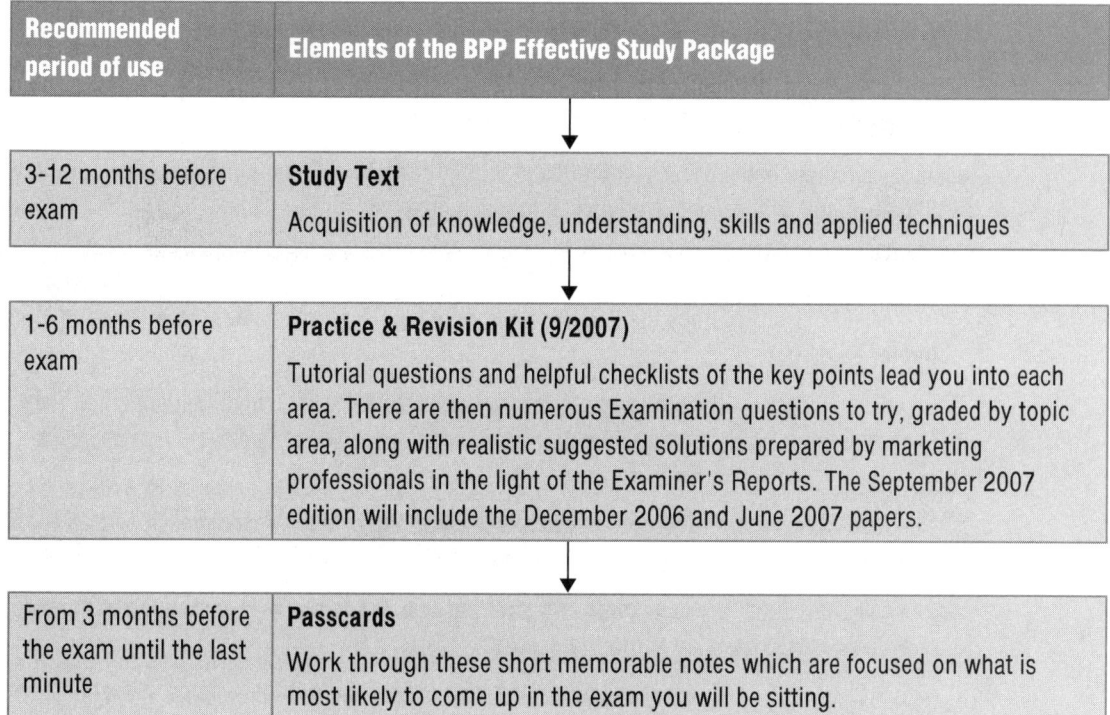

Recommended period of use	Elements of the BPP Effective Study Package
3-12 months before exam	**Study Text** Acquisition of knowledge, understanding, skills and applied techniques
1-6 months before exam	**Practice & Revision Kit (9/2007)** Tutorial questions and helpful checklists of the key points lead you into each area. There are then numerous Examination questions to try, graded by topic area, along with realistic suggested solutions prepared by marketing professionals in the light of the Examiner's Reports. The September 2007 edition will include the December 2006 and June 2007 papers.
From 3 months before the exam until the last minute	**Passcards** Work through these short memorable notes which are focused on what is most likely to come up in the exam you will be sitting.

Settling down to study

By this stage in your career you may be a very experienced learner and taker of exams. But have you ever thought about *how* you learn? Let's have a quick look at the key elements required for effective learning. You can then identify your learning style and go on to design your own approach to how you are going to study this text – your personal Study Plan.

Key element of learning	Using the BPP Study Text
Motivation	You can rely on the comprehensiveness and technical quality of BPP. You've chosen the right Study Text – so you're in pole position to pass your exam!
Clear objectives and standards	Do you want to be a prizewinner or simply achieve a moderate pass? Decide.
Feedback	Follow through the examples in this text and do the Action Programme and the Quick Quizzes. Evaluate your efforts critically – how are you doing?
Study Plan	You need to be honest about your progress to yourself – don't be over-confident, but don't be negative either. Make your Study Plan (see below) and try to stick to it. Focus on the short-term objectives – completing two chapters a night, say – but beware of losing sight of your study objectives.
Practice	Use the Quick Quizzes and Chapter Roundups to refresh your memory regularly after you have completed your initial study of each chapter.

These introductory pages let you see exactly what you are up against. However you study, you should:

- **Read through the syllabus** – this will help you to identify areas you have already covered, perhaps at a lower level of detail, and areas that are totally new to you
- **Study the examination paper section**, where we show you the format of the exam (how many and what kind of questions and so on)

Key study steps

The following steps are, in our experience, the ideal way to study for professional exams. You can of course adapt it for your particular learning style (see below).

Tackle the chapters in the order you find them in the Study Text. Taking into account your individual learning style, follow these key study steps for each chapter.

Key study steps	Activity
Step 1 **Chapter Topic list**	Study the list. Each numbered topic denotes a **numbered section** in the chapter.
Step 2 **Introduction**	Read it through. It is designed to show you **why the topics in the chapter need to be studied** – how they lead on from previous topics, and how they lead into subsequent ones.
Step 3 **Explanations**	Proceed **methodically** through the chapter, reading each section thoroughly and making sure you understand.
Step 4 **Key Concepts**	**Key concepts** can often earn you **easy marks** if you state them clearly and correctly in an appropriate exam.
Step 5 **Exam Tips**	These give you a good idea of how the examiner tends to examine certain topics – pinpointing **easy marks** and highlighting **pitfalls**.
Step 6 **Note taking**	Take **brief notes** if you wish, avoiding the temptation to copy out too much.
Step 7 **Marketing at Work**	Study each one, and try if you can to add flesh to them from your **own experience** – they are designed to show how the topics you are studying come alive (and often come unstuck) in the **real world**. You can also update yourself on these companies by going on to the Internet.
Step 8 **Action Programme**	Make a very good attempt at each one in each chapter. These are designed to put your **knowledge into practice** in much the same way as you will be required to do in the exam. Check the answer at the end of the chapter in the **Action Programme review**, and make sure you understand the reasons why yours may be different.
Step 9 **Chapter Roundup**	Check through it very carefully, to make sure you have grasped the **major points** it is highlighting
Step 10 **Quick Quiz**	When you are happy that you have covered the chapter, use the **Quick Quiz** to check your recall of the topics covered. The answers are in the paragraphs in the chapter that we refer you to.
Step 11 **Illustrative question(s)**	Either at this point, or later when you are thinking about revising, make a full attempt at the **illustrative questions**. You can find these at the end of the Study Text, along with the **Answers** so you can see how you did.

Developing your personal Study Plan

Preparing a Study Plan (and sticking closely to it) is one of the key elements in learning success.

First you need to be aware of your style of learning. There are four typical learning styles. Consider yourself in the light of the following descriptions. and work out which you fit most closely. You can then plan to follow the key study steps in the sequence suggested.

Learning styles	Characteristics	Sequence of key study steps in the BPP Study Text
Theorist	Seeks to understand principles before applying them in practice	1, 2, 3, 7, 4, 5, 8, 9, 10, 11 (6 continuous)
Reflector	Seeks to observe phenomena, thinks about them and then chooses to act	
Activist	Prefers to deal with practical, active problems; does not have much patience with theory	1, 2, 8 (read through), 7, 4, 5, 9, 3, 8 (full attempt), 10, 11 (6 continuous)
Pragmatist	Prefers to study only if a direct link to practical problems can be seen; not interested in theory for its own sake	8 (read through), 2, 4, 5, 7, 9, 1, 3, 8 (full attempt), 10, 11 (6 continuous)

Next you should complete the following checklist.

Am I motivated? (a) ☐

Do I have an objective and a standard that I want to achieve? (b) ☐

Am I a theorist, a reflector, an activist or a pragmatist? (c) ☐

How much time do I have available per week, given: (d) ☐

- The standard I have set myself
- The time I need to set aside later for work on the Practice and Revision Kit
- The other exam(s) I am sitting, and (of course)
- Practical matters such as work, travel, exercise, sleep and social life?

Now:

- Take the time you have available per week for this Study Text (d), and multiply it by the number of weeks available to give (e) (e) ☐
- Divide (e) by the number of chapters to give (f) (f) ☐
- Set about studying each chapter in the time represented by (f), following the key study steps in the order suggested by your particular learning style

This is your personal **Study Plan**.

Short of time?

Whatever your objectives, standards or style, you may find you simply do not have the time available to follow all the key study steps for each chapter, however you adapt them for your particular learning style. If this is the case, follow the Skim Study technique below (the icons in the Study Text will help you to do this).

Skim Study technique

Study the chapters in the order you find them in the Study Text. For each chapter, follow the key study steps 1–2, and then skim-read through step 3, Jump to step 9 and then go back to steps 4–5. Follow through step 7, and prepare outline Answers to the Action Programme (step 8). Try the Quick Quiz (step 10), following up any items you can't answer, then do a plan for the illustrative question (step 11), comparing it against our answers. You should probably still follow step 6 (note-taking).

Moving on...

However you study, when you are ready to embark on the practice and revision phase of the BPP Effective Study Package, you should still refer back to this Study Text:

- As a source of **reference** (you should find the list of key concepts and the index particularly helpful for this)
- As a **refresher** (the Chapter Roundups and Quick Quizzes help you here)

A note on pronouns

On occasions in this Study Text, 'he' is used for 'he or she', 'him' for 'him or her' and so forth. Whilst we try to avoid this practice it is sometimes necessary for reasons of style. No prejudice or stereotyping according to sex is intended or assumed.

Syllabus

Aims and objectives

The **Marketing Research and Information** module covers the first part of strategic marketing in a strategic and global context. It aims to provide participants with the knowledge and skills required to undertake strategic analysis and evaluation of the organisation's current situation as a foundation for making strategic marketing decisions. It sets strategic marketing in context as a key creator of stakeholder value and deals with strategic insights into the organisation, its customers and the challenges it faces.

Learning outcomes

Participants will be able to:

- Identify appropriate marketing information and marketing research requirements for business decision-making
- Plan for and manage the acquisition, storage, retrieval and reporting of information on the organisation's market and customers
- Explain the process involved in purchasing market research and the development of effective client supplier relationships
- Write a research brief to meet the requirements of an organisation to support a specific plan or business decision
- Develop a research proposal to fulfil a given research brief
- Evaluate the appropriateness of different qualitative and quantitative research methodologies to meet different research situations
- Design and plan a research programme
- Design a questionnaire and discussion guide
- Interpret quantitative and qualitative data and present coherent and appropriate recommendations that lead to effective marketing and business decisions
- Critically evaluate the outcomes and quality of a research project
- Explain the legal, regulatory, ethical and social responsibilities of organisations involved in gathering, holding and using information

Knowledge and skill requirements

Element 1: Information and research for decision-making (15%)		Covered in Chapter
1.1	Demonstrate a broad appreciation of the need for information in marketing management and its role in the overall marketing process.	1
1.2	Explain the concept of knowledge management and its importance in a knowledge-based economy.	1, 2
1.3	Explain how organisations determine their marketing information requirements and the key elements of user specifications for information.	1, 2
1.4	Demonstrate an understanding of marketing management support systems and their different formats and components.	2

Element 2: Customer databases (15%)		Covered in Chapter
2.1	Demonstrate an understanding of the application, and role of customer relationship management (CRM) and the benefits of customer databases.	2, 3
2.2	Describe the process for setting up a database.	3
2.3	Explain how organisations profile customers and prospects.	3
2.4	Explain the principles of data warehouses, data marts and data mining.	3
2.5	Explain the relationship between database marketing and marketing research.	3

Element 3: Marketing research in context (25%)		Covered in Chapter
3.1	Describe the nature and structure of the market research industry.	4
3.2	Explain the stages of the market research process.	4
3.3	Describe the procedures for selecting a market research supplier.	4
3.4	Identify information requirements to support a specific business decision in an organisation and develop a research brief to meet those requirements.	5
3.5	Develop a research proposal to fulfil a given research brief.	5
3.6	Explain the ethical and social responsibilities inherent in the market research task.	4

Element 4: Research methodologies (30%)		Covered in Chapter
4.1	Explain the uses, benefits and limitations of secondary data.	6
4.2	Recognise the key sources of primary and secondary data.	6, 7, 8
4.3	Describe and compare the various procedures for observing behaviour.	7, 8
4.4	Describe and compare the various methods for collecting qualitative and quantitative data.	6, 7, 8
4.5	Design a questionnaire and discussion guide to meet a project's research objectives.	8
4.6	Explain the theory and processes involved in sampling.	9

Element 5: Presenting and evaluating information to develop business advantage (15%)		Covered in Chapter
5.1	Demonstrate an ability to use techniques for analysing qualitative and quantitative data	10
5.2	Write a research report aimed at supporting marketing decisions	11
5.3	Plan and design an oral presentation of market research results	11
5.4	Use research and data to produce actionable recommendations for a marketing plan or to support a business decision	10, 11

Related skills for marketers

There is only so much that a syllabus can include. The syllabus itself is designed to cover the knowledge and skills highlighted by research as core to professional marketers in organisations. However, marketing is performed in an organisational context so there are other broader business and organisational skills that marketing professionals should also posses. The 'key skills for marketers' are therefore an essential part of armoury of the 'complete marketer' in today's organisations. They have been identified from research carried out in organisations where marketers are working.

'Key skills for marketers' are areas of knowledge and competency common to business professionals. They fall outside the CIM's syllabus, providing underpinning knowledge and skills. As such they will be treated as systemic to all marketing activities, rather than subjects treated independently in their turn. While it is not intended that the key skills are formally taught as part of programmes, it is expected that tutors will encourage participants to demonstrate the application of relevant key skills through activities, assignments and discussions during learning.

Using ICT and the Internet

Planning and using different sources to search for and select information; explore, develop and exchange information and derive new information; and present information including text, numbers and images.

Using financial information and metrics

Planning and interpreting information from different sources; carrying out calculations; and presenting and justifying findings.

Presenting information

Contributing to discussions; making a presentation; reading and synthesising information and writing different types of document.

Improving own learning and performance

Agreeing targets and planning how these will be met; using plans to meet targets; and reviewing progress.

Working with others

Planning work and agreeing objectives, responsibilities and working arrangements; seeking to establish and maintain co-operative working relationships; and reviewing work and agreeing ways of future collaborative work.

Problem solving

Exploring problems, comparing different ways of solving them and selecting options; planning and implementing options; and applying agreed methods for checking problems have been solved.

Applying business law

Identifying, applying and checking compliance with relevant law when undertaking marketing activities.

Assessment

CIM will normally offer two forms of assessment for this module from which centres or participants may choose: written examination and continuous assessment. CIM may also recognise, or make joint awards for, modules at an equivalent level undertaken with other professional marketing bodies and educational institutions.

Marketing journals

In addition to reading core and supplementary textbooks participants will be expected to acquire a knowledge and understanding of developments in contemporary marketing theory, practice and issues. The most appropriate sources of information for this include specialist magazines eg *Marketing*, *Marketing Week*, *Campaign and Revolution*; dedicated CIM publications eg *Marketing Business*; and business magazines and newspapers eg *The Economist*, *Management Today*, *Business Week*, *The Financial Times*, and the business pages and supplements of the quality press. A flavour of developments in academic marketing can be derived from the key marketing journals including:

Admap
European Journal of Marketing
Journal of the Academy of Marketing Science
Journal of Consumer Behaviour: An International Research Review
Journal of Consumer Research
Marketing Intelligence and Planning
Journal of Marketing
Journal of Marketing Management

Websites

The Chartered Institute of Marketing	
www.cim.co.uk	CIM website with information and access to learning support for participants.
www.cim.co.uk/learningzone	Direct access to information and support materials for all levels of CIM qualification
www.cim.co.uk/tutors	Access for Tutors
www.shapetheagenda.com	Quarterly agenda paper from CIM

Publications on line	
www.ft.com	Extensive research resources across all industry sectors, with links to more specialist reports. (Charges may apply)
www.thetimes.co.uk	One of the best online versions of a quality newspaper.
www.economist.com	Useful links, and easily-searched archives of articles from back issues of the magazine.
www.mad.co.uk	Marketing Week magazine online.
www.brandrepublic.com	Marketing magazine online.
www.westburn.co.uk	Journal of Marketing Management online, the official Journal of the Academy of Marketing and Marketing Review.
http://smr.mit.edu/smr/	Free abstracts from Sloan Management Review articles
www.hbsp.harvard.edu	Free abstracts from Harvard Business Review articles
www.ecommercetimes.com	Daily enews on the latest ebusiness developments
www.cim.co.uk/knowledgehub	3000 full text journals titles are available to members via the Knowledge Hub – includes the range of titles above - embargoes may apply.
www.cim.co.uk/cuttingedge	Weekly round up of marketing news (available to CIM members) plus list of awards and forthcoming marketing events.

Sources of useful information	
www.1to1.com	The Peppers and Rogers One-to-One Marketing site which contains useful information about the tools and techniques of relationship marketing
www.balancetime.com	The Productivity Institute provides free articles, a time management email newsletter, and other resources to improve personal productivity
www.bbc.co.uk	The Learning Zone at BBC Education contains extensive educational resources, including the video, CD Rom, ability to watch TV programmes such as the News online, at your convenience, after they have been screened
www.busreslab.com	Useful specimen online questionnaires to measure customer satisfaction levels and tips on effective Internet marketing research
www.lifelonglearning.co.uk	Encourages and promotes Lifelong Learning through press releases, free articles, useful links and progress reports on the development of the University for Industry (UFI)
www.marketresearch.org.uk	The Market Research Society. Contains useful material on the nature of research, choosing an agency, ethical standards and codes of conduct for research practice
www.nielsen-netratings.com	Details the current levels of banner advertising activity, including the creative content of the ten most popular banners each week (within Top Rankings area)
www.open.ac.uk	Some good Open University videos available for a broad range of

Sources of useful information

	subjects
www.direct.gov.uk	Gateway to a wide range of UK government information
www.srg.co.uk	The Self Renewal Group – provides useful tips on managing your time, leading others, managing human resources, motivating others etc
www.statistics.gov.uk	Detailed information on a variety of consumer demographics from the Government Statistics Office
www.durlacher.com	The latest research on business use of the Internet, often with extensive free reports
www.cyberatlas.com	Regular updates on the latest Internet developments from a business perspective
http://ecommerce.vanderbilt.edu	eLab is a corporate sponsored research centre at the Owen Graduate School of Management, Vanderbilt University
www.kpmg.co.uk www.ey.com/uk www.pwcglobal.com	The major consultancy company websites contain useful research reports, often free of charge
http://web.mit.edu	Massachusetts Institute of Technology site has extensive research resources
www.adassoc.org.uk	Advertising Association
www.dma.org.uk	The Direct Marketing Association
www.theidm.co.uk	Institute of Direct Marketing
www.export.org.uk	Institute of Export
www.bl.uk	The British Library, with one of the most extensive book collections in the world
www.managers.org.uk	Chartered Management Institute
www.cipd.co.uk	Chartered Institute of Personnel and Development
www.emerald-library.com	Article abstracts on a range of business topics (fees apply)
www.w3.org	An organisation responsible for defining worldwide standards for the Internet

Case studies

www.1800flowers.com	Flower and gift delivery service that allows customers to specify key dates when they request the firm to send them a reminder, together with an invitation to send a gift
www.amazon.co.uk	Classic example of how Internet technology can be harnessed to provide innovative customer service
www.broadvision.com	Broadvision specialises in customer 'personalisation' software. The site contains many useful case studies showing how communicating through the Internet allow you to find out more about your customers
www.doubleclick.net	DoubleClick offers advertisers the ability to target their advertisements on the web through sourcing of specific interest groups, ad display only at certain times of the day, or at particular geographic locations, or on certain types of hardware
www.facetime.com	Good example of a site that overcomes the impersonal nature of the Internet by allowing the establishment of real time links with a customer service representative
www.hotcoupons.com	Site visitors can key in their postcode to receive local promotions, and advertisers can post their offers on the site using a specially designed software package
www.superbrands.org	Access to case studies on international brands

The Exam Paper

Assessment methods and format of the paper

		Number of marks
Part A:	One compulsory question based on an industry scenario or a company mini-case study: this question will be broken down into parts, typically three	50
Part B:	Choice of two questions from four	50
		100

The examination will be based on the stated learning outcomes and every examination will cover at least 80% of the syllabus content.

Time allowed: 3 hours

Analysis of past papers

June 2007

Part A (compulsory question worth 50 marks)

1 Holiday company is commissioning market research to understand why there was an unusually high level of complaints in the previous year.

(a) Identify further information that would be required prior to writing a research proposal
(b) Produce a proposal to address the research needs of the company

Part B (two from four questions, 25 marks each)

2 Developing a customer database – four main types of customer data used in construction; ethical issues in merging information from MR study with the database

3 Designing a questionnaire to meet research objectives

4 Different types of non-sampling error and how they can be reduced

5 Organising qualitative data for analysis purposes; structuring and writing market research reports

December 2006

Part A (compulsory case study: 50 marks)

1 Thriving luxury ice-cream maker which sells its products through major retailers wants to maintain its position in the market in the face of growing competition. It has commissioned market research in order to better understand customer attitudes.

(a) Identify further information that would be required prior to writing a research proposal
(b) Produce a proposal to address the research needs of the company

Part B (two from four questions, 25 marks each)

2 Secondary research and data – importance and limitations
3 Discussion guide and projective techniques for use in group discussions
4 Product testing techniques – hall tests, placement tests, simulated test markets, panels
5 Preparation of written report for client; oral presentation of research findings

June 2006

Part A (compulsory question worth 50 marks)

1 Sealux Cruises wishes to examine the effectiveness of their direct advertising messages.

(a) Identify further information that would be required prior to writing a research proposal
(b) Produce a proposal to address the research needs of the company

Part B (two from four questions, 25 marks each)

2 Information gathering for a database; benefits and ethics
3 Projective techniques in group discussions
4 Customer satisfaction and attitude measuring scales
5 Disadvantages of postal surveys; advantages and disadvantages of email

December 2005

Part A (compulsory case study: 50 marks)

1 Perfume manufacturer seeking to increase market share for one of its fragrances by re-designing the packaging. Need to investigate customer attitudes and awareness.

(a) Identify further information requirements prior to writing a research proposal
(b) Produce a proposal to address the research needs of the company

Part B (two from four questions, 25 marks each)

2 Developing a customer database – benefits, data collection and ethical issues
3 Discussion guide and projective techniques for use in group discussions
4 Sample size, sampling error and non-sampling error
5 Panels of respondents and falling response rates

June 2005

Part A (compulsory question worth 50 marks)

1 Spanish cosmetics company planning to open its first UK store. Needs to undertake research into the attitudes of British consumers before designing the outlet and determining products and promotional activity.

(a) Identify further information requirements prior to writing a proposal
(b) Produce a research proposal

Part B (two from four questions, 25 marks each)

2 Roles of marketing information; remit of marketing research departments
3 Discussion guide and projective techniques for use in group discussions
4 Hall tests and placement tests
5 Writing reports, using tables and preparing oral presentation

December 2004

Part A (compulsory question worth 50 marks)

1 The case study scenario relates to a clothing retailer trying to improve sales performance.

(a) Identification of information to be gathered
(b) Proposal to address the research needs of the company

Part B (two from four questions, 25 marks each)

2 (a) Differences between a marketing decision support system and a customer database
(b) Issues in creating a customer database
(c) Using a loyalty card scheme to create a database

3 Projective techniques for use in group discussions

4 (a) Issues involved in observing customer behaviour in retail environment
(b) Running a mystery shopper programme

5 Issues about determining sample size

June 2004

Part A (compulsory question worth 50 marks)

1 A local authority (municipality) has been given targets to ensure the recycling of material and wishes to find out about the resident's attitude to recycling.

(a) Further information
(b) Research proposal

Part B (two from four questions, 25 marks each)

2 Sampling
3 Questionnaire
4 Classification of technical issues
5 Oral presentation

December 2003

Part A (compulsory question worth 50 marks)

1 Small hotel chain seeking to expand its 'leisure traveller' customer base: research needed into customer attitudes.

(a) Further information requirements
(b) Research proposal

Part B (two from four questions, 25 marks each)

2 Customer database: information, benefits and merging with market research information
3 Use of projective techniques
4 'Mystery shopping'
5 Response rates in marketing research

Analysis of Pilot Paper

Part A (compulsory question worth 50 marks)

1 Builders' merchants with need for customer information.

(a) Additional information needed prior to writing a research proposal *(10 marks)*

(b) Write a research proposal *(40 marks)*

Part B (two from four questions, 25 marks each)

2 Customer databases

3 Design a questionnaire

4 Agency selection; professional codes and researcher/client relationship

5 Analysing qualitative data; audience thinking sequence

The Pilot paper and BPP's suggested answer plans are reproduced at the back of this Study Text.

Guide to the Assignment Route

- Aims and objectives of this guide
- Introduction
- Assignment route, structure and process
- Preparing for assignments: general guide
- Presentation
- Time management
- Tips for writing assignments
- Writing reports
- Resources to support Assignment Based Assessment

Aims and objectives of this Guide to the Assignment Route

- To understand the scope and structure of the Assignment Route process
- To consider the benefits of learning through the Assignment Route
- To assist students in preparation of their assignments
- To consider the range of communication options available to students
- To look at the range of potential assignment areas that assignments may challenge
- To examine the purpose and benefits of reflective practice
- To assist with time-management within the assignment process

Introduction

At time of writing, there are over 80 CIM Approved Study Centres that offer the Assignment Route option as an alternative to examinations. This change in direction and flexibility in assessment was externally driven by industry, students and tutors alike, all of whom wanted a test of practical skills as well as a knowledge-based approach to learning.

At Stage 2, all modules are available via this Assignment Route. The Assignment Route is however optional, and examinations are still available. This will of course depend upon the nature of delivery within your chosen Study Centre.

Clearly, all of the Stage 2 subject areas lend themselves to assignment-based learning, due to their practical nature. The assignments that you will undertake provide you with an opportunity to be **creative in approach and in presentation.** They enable you to give a true demonstration of your marketing ability in a way that perhaps might be inhibited in a traditional examination situation.

The Assignment Route offers you considerable scope to produce work that provides existing and future **employers** with **evidence** of your **ability.** It offers you a **portfolio** of evidence which demonstrates your abilities and your willingness to develop continually your knowledge and skills. It will also, ultimately, help you frame your continuing professional development in the future.

It does not matter what type of organisation you are from, large or small, as you will find substantial benefit in this approach to learning. In some cases, students have made their own organisation central to their assessment and produced work to support their organisation's activities, resulting in subsequent recognition and promotion: a success story for this approach.

So, using your own organisation can be beneficial (especially if your employer sponsors you). However, it is equally valid to use a different organisation, as long as you are familiar enough with it to base your assignments on it. This is particularly useful if you are between jobs, taking time out, returning to employment or studying at university or college.

To take the Assignment Route option, you are required to register with a CIM Accredited Study Centre (ie a college, university, or distance learning provider). **Currently you would be unable to take the Assignment Route option as an independent learner**. If in doubt you should contact the CIM Education Division, the awarding body, who will provide you with a list of local Accredited Centres offering the Assignment Route.

Structure and process

The **assignments** that you will undertake during your studies are normally set **by CIM centrally** and not usually by the study centre. All assignments are validated to ensure a structured, consistent, approach. This standardised approach to assessment enables external organisations to interpret the results on a consistent basis.

Each module at Stage 2 has one assignment, with four separate elements within it. This is broken down as follows.

- The **Core Section** is compulsory and worth 40% of your total mark.
- The **Elective Section** has four options, from which you must complete **two**. Each of these options is worth 25% of your total mark. Please note here that it is likely that in some Study Centres the option may be chosen for you. This is common practice and is done in order to maximise resources and support provided to students.
- The **Reflective Statement** is also compulsory. It is worth 10%. It should reflect what you feel about your learning experience during the module and how that learning has helped you in your career both now and in the future.

The purpose of each assignment is to enable you to demonstrate your ability to research, analyse and problem-solve in a range of different situations. You will be expected to approach your assignment work from a professional marketer's perspective, addressing the assignment brief directly, and undertaking the tasks required. Each assignment will relate directly to the syllabus module and will be applied against the content of the syllabus.

All of the assignments clearly indicate the links with the syllabus and the assignment weighting (ie the contribution each assignment makes to your overall marks).

Once your assignments have been completed, they will be marked by your accredited centre, and then **moderated** by a CIM External Moderator. When all the assignments have been marked, they are sent to CIM for further moderation. After this, all marks are forwarded to you by CIM (not your centre) in the form of an examination result. Your **centre** will be able to you provide you with some written feedback on overall performance, but **will not** provide you with any detailed mark breakdown.

Preparing for Assignments: general guide

The whole purpose of this guide is to assist you in presenting your assessment professionally, both in terms of presentation skills and overall content. In many of the assignments, marks are awarded for presentation and coherence. It might therefore be helpful to consider how best to present your assignment. Here you should consider issues of detail, protocol and the range of communications that could be called upon within the assignment.

Presentation of the Assignment

You should always ensure that you prepare two copies of your assignment, keeping a soft copy on disc. On occasions assignments go missing, or second copies are required by CIM.

- Each assignment should be clearly marked up with your name, your study centre, your CIM Student registration number and ultimately at the end of the assignment a word count. The assignment should also be word-processed.
- The assignment presentation format should directly meet the requirements of the assignment brief, (ie reports and presentations are the most called for communication formats). You **must** ensure that you assignment does not appear to be an extended essay. If it does, you will lose marks.
- The word limit will be included in the assignment brief. These are specified by CIM and must be adhered to.
- Appendices should clearly link to the assignment and can be attached as supporting documentation at the end of the report. However failure to reference them by number (eg Appendix 1) within the report and also marked up on the Appendix itself will lose you marks. Only use an Appendix if it is essential and clearly adds value to the overall assignment. The Appendix is not a waste bin for all the materials you have come across in your research, or a way of making your assignment seem somewhat heavier and more impressive than it is.

Time management for Assignments

One of the biggest challenges we all seem to face day-to-day is that of managing time. When studying, that challenge seems to grow increasingly difficult, requiring a balance between work, home, family, social life and study life. It is therefore of pivotal importance to your own success for you to plan wisely the limited amount of time you have available.

Step 1 **Find out how much time you have**

Ensure that you are fully aware of how long your module lasts, and the final deadline. If you are studying a module from September to December, it is likely that you will have only 10-12 weeks in which to complete your assignments. This means that you will be preparing assignment work continuously throughout the course.

Step 2 **Plan your time**

Essentially you need to **work backwards** from the final deadline, submission date, and schedule your work around the possible time lines. Clearly if you have only 10-12 weeks available to complete three assignments, you will need to allocate a block of hours in the final stages of the module to ensure that all of your assignments are in on time. This will be critical as all assignments will be sent to CIM by a set day. Late submissions will not be accepted and no extensions will be awarded. Students who do not submit will be treated as a 'no show' and will have to resubmit for the next period and undertake an alternative assignment.

Step 3 **Set priorities**

You should set priorities on a daily and weekly basis (not just for study, but for your life). There is no doubt that this mode of study needs commitment (and some sacrifices in the short term). When your achievements are recognised by colleagues, peers, friends and family, it will all feel worthwhile.

Step 4 **Analyse activities and allocate time to them**

Consider the **range** of activities that you will need to undertake in order to complete the assignment and the **time** each might take. Remember, too, there will be a delay in asking for information and receiving it.

- Preparing terms of reference for the assignment, to include the following.

  1. A short title
  2. A brief outline of the assignment purpose and outcome
  3. Methodology – what methods you intend to use to carry out the required tasks
  4. Indication of any difficulties that have arisen in the duration of the assignment
  5. Time schedule
  6. Confidentiality – if the assignment includes confidential information ensure that this is clearly marked up and indicated on the assignment
  7. Literature and desk research undertaken

This should be achieved in one side of A4 paper.

- A literature search in order to undertake the necessary background reading and underpinning information that might support your assignment
- Writing letters and memos asking for information either internally or externally
- Designing questionnaires
- Undertaking surveys
- Analysis of data from questionnaires
- Secondary data search
- Preparation of first draft report

Always build in time to spare, to deal with the unexpected. This may reduce the pressure that you are faced with in meeting significant deadlines.

Warning!

The same principles apply to a student with 30 weeks to do the work. However, a word of warning is needed. Do not fall into the trap of leaving all of your work to the last minute. If you miss out important information or fail to reflect upon your work adequately or successfully you will be penalised for both. Therefore, time management is important whatever the duration of the course.

Tips for writing Assignments

Everybody has a personal style, flair and tone when it comes to writing. However, no matter what your approach, you must ensure your assignment meets the **requirements of the brief** and so is comprehensible, coherent and cohesive in approach.

Think of preparing an assignment as preparing for an examination. Ultimately, the work you are undertaking results in an examination grade. Successful achievement of all four modules in a level results in a qualification.

There are a number of positive steps that you can undertake in order to ensure that you make the best of your assignment presentation in order to maximise the marks available.

Step 1 **Work to the brief**

Ensure that you identify exactly what the assignment asks you to do.

- If it asks you to be a marketing manager, then immediately assume that role.
- If it asks you to prepare a report, then present a report, not an essay or a letter.
- Furthermore, if it asks for 2,500 words, then do not present 1,000 or 4,000 unless it is clearly justified, agreed with your tutor and a valid piece of work.

Identify whether the report should be **formal or informal**; who it should be **addressed to**; its **overall purpose** and its **potential use** and outcome. Understanding this will ensure that your assignment meets fully the requirements of the brief and addresses the key issues included within it.

Step 2 **Addressing the tasks**

It is of pivotal importance that you address **each** of the tasks within the assignment. **Many students fail to do this** and often overlook one of the tasks or indeed part of the tasks.

Many of the assignments will have two or three tasks, some will have even more. You should establish quite early on, which of the tasks:

- Require you to collect information
- Provides you with the framework of the assignment, i.e. the communication method.

Possible tasks will include the following.

- *Compare and contrast.* Take two different organisations and compare them side by side and consider the differences ie the **contrasts** between the two.
- *Carry out primary or secondary research.* Collect information to support your assignment and your subsequent decisions
- *Prepare a plan.* Some assignments will ask you to prepare a plan for an event or for a marketing activity – if so provide a step-by-step approach, a rationale, a time-line, make sure it is measurable and achievable. Make sure your actions are very specific and clearly explained. (Make sure your plan is SMART.)
- *Analyse a situation.* This will require you to collect information, consider its content and present an overall understanding of the situation as it exists. This might include looking at internal and external factors and how the current situation evolved.
- *Make recommendations.* The more advanced your get in your studies, the more likely it is that you will be required to make recommendations. Firstly **considering and evaluating your options** and then making justifiable **recommendations**, based on them.
- *Justify decisions.* You may be required to justify your decision or recommendations. This will require you to explain fully how you have arrived at as a result and to show why, supported by relevant information. In other words, you should not make decisions in a vacuum; as a marketer your decisions should always be informed by context.
- *Prepare a presentation.* This speaks for itself. If you are required to prepare a presentation, ensure that you do so, preparing clearly defined PowerPoint or

overhead slides that are not too crowded and that clearly express the points you are required to make.

- *Evaluate performance.* It is very likely that you will be asked to evaluate a campaign, a plan or even an event. You will therefore need to consider its strengths and weaknesses, why it succeeded or failed, the issues that have affected it, what can you learn from it and, importantly, how can you improve performance or sustain it in the future.

All of these points are likely requests included within a task. Ensure that you identify them clearly and address them as required.

Step 3 Information Search

Many students fail to realise the importance of collecting information to **support** and **underpin** their assignment work. However, it is vital that you demonstrate to your centre and to the CIM your ability to **establish information needs**, obtain **relevant information** and **utilise it sensibly** in order to arrive at appropriate decisions.

You should establish the nature of the information required, follow up possible sources, time involved in obtaining the information, gaps in information and the need for information.

Consider these factors very carefully. CIM are very keen that students are **seen** to collect information, **expand** their mind and consider the **breadth** and **depth** of the situation. In your *Personal Development Portfolio,* you have the opportunity to complete a **Resource Log**, to illustrate how you have expanded your knowledge to aid your personal development. You can record your additional reading and research in that log, and show how it has helped you with your portfolio and assignment work.

Step 4 Develop an Assignment Plan

Your **assignment** needs to be structured and coherent, addressing the brief and presenting the facts as required by the tasks. The only way you can successfully achieve this is by **planning the structure** of your Assignment in advance.

Earlier on in this unit, we looked at identifying your tasks and, working backwards from the release date, in order to manage time successfully. The structure and coherence of your assignment needs to be planned with similar signs.

In planning out the Assignment, you should plan to include **all the relevant information as requested** and also you should plan for the use of models, diagrams and appendices where necessary.

Your plan should cover your:

- Introduction
- Content
- Main body of the assignment
- Summary
- Conclusions and recommendations where appropriate

Step 5 Prepare Draft Assignment

It is good practice to always produce a **first draft** of a report. You should use it to ensure that you have met the aims and objectives, assignment brief and tasks related to the actual assignment. A draft document provides you with scope for improvements, and enables you to check for accuracy, spelling, punctuation and use of English.

Step 6 **Prepare Final Document**

In the section headed 'Presentation of the Assignment' in this unit, there are a number of components that should always be in place at the beginning of the assignment documentation, including **labelling** of the assignment, **word counts, appendices** numbering and presentation method. Ensure that you **adhere to the guidelines presented**, or alternatively those suggested by your Study Centre.

Writing reports

Students often ask 'what do they mean by a report?' or 'what should the report format include?'.

There are a number of approaches to reports, formal or informal: some report formats are company specific and designed for internal use, rather than external reporting.

For Continuous Assessment process, you should stay with traditional formats.

Below is a suggested layout of a Management Report Document that might assist you when presenting your assignments.

- *A Title Page* includes the title of the report, the author of the report and the receiver of the report
- *Acknowledgements* – this should highlight any help, support, or external information received and any extraordinary co-operation of individuals or organisations
- *Contents page* provides a clearly structured pathway of the contents of the report – page by page.
- *Executive summary* – a brief insight into purpose, nature and outcome of the report, in order that the outcome of the report can be quickly established
- *Main body of the report divided into sections, which are clearly labelled.* Suggested labelling would be on a numbered basis eg:
  - 1.0 Introduction
  - 1.1 Situation Analysis
  - 1.1.1 External Analysis
  - 1.1.2 Internal Analysis
- *Conclusions* – draw the report to a conclusion, highlighting key points of importance, that will impact upon any recommendations that might be made
- *Recommendations* – clearly outline potential options and then recommendations. Where appropriate justify recommendations in order to substantiate your decision
- *Appendices* – ensure that you only use appendices that add value to the report. Ensure that they are numbered and referenced on a numbered basis within the text. If you are not going to reference it within the text, then it should not be there
- *Bibliography* – whilst in a business environment a bibliography might not be necessary, for an **assignment-based report it is vital**. It provides an indication of the level of research, reading and collecting of relevant information that has taken place in order to fulfil the requirements of the assignment task. Where possible, and where relevant, you could provide academic references within the text, which should of course then provide the basis of your bibliography. References should realistically be listed alphabetically and in the following sequence
  - Author's name and edition of the text
  - Date of publication
  - Title and sub-title (where relevant)
  - Edition 1st, 2nd etc

- Place of publication
- Publisher
- Series and individual volume number where appropriate.

Resources to support Assignment Based Assessment

The aim of this guidance is to present you with a range of questions and issues that you should consider, based upon the assignment themes. The detail to support the questions can be found within your BPP Study Text and the 'Core Reading' recommended by CIM.

Additionally you will find useful support information within the CIM Student website www.cim.co.uk -: www.cimvirtualinstitute.com, where you can access a wide range of marketing information and case studies. You can also build your own workspace within the website so that you can quickly and easily access information specific to your professional study requirements. Other websites you might find useful for some of your assignment work include www.wnim.com - (What's New in Marketing) and also www.connectedinmarketing.com - another CIM website.

Other websites include:

www.mad.com	– Marketing Week
www.ft.com	– Financial Times
www.thetimes.com	– The Times newspaper
www.theeconomist.com	– The Economist magazine
www.marketing.haynet.com	– Marketing magazine
www.ecommercetimes.com	– Daily news on e-business developments
www.open.gov.uk	– Gateway to a wide range of UK government information
www.adassoc.org.uk	– The Advertising Association
www.marketresearch.org.uk	– The Marketing Research Society
www.amazon.com	– Online Book Shop
www.1800flowers.com	– Flower and delivery gift service
www.childreninneed.com	– Charitable organisation
www.comicrelief.com	– Charitable organisation
www.samaritans.org.uk	– Charitable organisation

Part A

Information and research for decision making

1

Information in marketing management

Chapter topic list

Syllabus content – knowledge and skills requirements

- 1.1: The need for information in marketing management and its role in the overall marketing process
- 1.2: The concept of knowledge management and its importance in a knowledge-based economy
- 1.3: How organisations determine their marketing information requirements and the key elements of user specifications for information

Introduction

Without **information**, no-one in an organisation could take effective action. Managers **gather** information about tasks or problems, **process** the information to decide what needs to be done, and then **communicate** their decisions in the form of instructions to their staff. This goes on constantly throughout the organisation, from the very top levels to the most junior.

The 'Information Age'

There's nothing new about using information to get things done, but you will often hear that we now live in the **'Information Age'**. That suggests that information is more important than ever before – perhaps **the** most important thing in modern life.

- At one time organisations could be successful simply by investing in physical resources – bigger and better factories, nearer to customers than their competitors' factories, for example. The problem was producing enough to satisfy demand.
- As competition has increased and become more global there is no significant difference between, say, a Ford factory in Chicago and a Nissan factory in Wales. The problem now is creating enough demand in the first place.

In a **knowledge-based economy** economic factors such as land and capital are not vital for success. Organisations now compete by **knowing** more about the markets they serve, who the best suppliers are, how to do things, and – above all – by having the best new ideas. In other words they compete by **gathering information** and **using it intelligently**.

1 Information for competitive advantage 12/04

Information is a **marketing asset**. It impacts on performance in several ways.

- It helps to increase **responsiveness** to customer demands.
- It helps to identify **new customer opportunities** and new product/service demands.
- It helps to **anticipate competitive attacks** and threats.

FAST FORWARD

In a **knowledge-based economy** organisations compete by obtaining **superior information**. The more information that a firm can obtain about competitors and customers, the more it should be able to adapt its product/service offerings to meet the needs of the market place.

Firms are becoming increasingly aware of the competitive advantage that may be achieved through the use of information. Information systems can affect the way the firm approaches **customer service** – the very essence of the **marketing concept** – and can provide advantages over competitor approaches. Superior customer service can only be achieved by being able to anticipate and satisfy customer needs. In order to meet this objective, **information** which is **up-to-date**, **accurate**, **relevant** and **timely** is essential.

The more information that a firm can obtain about competitors and customers, the more it should be able to adapt its product/service offerings to meet the needs of the market place through strategies such as **differentiation**. For example, mail order companies that are able to store data about customer buying habits can exploit this data by recognising patterns of buying behaviour, and offering products at likely buying times that are in line with the customer's profile.

Good information systems may alter the way business is done and may provide organisations with **new opportunities**.

Marketing at Work

Let us take the example of a theatre which is in a tourist city and which wants to build a **database**. The types of data it may wish to have are as follows.

(a) Analysis of theatregoers by specific **characteristics**: age, sex, home address

(b) How many **performances** each theatre customer sees in the year

(c) How many days visitors stay in the city and how they choose a day or night at the theatre

(d) **Types of production** customers like to watch

(e) **Factors** important to their decision to visit the theatre, such as price, location, play, cast, facilities

(f) Where they obtained **information** on the theatre and its productions: press, hotel, leaflets, mailings and so on

(g) **Other purchases** customers make when visiting the theatre

(h) **Other entertainment** that theatregoers choose to spend their money on

This data could then be used by the theatre marketing management to build relationships with customers and to exploit sales and promotional opportunities.

Exam tip

Information requirements for a given research brief are likely to feature regularly in the exam. You will probably be asked to identify additional information that is needed.

1.1 Information, technology, markets and marketing

FAST FORWARD

Information and communications technology (ICT) is changing the way markets are structured and it has created **new marketing techniques** and **new marketing channels**.

Take the clothing industry as an example. It is now possible for a retail organisation in England to develop designs and production specifications which may be sent electronically to a remote manufacturer off-shore. The manufacturer will put the garments into production, organise transportation, inform the customer, invoice the customer and despatch the goods – all within a matter of days rather than the weeks or months that this might have taken not so long ago.

This not only opens up new market opportunities but may also present competitor threats. New technologies increase the opportunities to develop **global markets** for what once may only have been local products or services.

ICT has also created new **marketing techniques** and new **marketing channels**. As we'll see in much more detail later in this book, **database marketing** allows vast amounts of customer data to be stored and analysed and used to produce more accurate targeting as well as other marketing tactics. This is significant when a firm is able to gain an advantage over competitors by accessing and applying technologies that the competitor has not yet developed, information that the competitor do not possess, and ideas that have not occurred to others.

Marketing at Work

'... advances in software mean that marketers can burrow down into vast stores of information and retrieve exactly what they want with the click of a mouse.

Such technology can be very effective. A case in point is cider maker HP Bulmer. Over the past few years, the company has undertaken an IT overhaul in order to make profit rather than volume the driver of the business. On top of a powerful database it has installed a financial management system that allows it to calculate precisely the profit contribution from different products and different customers. Under the previous system, such detailed information would have been hard, if not impossible, to determine. Now marketing staff can begin to make far more informed decisions about the product mix, which will help them streamline the portfolio and focus on higher margins.

Similarly, at snacks group Golden Wonder, marketers have software programmes that enable them to integrate sales and marketing data from both internal and external sources with a range of *ad hoc* and reporting tools. They can also analyse various scenarios by cross-referencing bits of data and asking a wide variety of "what-if" type questions. Less tangibly, but equally as important, planning and implementation of marketing activity is improving, along with greater effectiveness in promotional spend.'

Laura Mazur, Accountability, *Marketing Business*

2 Marketing management and information

FAST FORWARD

Information is required by marketing and sales management for **analysis**, **planning**, **implementation** and **control**: APIC.

2.1 Analysis, planning, implementation, control: APIC

To carry out marketing management activities, **marketing managers need information**. They need to:

- Anticipate changes in demand
- Introduce, modify or discontinue products or services
- Evaluate profitability
- Set prices
- Undertake promotional activity
- Plan budgets
- Control costs

Marketing management activities have been summarised using the acronym **APIC** (Kotler *et al (1991)*).

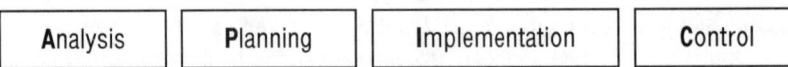

Analysis	**P**lanning	**I**mplementation	**C**ontrol

(a) **Analysis**. 'Managing the marketing function begins with a complete analysis of the company's situation. The company must analyse its markets and marketing environment to find attractive opportunities and to avoid environmental threats. It must analyse company strengths and weaknesses, as well as current and possible marketing actions, to determine which opportunities it can best pursue. Marketing analysis feeds information and other inputs to each of the other marketing management functions.'

(b) **Planning**. 'Through strategic planning, the company decides what it wants to do with each business unit. Marketing planning involves deciding on marketing strategies that will help the company attain its overall strategic objectives.'

(c) **Implementation**. 'Good marketing analysis and planning are only a start toward successful company performance – the marketing plans must be carefully implemented. It is often easier to design good marketing strategies than put them into action.

People at all levels of the marketing system must work together to implement marketing strategy and plans. People in marketing must work closely with people in finance, purchasing, manufacturing and other company departments. And many outside people and organisations must help with implementation – suppliers, resellers, advertising agencies, research firms, the advertising media. All must work together effectively to implement the marketing program.'

(d) **Control**. 'Many surprises are likely to occur as marketing plans are being implemented. The company needs control procedures to make certain that its objectives will be achieved. Companies want to make sure that they are achieving the sales, profits, and other goals set in their annual plans. This control involves measuring ongoing market performance, determining the causes of any serious gaps in performance, and deciding on the best corrective action to take to close the gaps. Corrective action may call for improving the ways in which the plan is being implemented or even changing the goals.

Companies should also stand back from time to time and look at their overall approach to the marketplace. The purpose is to make certain that the company's objectives, policies, strategies, and programs remain appropriate in the face of rapid environmental changes.'

Action Programme 1

You should spend about 10 minutes, before you carry on reading, thinking about information you use at work and then try and classify it into the major marketing and selling activities described under ACTIVITY. (Use a separate sheet of paper if necessary.) The second column headed INFORMATION should describe the type of information, for example: control chart, written report, oral report, telephone call, database and so on. The third column is for you to describe what you USE the information for. You may find that you use certain types of information to do more than one marketing or sales management activity, in which case feel free to list it more than once.

ACTIVITY	INFORMATION	USE
Analysing		
Planning		
Implementing		
Controlling		

2.2 The organisation's marketing information requirements

Here is a list of questions that marketing managers might need answered.

(a) **Markets**. Who are our customers? What are they like? How are buying decisions made?

(b) **Share of the market**. What are total sales of our product? How do our sales compare with competitors' sales?

(c) **Products**. What do customers think of our product? What do they do with it? Are our products in a 'growth' or 'decline' stage of their life cycle? Should we extend our range?

(d) **Price**. How do our prices compare with others: higher, average, lower? Is the market sensitive to price?

(e) **Distribution**. Should we distribute directly, indirectly or both? What discounts are required?

(f) **Sales force**. Do we have enough/too many salespeople? Are their territories equal to their potential? Are they contacting the right people? Should we pay commission?

(g) **Advertising**. Do we use the right media? Do we communicate the right message? Is it effective?

(h) **Customer attitudes**. What do they think of our product/firm/service/delivery?

(i) **Competitors' activities**. Who are our competitors? Are they more or less successful businesses? Why are they more or less successful?

(j) **Environmental factors**. What factors impact on marketing planning (SLEPT factors)?

Another way of viewing information needs in marketing management is to consider the **four key strategic questions**.

Question	Examples of information needed	Sources of information: forms of marketing research
Where are we now? Strategic, financial and marketing analysis	Current sales by product/market Market share by product/market Competitors' market shares Customer attitudes and behaviour Corporate image versus competitors' image Company strengths and weaknesses	Accounting system Customer database Market analysis/surveys Competitor intelligence Customer surveys Internal/external analyses
Where do we want to be? Strategic direction and strategy formulation	Market forecasts by segment Environmental changes Growth capabilities Opportunities and threats Competitor response New product/market potentials	Industry forecasts/surveys SLEPT analysis PIMS Competitor research Product/market research
How might we get there? Strategic choice and evaluation	Marketing mix evaluation Buying behaviour New product development Risk evaluation Alternative strategic options	Internal/external audits Customer research Concept testing/test marketing Feasibility studies/competitor response modelling/focus groups/marketing mix research

Question	Examples of information needed	Sources of information: forms of marketing research
How can we ensure arrival? Strategic implementation and control	Budgets Performance evaluation	Internal accounting, production and human resource systems Marketing information systems Marketing audit Benchmarking External (financial) auditing

2.3 Descriptive, comparative, diagnostic and predictive information

FAST FORWARD

Marketing information may have four roles: **descriptive**, **comparative**, **diagnostic** and **predictive**.

Alan Wilson (2002) distinguishes four roles for marketing information.

(a) **Descriptive information** answers questions such as which products are customers buying and where are they buying them.

(b) **Comparative information** looks at how one factor compares with another, for instance how good an organisation's after-sales support is when compared with its competitors.

(c) **Diagnostic information** is intended to explain customer behaviour: why are they buying less of product A?

(d) **Predictive information** attempts to determine the outcome of marketing actions. How would customers respond if Product A were made available in larger sized packs?

Action Programme 2

Try to assign the examples of information needs listed in the second column of the table above to the categories *descriptive*, *comparative*, *diagnostic* and *predictive*.

2.4 Information and decision making

FAST FORWARD

Information is required for **strategic**, **tactical** and **operational decisions** relating to matters such as markets and market share, products, prices, distribution, sales force organisation, advertising, customer attitudes, competitors' activities and SLEPT factors.

The APIC activities described by Kotler *et al* (1991) culminate in marketing and selling **decisions** being taken. Information is required for all levels of decision making within an organisation, whether **strategic**, **tactical** or **operational**. Decision-making levels, and the types of marketing and selling decisions taken at these levels, are shown in the following table.

Levels of decision making	Marketing and selling decisions
Strategic	Product/market decisions Product life cycles Product development Entry into new markets Investment in new technology to provide better information Database development
Tactical	Setting short term prices Discounting Promotional campaigns Advertising Distribution Product service levels Customer service levels Packaging Planning sales territories Short-term agency agreements
Operational	Pricing, including discounting Competitor tracking Customer research Consumer research Distribution channels and logistical choices Sales and marketing budgets and sub-budgets, eg promotion/advertising Database management

2.5 User specifications for information

FAST FORWARD

Key elements of user specifications for information include: **rationale**, **budget**, **timescale**, **objectives**, **methods** and **reports**.

We will consider the place of a **research brief** in the marketing research process in more detail in Part C, but it is worth stressing from the outset of this book how important it is that the **users of new information specify in advance what their information needs are**. It can be very wasteful of time and money to collect answers to questions that did not need to be asked or which are the **wrong questions**!

Key elements of user specifications will include the following.

(a) **Rationale**. How the need for information arose and what the users intend to do with the information when they have it. What decisions will be taken?

(b) **Budget**. In general the benefits of collecting information should be greater than the costs of collecting it, but benefits in particular are not always easy to quantify. In any case the budget may be limited by other organisational factors such as availability of cash or a head office allocation of, say, £5,000 per annum for marketing research purposes. Clearly this will affect the scale and type of information search that can be carried out.

(c) **Timescale**. Quite obviously, if the decisions have to be made by May then the information needs to be collected and analysed before then. Once again this will have an impact on the scale and type of information search that can be carried out.

(d) **Objectives**. The precise information needed, set out as clearly as possible. For instance 'To determine customer response to a price reduction of £250 in terms of repeat purchasing, word-of-mouth recommendations and willingness to purchase our other products and services'. The objectives should relate **only** to the rationale: it might be 'nice to know' what type of car customers drive, but if this will make no difference to the decisions that will be taken once the information has been collected, there is no need to know about customers' cars in the first place.

(e) **Methods**. This need only be an outline, setting out, for instance, the scale of the search, the mix of quantitative and qualitative information needed, the segments of the market to be included.

(f) **Reports**. How the final information should be presented. Considerations here might include style of reports, degree of summarisation, use of charts and other graphics, format for quantitative information (eg in Excel spreadsheets, for ease of further analysis).

3 Knowledge management

FAST FORWARD

In a knowledge-based economy knowledge must be actively managed. Knowledge includes **tacit knowledge** in employees' heads as well as **formally recorded facts**, transactions and so on.

Key concepts

Knowledge is information within people's minds. It may or may not be recorded in the form of generally accessible information.

A **knowledge-based economy** is an economy based on application of knowledge. Organisations' capabilities and efficiency in using their knowledge override other, more traditional, economic factors such as land and capital.

As we noted at the beginning of this chapter, modern organisations operate in a **knowledge-based economy**. It is an age in which the competitiveness of organisations depends on the accumulation of knowledge and its rapid mobilisation to produce goods and services.

(a) Producing unique products or services or producing products or services at a lower cost than competitors is based on **superior knowledge**.

(b) Knowledge is especially valuable as it may be used to create **new ideas**, insights and interpretations and for decision making.

(c) However knowledge, like information, is of no value unless it is **applied**.

As the importance of knowledge increases, the success of an organisation becomes increasingly dependent on its ability to gather, produce, hold and disseminate knowledge.

FAST FORWARD

Knowledge management entails identifying knowledge and using a variety of organisational and technological means to ensure that it is **shared**.

Key concepts

Knowledge management involves the identification and analysis of available and required knowledge, and the subsequent planning and control of actions to develop knowledge assets so as to fulfil organisational objectives.

Knowledge assets are the sum of the knowledge regarding markets, products, technologies, resources, skills and systems that a business owns or controls and which enable it to achieve its objectives.

Knowledge management programmes are attempts at:

(a) Designing and installing techniques and processes to create, protect and use **explicit knowledge** (knowledge that the company knows that it has). Explicit knowledge includes facts, transactions and events that can be clearly stated and stored in management information systems.

(b) Designing and creating environments and activities to discover and release **tacit knowledge** (explained below).

Tacit knowledge is expertise held by people within the organisation that has not been formally documented.

(a) Tacit knowledge is a difficult thing to manage because it is **invisible** and **intangible**. We do not know what knowledge exists within a person's brain, and whether he or she chooses to share knowledge is a matter of choice.

(b) The **motivation to share** hard-won experience is sometimes low; the individual is 'giving away' their value and may be very reluctant to lose a position of influence and respect by making it available to everyone.

For these two reasons **an organisation may never fully know what knowledge it possesses** and could exploit. Knowledge management is an attempt to address this problem. It attempts to turn all relevant knowledge, including personal knowledge, into corporate **knowledge assets** that can be easily and widely shared throughout an organisation and appropriately applied.

Marketing at Work

Here are some examples of 'knowledge management' in business.

BP – introduced virtual teamworking (using videoconferencing) to solve problems.

Hewlett Packard – shares existing expertise to bring new products to the market faster.

Dow Chemical – exploits its patents to generate more revenue, by managing its patent portfolio more effectively.

(*www.skyrme.com* – Accessed 10 February 2004)

3.1 Where does knowledge reside?

There are various actions that can be taken to try to determine the prevalence of knowledge in an organisation.

One is the **identification and development of informal networks** and communities of practice within organisations. These self-organising groups share common work interests, usually cutting across a company's functions and processes. People exchange what they know and develop a shared language that allows knowledge to flow more efficiently.

Another means of establishing the prevalence of knowledge is to look at knowledge-related business **outcomes**. One example is **product development and service innovation**. While the knowledge embedded within these innovations is invisible, the products themselves are tangible.

3.2 Customer knowledge within the organisation

Many business functions deal with customers, including marketing, sales, service, logistics and financial functions. Each function will have its own reasons for being interested in customer information, and may have its own way of recording what it learns and even its own customer information system. The diverse interests of different departments make it **difficult to pull together** customer knowledge in one common format and place and the problem is magnified because all have some political reason to keep control of what they know about customers.

While much of this book is about the processes of **market research** (which generates **explicit knowledge**, often by going outside the organisation), it is also worth remembering the necessity to **motivate employees to record, share and use** knowledge gained in a **less formal** manner. This includes experiential observations, comments made, lessons learned, interactions among people, impressions formed and so on.

Organisational means of encouraging sharing include emphasising it in the corporate **culture**, **evaluating** people on the basis of their knowledge behaviour and **rewarding** those who display good knowledge-sharing practice.

On a more practical level, **information and communications technology** can be of great assistance too, as we will see in the next chapter.

Marketing at Work

A New Orleans university whose archived records were damaged by Hurricane Katrina decided to embark upon a large digital imaging project to restore them. Grantham University was faced with the task of digitising more than 377,000 pages of records from 48 waterlogged filing cabinets.

Grantham has already begun storing new information on remote servers, and this data was spared from the hurricane. A portion of the older records of former students and graduates, however, had not been processed into the knowledge management system. They existed only on paper, and needed to be digitised so that they could be made available.

(*www.kmworld.com* – accessed 6 April 2006)

4 Marketing research: an introduction

FAST FORWARD

Marketing research is made up of **market research**, **product research**, **price research**, **sales promotion research** and **distribution research**.

Strictly speaking **marketing** research is any kind of information gathering and analysis that aids the **marketing process** as a whole (a study of competitors' strengths and weaknesses) while **market** research is research into the characteristics of a **market** (France as opposed to India, or people aged under 30 as opposed to people aged over 65).

Key concepts

Marketing research. 'The collection, analysis and communication of information undertaken to assist decision making in marketing.' (Alan Wilson, 2002). Market-**ing** research includes market research, price research and so on (see below).

Market research. Sometimes used synonymously with marketing research; strictly speaking, however, it refers to the acquisition of primary data about customers and customer attitudes.

FAST FORWARD

In brief, the marketing research process has the following stages.

- Define the problem and research **objectives**
- Develop the research **plan**
- Collect and process **data**
- **Analyse and interpret** information
- **Report** on the findings

To give you an idea of the **scope** of marketing research, the various components are summarised below, under the acronym 'MPPSD':

Research type	Application
Market research	Forecasting demand (new and existing products) Sales forecast by segment Analysis of market shares Market trends Industry trends Acquisition/diversification studies
Product research	Likely acceptance of new products Analysis of substitute products Comparison of competitors products Test marketing Product extension Brand name generation and testing Product testing of existing products Packaging design studies
Price research	Competitor prices (analysis) Cost analysis Profit analysis Market potential Sales potential Sales forecast (volume) Customer perception of price Effect of price change on demand (elasticity of demand) Discounting Credit terms

Research type	Application
Sales promotion research	Analysing the effect of campaigns Monitoring/analysing advertising media choice Evaluation of sales force performance To decide on appropriate sales territories and make decisions as to how to cover the area Copy research Public image studies Competitor advertising studies Studies of premiums, coupons, promotions
Distribution research	Planning channel decisions Design and location of distribution centres In-house versus outsourced logistics Export/international studies Channel coverage studies

The following diagram summarises the marketing research process. This process will be discussed in more detail in Parts C to E of this Study Text.

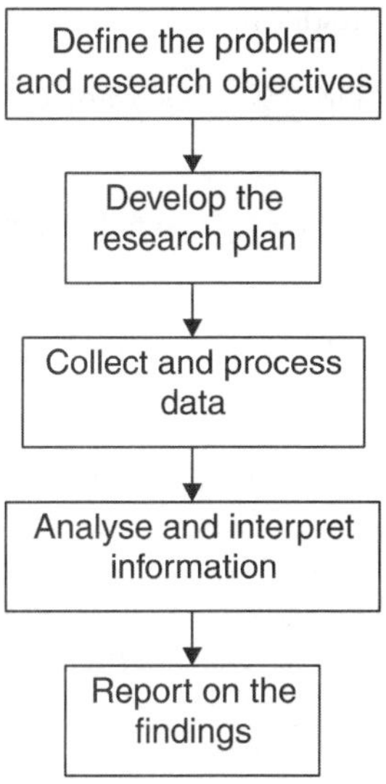

In putting together the research plan, decisions need to be made under the following headings.

Data sources	Primary data (data the organisation collects itself for the purpose) Secondary data (collected by someone else for another purpose which may provide useful information)
Type of data required	Continuous/ad hoc Quantitative (numbers) Qualitative (important insights)
Research methods	Observation Focus groups Survey Experiment

Research tools	Interviews (semi-structured, structured, unstructured; open v closed questions) Questionnaires Mechanical tools (video, audio)
Sampling plan (if required)	Sampling unit Sample size Sample procedure
Contact methods	Telephone Mail Face to face

Chapter Roundup

- In a **knowledge-based economy** organisations compete by obtaining **superior information**. The more information that a firm can obtain about competitors and customers, the more it should be able to adapt its product/service offerings to meet the needs of the market place.
- **Information and communications technology** (ICT) is changing the way markets are structured and it has created **new marketing techniques** and **new marketing channels**.
- Information is required by marketing and sales management for **analysis**, **planning**, **implementation** and **control**: APIC.
- Marketing information may have four roles: **descriptive**, **comparative**, **diagnostic** and **predictive**.
- Information is required for **strategic**, **tactical** and **operational decisions** relating to matters such as markets and market share, products, prices, distribution, sales force organisation, advertising, customer attitudes, competitors' activities and SLEPT factors.
- Key elements of user specifications for information include: **rationale**, **budget**, **timescale**, **objectives**, **methods** and **reports**.
- In a knowledge-based economy knowledge must be actively managed. Knowledge includes **tacit knowledge** in employees' heads as well as **formally recorded facts**, transactions and so on.
- Knowledge management entails identifying knowledge and using a variety of organisational and technological means to ensure that it is **shared**.
- Marketing research is made up of **market research**, **product research**, **price research**, **sales promotion research** and **distribution research**.
- In brief, the marketing research process has the following stages.
  - Define the problem and research **objectives**
  - Develop the research **plan**
  - Collect and process **data**
  - **Analyse and interpret** information
  - **Report** on the findings

Quick Quiz

1 Information helps the marketing manager to increase .... to customer demands, identifying ....and new product/service demands, and to anticipate .... and threats.

Fill in the gaps.

2 Information and communications technology only creates opportunities, it does not pose threats. True or false?

3 What are the activities involved in marketing management, in broad terms?

4 What questions might an organisation need to answer under the following headings?

Products ....

Advertising ....

5 The roles of information may be summarised by the acronym DCDP. What do the letters stand for?

6 What key points would you make about the following elements of a user specification for information?

Objectives ....

Methods ....

7 Define knowledge management.

8 What are the two main reasons why tacit knowledge is hard to manage?

9 What does MPPSD stand for?

10 Draw a diagram summarising the marketing research process.

Answers to Quick Quiz

1 Information helps the marketing manager to increase **responsiveness** to customer demands, by identifying **new customer opportunities** and new product/service demands, and to anticipate **competitive attacks** and threats

2 False. If your firm has the technology others can acquire that technology too, or develop better technology. Communications technology has created global competition.

3 APIC: Analysis, Planning, Implementation and Control

4 **Products**. What do customers think of our product? What do they do with it? Are our products in a 'growth' or 'decline' stage of their life cycle? Should we extend our range?

Advertising. Do we use the right media? Do we communicate the right message? Is it effective?

You may have thought of other examples.

5 Descriptive, Comparative, Diagnostic, Predictive

6 **Objectives** should set out the precise information needed, as **clearly as possible**. The objectives should relate **only** to the original rationale for seeking the information, not what it might be 'nice to know'.

Methods would outline matters such as the scale of the search, the mix of quantitative and qualitative information needed, the segments of the market to be included.

7 Knowledge management involves the identification and analysis of available and required knowledge, and the subsequent planning and control of actions to develop knowledge assets so as to fulfil organisational objectives.

8 Tacit knowledge is hard to manage because the organisation cannot know that it exists (even the possessor of the information may not realise why it is that he or she is better at doing something than others), and because people may be reluctant to share it.

9 Market, Product, Price, Sales promotion, Distribution

10

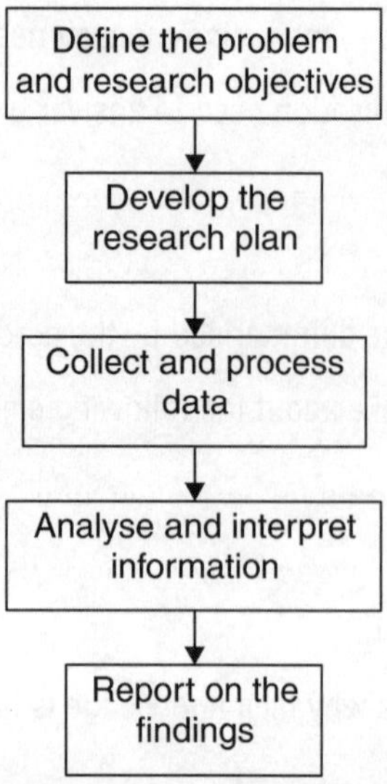

Now try Question 1 at the end of the Study Text

2

Marketing management support systems

Chapter topic list

Syllabus content – knowledge and skill requirements

- 1.2: The concept of knowledge management and its importance in a knowledge-based economy
- 1.3: How organisations determine their marketing information requirements and the key elements of user specifications for information
- 1.4: Marketing management support systems and their different formats and components
- 2.1: The application and role of customer relationship management (CRM) and the benefits of customer databases

Introduction

A 'marketing management support system' may be a personal organiser, or one or two **assistant** personnel who look after matters when the marketing manager can't be in the office or has too much else to do, or even a full **customer relationship management** (CRM) system or **enterprise resource planning** (ERP) system with dozens of software modules and a customer database spanning most of the world. Each may be equally effective, depending on the circumstances and the size and complexity of the business.

Pretty much everything to do with marketing support in medium to large organisations is given the **'CRM' label** these days. No doubt system vendors think it is sexier to add the CRM tag to things that in the late 1980s/early 1990s might have been described with a name like **'executive information system'** (for instance). However, the older **generic names** are still valid, so that is where we begin this chapter. We'll also consider systems that encourage knowledge sharing and collaboration. None of these are **exclusively** for the support of marketing management, of course, but they support marketing management just as much as they support other functions in the organisation.

We will then look at what used to be described as **Marketing Information Systems (MkIS)**: the term is less common these days, perhaps because the customer-focused marketing concept has taken hold, or perhaps because the thought of a system entirely devoted to the marketing function is too insular an approach in a modern organisation. Nevertheless the ideas behind a MkIS provide a good introduction both to the use of databases in marketing and to the broader perspective of CRM systems.

You will often read that the **customer database** is the most important component of CRM, and it is certainly important enough in the context of this syllabus to merit an entire section to itself (See Part B). However, databases are just the **means**. The really important thing about CRM systems is that they **integrate** systems right across the organisation and facilitate their use as a source of management information from one central point.

1 Formats and components

FAST FORWARD

In general terms information systems in organisations consist of **transaction processing systems**, **expert systems**, **decision support systems** and **executive information systems**.

We are **not**, of course, talking about **hardware components** (keyboard, mouse etc) in this section, although it is worth noting in passing that there is an ever wider range of devices that can be used in conjunction with an information system, thanks largely to developments in **communications technology** such as mobile telephony and wireless technologies.

Information systems in all but the smallest organisations are conventionally divided into several broad categories.

(a) **Transaction processing systems** do the essential number crunching.

(b) **Expert systems** are used principally at the **operational** level and assist in structured problems that can be solved by applying the relevant business rules.

(c) **Decision support systems** are used by **middle managers** for routine modelling, but also to analyse unstructured problem situations where there is no precedent that can be used as a universal guideline.

(d) **Executive information systems** are used at **strategic** level, for unstructured problems, or to identify new opportunities.

1.1 Transaction processing systems

FAST FORWARD

Transaction processing systems are essential for the everyday operation of the business and they also provide the raw material for other systems. **Data capture** is potentially highly time-consuming and expensive for organisations so every effort should be made to automate it.

Transaction processing systems represent the lowest level in an organisation's use of information systems. They are essential for day-to-day operational and financial management, and they also provide **raw material** which can then be used at higher levels to generate information such as reports on cumulative sales figures, response to sales promotions, sales by type of customer, and so on: information that gives rise to marketing management decisions and new actions.

Key concept

Transaction processing systems are used for **routine tasks** in which data items or transactions must be processed so that operations can continue. Handling sales orders, purchase orders, payroll items and stock records are typical examples.

Action Programme 1

How much do you know about the accounting systems used in your organisation? You may have access to only a part of the system, but you should appreciate the range of marketing and sales related information it contains and hopefully know how to get reports on matters of relevance to your job. Find out as much as you can because this may provide you with practical examples to use in exam answers.

1.1.1 Modern developments

The capture of transaction data via **barcodes** and scanners is commonplace these days. The combination of Electronic Point of Sale (**EPOS**), Electronic Funds Transfer at Point of Sale (**EFTPOS**) and possibly a **loyalty card** scheme enables individual transactions and individual purchasers to be tracked, identified and linked. This helps to build up a very detailed picture of the buying habits of individual customers, as well as serving the practical purpose of updating stock records and financial accounts.

Barcode technology is well-established and is especially suitable for retailers, but the capture of data is still so time consuming and expensive for many organisations that new applications and developments will continue to emerge.

(a) The **Internet** offers the possibility for customers to do all the data entry themselves as well as allowing organisations to track browsing behaviour. You may think that the Internet is a familiar tool, but Tim Berners-Lee, the 'inventor' of the World Wide Web, still considers the technology and the possible applications to be at infant stage.

(b) **Voice recognition software** already enables computers to interpret and respond to human speech to a limited extent and the technology is steadily improving.

(c) Better 'seeing' devices and software will capture **visual information** in ways that computers can understand. This will enable machines to carry out surveillance, checking and inspection activities with less human supervision.

Marketing at Work

There is already an 'Internet fridge' on the market:

"Watch TV, listen to music or surf the Internet using this titanium finish, state-of-the-art fridge freezer. It's the ultimate in kitchen technology with a built-in MP3 player for downloading and playing music from the Internet, email and video mail using a built-in camera and microphone. It even has full Internet access so you can restock the refrigerator online or check on the latest news and weather – all without leaving the kitchen. And it's great for storing food too ..."

(*www.lginternetfamily.co.uk*)

Action Programme 2

How could voice recognition be used in marketing research?

1.2 Expert systems

FAST FORWARD

Expert systems apply pre-defined business rules to data to find the answers to questions that would otherwise require specialised knowledge and a great amount of processing time. They are now common in customer support applications and can also be used for marketing planning decisions.

Key concept

Expert systems are computer programs which allow users to benefit from expert knowledge, information and advice.

Expert systems take advantage of a database holding **specialised data** on, for example, **technical customer support** matters, and **rules** that can be pre-defined and applied by computer. This means that relatively untrained customer support staff can enter key data about a problem and the program will produce a decision or an answer about something on which an expert's input would normally be required. This is why, for instance, you can now get quick decisions on loan applications that used to have to be processed by highly qualified actuaries.

1.2.1 Expert systems and marketing management

Expert systems are able to process very large amounts of inter-related data much more quickly and accurately than a human could. Let's consider the marketing management goal of **precision marketing** (the mass-customisation model in which the marketing approach is matched precisely to the needs of the individual).

Marketing at Work

In the USA, Sears-Roebuck targets those of its customers who have purchased domestic appliances without any associated maintenance cover, in a drive to sell them general maintenance contracts.

Precision marketing is problematic because of the difficulty of manipulating the vast quantities of data involved. Computers can easily handle the volume of data, although they cannot take decisions without being fed sets of rules to govern every possible situation.

A well-designed expert system is a possible solution to this kind of dilemma. With an expert system, the computer can be taught how to make the necessary decisions using **artificial intelligence**. It may even 'learn from experience' in some circumstances.

There are other less complex applications which still allow some of the benefits of expert systems to be realised.

(a) **Aggregation**. Customers are aggregated with others who share broadly similar behaviour patterns. This is the principle on which ACORN (A Classification of Residential Neighbourhoods) works. The precision is limited, but at least 'individual' approaches are possible at the group level. There is more on this later in this book.

(b) **Simple decisions**. Automatic decisions can be made to relate to relatively simple factors, as in the example of the Sears Roebuck maintenance contracts. This approach can be developed incrementally, adding new decisions based upon simple combinations of factors revealed by experience.

Action Programme 3

Does your organisation use expert systems of any kind (it probably won't be called an 'expert system')? If so make brief notes on how it uses such systems, or if not try to think of ways in which expert systems might make your job easier and improve the service given to your customers.

1.3 Decision support systems 12/04

FAST FORWARD

Decision support systems help managers to consider and evaluate alternative answers to problems that cannot be reduced to rules.

Decision support systems are used by management to assist them in making decisions on issues which are not as clear-cut as those that can be dealt with by expert systems. The objective is to allow the manager to consider a number of **alternatives** and **evaluate** them under a variety of potential conditions.

Key concept

A **marketing decision support system** is a coordinated collection of data systems, tools and techniques with supporting **software and hardware** which is used for gathering and interpreting relevant information from the business and its environment, which may be used as a basis for marketing decisions and action. It is used by management to aid decision making on unstructured, complex, uncertain or ambiguous issues.

A Marketing Decision Support System

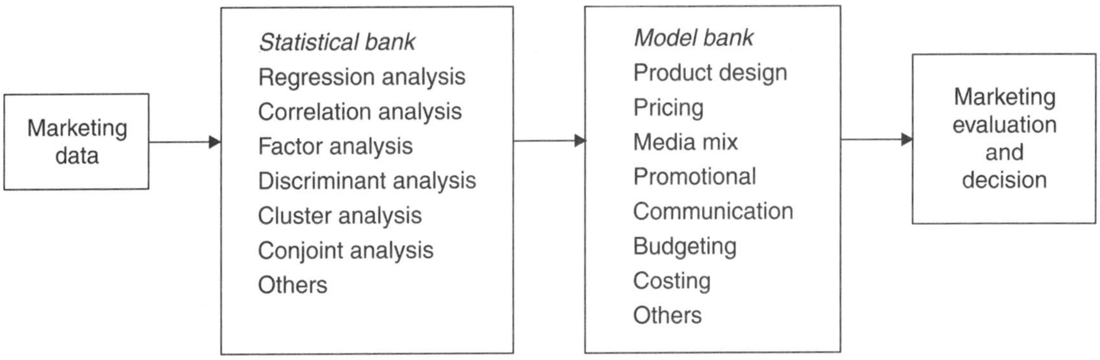

In fact a simple **spreadsheet** 'what if' model, using data extracted from an accounting package, is one form of decision support tool: you may have devised one of your own without realising how clever you were being! However, there are also many specialised software packages that enable **computer modelling** of **complex marketing management problems**. We'll look at some recent examples later in this chapter.

1.4 Executive information systems

FAST FORWARD

Executive information systems offer summary level data that is easy to access, manipulate and understand at a glance.

Key concept

An **executive information system** (EIS) is an 'information system which gives the executive easy access to key internal and external data'.

An EIS is likely to have the following features.

(a) Provision of **summary-level data**, captured from the organisation's transaction processing or other systems.

(b) A facility which allows the executive to '**drill down**' from higher to lower levels of information for more details, usually using hyperlinks and clickable images, as on a website.

(c) **Data manipulation facilities** (such as comparison with budget or prior year data, trend analysis),

(d) **Graphics**, for user-friendly presentation of data.

The basic design philosophy of executive information systems is that they should:

(a) Be **easy to use** as an EIS may be consulted during a meeting

(b) Make **data easy to access**, so that it describes the organisation from the executive's point of view, not just in terms of its data flows

(c) Provide **tools for analysis** such as forecasts and trends

(d) Provide **presentational aids** so that information can be converted into graphs, charts and tables at the click of the mouse

2 Systems that aid knowledge management

FAST FORWARD

Knowledge management is **aided by software** that encourages and facilitates collaboration and sharing of information. Examples range from basic 'Office' and e-mail packages on a network, to formal groupware such as Lotus Notes or Microsoft Exchange, which aids scheduling and workflow as well as communication.

Any system – even a basic e-mail system – that helps and encourages people to work together and share information and knowledge will aid knowledge management. We have already covered expert systems, which may help to solve specific marketing problems, but marketing management is also likely to have the support of more general information sharing tools.

2.1 Groupware

Key concept

Groupware is a term used to describe software that provides functions for the use of collaborative work groups.

Typically, groups utilising groupware are small project-oriented teams that have important tasks and tight deadlines. Perhaps the best-known general purpose groupware product is **Lotus Notes**. However, the components of **Microsoft Exchange** used on a networked system could also be considered to be a form of groupware, as could a CRM system.

Features might include the following.

(a) A **scheduler** allowing users to keep track of their schedule and plan meetings with others

(b) An **address book**

(c) '**To do'** lists

(d) A **journal**, used to record interactions with important contacts, record items (such as e-mail messages) and files that are significant to the user, and record activities of all types and track them all without having to remember where each one was saved

(e) A **jotter** for jotting down notes as quick reminders of questions and ideas.

(f) File sharing and distribution utilities

There are clearly advantages in having such information available from the desktop at the touch of a button, rather than relying on scraps of paper, address books, and corporate telephone directories. However, it is when groupware is used to **share information** with colleagues that it comes into its own. Here are some of the features that may be found.

(a) **Messaging**, comprising an **e-mail** in-box which is used to send and receive messages from the office, home, or the road and **routing** facilities, enabling users to send a message to a single person, send it sequentially to a number of people (who may add to it or comment on it before passing it on), or sending it to everyone at once.

(b) Access to an **information database**, and customisable **'views'** of the information held on it, which can be used to standardise the way information is viewed in a workgroup.

(c) **Group scheduling**, to keep track of colleagues' itineraries. Microsoft Exchange Server, for instance, offers a 'Meeting Wizard' which can consult the diaries of everyone needed to attend a meeting and automatically work out when they will be available, which venues are free, and what resources are required.

(d) **Public folders**. These collect, organise, and share files with others on the team or across the organisation.

(e) One person (for instance a secretary or a stand-in during holidays or sickness) can be given **'delegate access'** to another's groupware folders and send mail on their behalf, or read, modify, or create items in public and private folders on their behalf.

(f) **Conferencing**. Participation in public, online discussions with others.

(g) **Assigning tasks**. A task request can be sent to a colleague who can accept, decline, or reassign the task. After the task is accepted, the groupware will keeps the task status up-to-date on a task list.

(h) **Voting** type facilities that can, say, request and tally responses to a multiple-choice question sent in a mail message (eg 'Here is a list of options for this year's Christmas party').

(i) **Hyperlinks** in mail messages. The recipient can click the hyperlink to go directly to a Web page or file server.

(j) **Workflow management** (see below) with various degrees of sophistication.

Workflow is a term used to describe the defined series of tasks within an organisation to produce a final outcome. Sophisticated workgroup computing applications allow the user to define different **workflows** for different types of jobs. For example, when preparing a brochure, a document might be automatically routed between writers and then on to an editor, a proofreader and finally the printers.

At **each stage** in the workflow, **one individual** or group is **responsible** for a specific task. Once the task is complete, the workflow software ensures that the individuals responsible for the **next** task are notified and receive the data they need to do their stage of the process.

Action Programme 4

What kind of systems do you use to facilitate collaboration with colleagues? How could they be improved?

2.2 Intranets

FAST FORWARD

An **intranet** is a mini-version of the Internet accessible only within a company. Intranets can be used for a wide variety of information-sharing purposes.

Key concept

An **intranet** is an internal network used to share information. Intranets utilise Internet technology and protocols. The firewall surrounding an Internet fends off unauthorised access.

Intranets use a combination of the organisation's own networked computers and Internet technology. Each employee has a browser, used to access a server computer that holds corporate information on a wide variety of topics, and in some cases also offers access to the Internet.

Potential applications include company newspapers, induction material, online procedures and policy manuals, employee web pages where individuals post details of their activities and progress, and **internal databases** of the corporate information store.

Most of the **cost** of an intranet is the **staff time** required to set up the system.

The **benefits** of intranets are diverse.

(a) Savings accrue from the **elimination of storage**, **printing** and **distribution** of documents that can be made available to employees on-line.

(b) Documents on-line are often **more widely used** than those that are kept filed away, especially if the document is bulky (eg training manual) and needs to be searched. This means that there are **improvements in productivity** and **efficiency**.

(c) It is much **easier to update** information in electronic form.

(d) Wider access to corporate information should open the way to **more flexible working patterns**, eg material available on-line may be accessed from remote locations.

2.3 Extranets

Key concept

An **extranet** is an intranet that is accessible to designated authorised outsiders.

Whereas an intranet is accessible only to people who are members of the same company or organisation, an extranet provides various levels of accessibility to outsiders.

Only those outsiders with a valid username and password can access an extranet, with varying levels of access rights enabling control over what people can view. Extranets are becoming a very popular means for **business partners to exchange information** for mutual benefit.

Extranets therefore allow better use of the knowledge held by an organisation – by facilitating access to that knowledge.

3 Marketing Information Systems (MkIS)

FAST FORWARD

A **marketing information system** is built up from several different systems which may not be directly related to marketing. Typical components are an **internal reporting system**, a **marketing intelligence system**, a **marketing research system** and an **analytical marketing system**.

In today's environment marketing managers cannot operate unless there is lots of information coming into the organisation from a wide variety of sources such as commissioned research, third-party continuous research, databases, secondary sources of all descriptions, sales figures, customer surveys, environmental scanning and so forth.

Key concept

The collection, organisation and analysis of marketing information is the responsibility of a **marketing information system** (MkIS), which in itself is part of the hierarchy of information systems that exist within an organisation. The information collected, organised and analysed by an MkIS will typically include the following.

- Details on consumers and markets
- Sales – past, current and forecast
- Production and marketing costs
- Data on the operating environment: competitors, suppliers, distributors and so on

Kotler (1991) defines a marketing information system as a 'continuing and interacting structure of people, equipment and procedures to gather, sort, analyse, evaluate, and distribute pertinent, timely, and accurate information for use by marketing decision makers to improve their marketing planning, implementation and control.'

Three aspects of the information-gathering system are of special significance here.

(a) **The speed of feedback**. The sooner the information is collected, the more accurate and useful it will be.

(b) **The length of the planning horizon**. The planning horizon is getting shorter and there is no value in having quicker response times in the marketing function if these are not matched by quicker response times in other parts of the organisation. In the retail world, for example, scanning and EPOS systems mean that retailers know very quickly if a product on the shelves is selling or not.

(c) **Planning how to do it** is becoming more important than planning **what to do**. To be able to react quickly to change, it is important to have a clear picture of how to respond in various eventualities so that when any given scenario emerges, action can be initiated rapidly.

3.1 Components of a MkIS

A MkIS is therefore built up from several different systems which **may not be directly related to marketing**. It is likely to contain the following **components**.

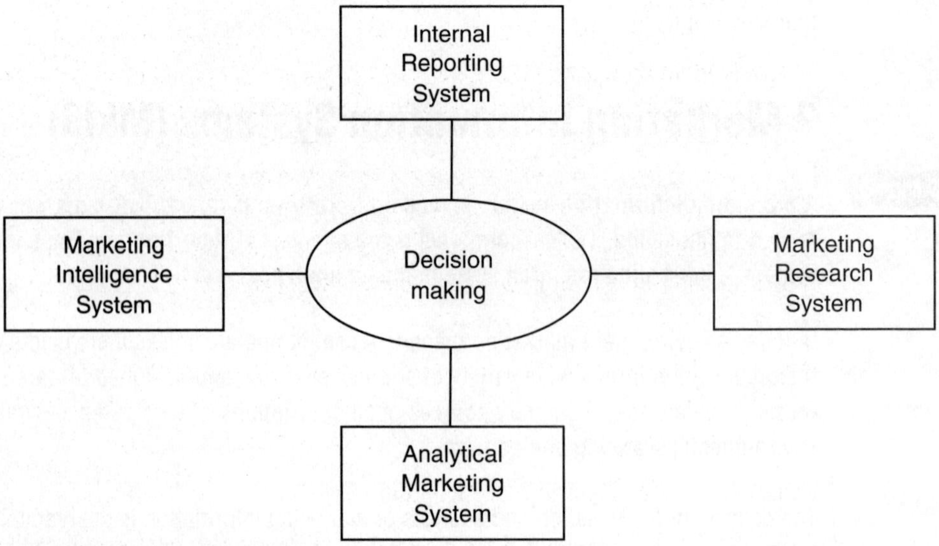

3.1.1 Internal Reporting System

This part of the MkIS utilises internal records of the company – information on costs, production schedules, orders, sales and some types of financial information relating to customers (such as credit ratings).

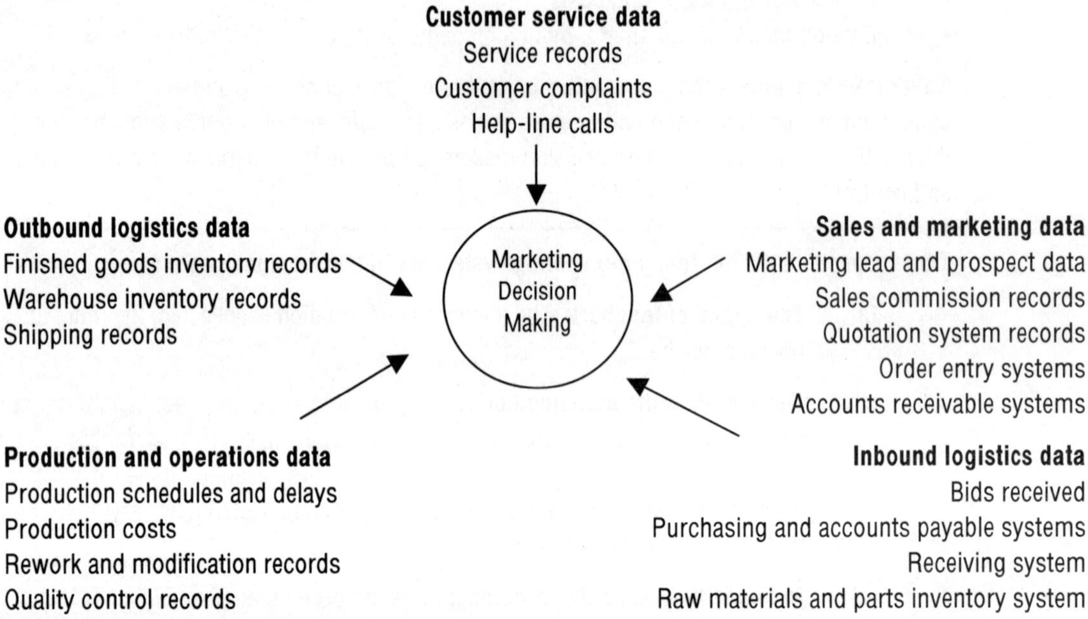

Although these records have been generated for some other purpose, they provide an invaluable insight into the current activity and performance of the company. Data such as sales records, invoices, production records and accounts are used in a system of this type. Many of these records are stored in computerised databases and therefore storage, retrieval and analysis of such records is relatively quick and easy.

The current operations of a business can be analysed and understood. It is good marketing practice to build any strategy or plan from an understanding of 'where we are now' and this system provides that understanding. For example, these records may be used to provide an understanding of size and growth of customer segments, buying patterns, product profitability and many other areas.

3.1.2 Marketing Intelligence System

Key concept

A **marketing intelligence system** is a set of procedures and sources used by managers to obtain everyday information about pertinent developments in the marketing environment.

This system collects and stores everyday information about the external environment – information such as industry reports, competitors' marketing materials and competitors' quotes. Information collected here allows a company to build a more accurate profile of the external environment. The data may take the form of press cuttings and information derived from websites, but can also incorporate subscriptions to external sources of competitive data.

This could allow a company to calculate market sizes and growth patterns, competitor positioning and pricing strategy. This information may help in decision making in many areas such as gap analysis, segmentation and targeting, market development and pricing strategy.

Managers can scan the environment in four ways.

(a) **Undirected viewing**: having general exposure to information with no specific purpose in view

(b) **Conditional viewing**: directed exposure

(c) **Informal search**: an unstructured effort to obtain specific information

(d) **Formal search**: a deliberate effort with a plan, procedure, or methodology to obtain specific information

Action Programme 5

Can you think of any dangers inherent in a marketing intelligence system?

3.1.3 Marketing Research System

This system uses marketing research techniques to gather, evaluate and report findings in order to minimise guesswork in business decisions. The system is used to fill essential information gaps which are not covered by the other components of the MkIS system. In this way it provides targeted and detailed information for the decision making problem at hand.

A company might use marketing research to provide detailed information on new product concepts, attitudes to marketing communication messages, testing advertising effectiveness and understanding customer perceptions of service delivery.

3.1.4 Analytical Marketing System

This comprises analytical techniques that enable marketing managers to make full use of the information provided by the other three sources. This analysis may range from simple financial ratios and projections of sales patterns to more complex statistical models, spreadsheets and other exercises in extrapolation.

An example would be a price sensitivity analysis tool using internal data from sales records together with market share and pricing information on competitors to calculate the price sensitivity of products.

4 Customer Relationship Management (CRM) systems

FAST FORWARD

CRM software integrates the entire marketing and sales process, bringing together all customer facing systems.

As noted at the beginning of this chapter **the label 'CRM'** now tends to be applied (especially by software vendors) to **any and all systems** designed to support marketing and sales.

Traditional 'vertical' organisation structures tended to create stand-alone systems developed for distinct functions or departments, which were responsible for the four main types of interaction with the customer: marketing, sales, fulfilment and after sales. The modern philosophy is that these systems need to be integrated into (or replaced by) central facilities that allow data to be accessed from and fed into the central system from other departments and applications (including Internet applications), so that all customer information can be kept up-to-date and shared.

A CRM system is above all an **integrated system,** covering the entire sales and marketing process. It brings together a number of marketing and customer facing systems within one strategy or homogeneous software application. The following features are usually associated with CRM:

- Data warehouses
- Customer service systems
- Call centres
- E-commerce
- Web marketing
- Operational systems (eg invoicing and payment)
- Sales systems (eg mobile communications)

Marketing at Work

PeopleSoft *(www.peoplesoft.com)* and Siebel *(www.Siebel.com)* are leading vendors of customer relationship management software. PeopleSoft was integrated with computer giant Oracle in June 2005, and Siebel was acquired by Oracle in January 2006. All information about their products and services is now available at *www.oracle.com.*

4.1 Self-support?

With an effective CRM system, each time a customer contacts a company – whether by telephone, in a retail outlet or online – the customer should be recognised and managed in the appropriate way, receiving appropriate information and attention. CRM software provides advanced personalisation and customised solutions to customer demands and gives marketing management a range of key information about each customer which can be applied to the transaction and future transactions.

However some commentators would argue that it is now **customers** who **manage** the relationship with **companies**, and not the other way around.

5 Designing an effective system

FAST FORWARD

Design considerations include **ease of access** and **use**, **cost**, **flexibility**, the **purity of data**, **reporting capabilities**, and **training needs**.

When marketing management support systems are being designed the following factors should be considered.

(a) Users should **understand** the systems and be in a position to evaluate and control them. Management's **access** to the information must be **easy and direct** and the true meaning of the information provided must be clear.

(b) The **cost** of data/information **gathering** should be **minimal**.

(c) **Data gathering** should not cause excessive inconvenience to information sources. Preferably the data will be gathered without customers having to make any extra effort (for example through analysis of supermarket checkout receipts which show consumer purchase patterns).

(d) **Data gathering should be regular and continuous** since a small amount of data gathered regularly can build a considerable database. Regular data gathering produces more reliable results because it reduces the likelihood of bias of one kind or another.

(e) The system must be **flexible**. It should be regularly **reviewed** and **improved** where possible.

Obviously the system needs to produce useful information in a useable format and it will only do so if the following matters are addressed.

(a) **Irrelevant and/or inaccurate content** must be eliminated. (This is discussed in more depth in the next chapter). In particular a system that suggests **answers** that are clearly **nonsense** (for instance because business rules are badly defined) will not be trusted and not be used.

(b) The system must allow for the easy and effective **storage and retrieval** of data and so consideration must be given to matters such as the following.

- Manual or computerised data, or both?
- The regularity of back up
- Cross referencing of data
- Data protection legislation considerations

(c) **Dissemination of the information**. Who needs to, or who should, receive information? Newsletters (or email or an intranet) can be used for standardised regular information, but ad hoc reports should be available to senior managers on demand.

There will of course be **cost** and **organisational implications** of any marketing management support system.

- **Training** of all staff will be necessary.
- Staff with **specialist skills** might have to be recruited or contracted from outside.
- **Software** and suitable networking and communications **hardware** may be very expensive.
- Organisational considerations might include the **reallocation of duties** or **redundancies**.

Marketing at Work

As a quick **example** of a marketing management support system in action, let us visualise a company that has identified **quality service** as a strategic priority. To meet this goal, the system must be capable of performing a wide range of tasks, including the following.

(a) Provide managers with **real time** information on how customers and staff **perceive the service** being given

(b) Measure quality of both service and customer care so as to provide evidence that they do matter

(c) Monitor how (if at all) the **customer base is changing**

(d) Perhaps, provide a basis on which marketing staff bonus payments can be determined

Chapter Roundup

- In general terms information systems in organisations consist of **transaction processing systems**, **expert systems**, **decision support systems** and **executive information systems**.
- **Transaction processing systems** are essential for the everyday operation of the business and they also provide the raw material for other systems. **Data capture** is potentially highly time-consuming and expensive for organisations so every effort should be made to automate it.
- **Expert systems** apply pre-defined business rules to data to find the answers to questions that would otherwise require specialised knowledge and a great amount of processing time. They are now common in customer support applications and can also be used for simple, and not so simple marketing planning decisions.
- **Decision support systems** help managers to consider and evaluate alternative answers to problems that cannot be reduced to rules.
- **Executive information systems** offer summary level data that is easy-to-access, manipulate and understand at a glance.
- **Knowledge management** is **aided by software** that encourages and facilitates collaboration and sharing of information. Examples range from basic 'Office' and e-mail packages on a network, to formal groupware such as Lotus Notes or Microsoft Exchange, which aids scheduling and workflow as well as communication.
- An **intranet** is a mini-version of the Internet accessible only within a company. Intranets can be used for a wide variety of information-sharing purposes. Extranets allow access to business partners' information systems.
- A **marketing information system** is built up from several different systems which may not be directly related to marketing. Typical components are an **internal reporting system**, a **marketing intelligence system**, a **marketing research system** and an **analytical marketing system**.
- **CRM software** integrates the entire marketing and sales process, bringing together all customer facing systems.
- Design considerations include **ease of access** and **use**, **cost**, **flexibility**, the **purity of data**, **reporting capabilities**, and **training needs**.

Quick Quiz

1 Expert systems designed for the use of production personnel do not form part of the marketing management support system. True or false? Explain your answer.

2 Decisions made by a decision support system are likely to be better than decisions made by a manager. True or false? Explain your answer.

3 List six ways in which groupware helps organisations to share information.

4 An extranet cannot be considered to be part of an organisation's marketing management support system because it involves other organisations. True or false? Explain your answer.

5 A marketing information system has four typical components. Fill in the gaps.

I .... R .... System

M .... I .... System

M .... R .... System

A .... M .... System

6 A marketing information system requires a complex statistical analysis package. True or false? Explain your answer.

7 What is the most important thing that is achieved by CRM systems as opposed to earlier types of system?

8 List five 'modules' that might be available in a customer relationship management package.

9 A web-enabled CRM system:

A Means that a company's employees can take more care of customers
B Is more impersonal because customers have to serve themselves
C Empowers customers to define the sort of relationship they want with an organisation

10 What are the possible consequences of failing to eliminate inaccurate or irrelevant information from a marketing management support system?

Answers to Quick Quiz

1 False. If a system helps with marketing management it can be considered to be part of the support system, no matter who actually 'owns' it.

2 False. Decision support systems do not make decisions, they help managers to weigh up the options. Managers make decisions.

3 The features mentioned in the text of the chapter are: messaging, access to databases, scheduling, shared public folders, delegate access, conferencing, task assignment, voting, and workflow management.

4 False. This is similar to question 1. If something helps with marketing management it can be considered to be part of the support system, no matter who actually 'owns' it.

5 Internal Reporting System
Marketing Intelligence System
Marketing Research System
Analytical Marketing System

6 False. Much of the analytical work may be done by fairly simple spreadsheets, although there are packages that make things even easier for those not familiar with analytical techniques.

7 Integration of information from all the systems that impact upon marketing.

8 Five possible examples are Field Sales Management, Call Centre Management, Order Capture, Customer Behaviour Modelling, Warehouse Management. Larger systems have modules for practically everything you can think of, so it is hard to get this question wrong!

9 C is the 'most' correct answer, although an argument could be made for options A and B, depending on the circumstances. For instance if the customer is doing most of the data entry this frees up the time of customer service staff, and that may mean that fewer customer service staff are needed or it may mean that they spend more time dealing with problems. Web technology allows the offer to the customer to be highly personalised, but many people still prefer explaining their needs to human beings and being reassured that they are ordering the right product.

10 The obvious immediate consequence is that incorrect data may lead to incorrect decisions and actions. Taking a longer term view just a few pieces of incorrect data may mean that users do not trust the system at all (even if the bad data is the exception) and so do not use it.

Action Programme Review

1 The answer will be specific to your circumstances. Don't neglect to do questions that ask you to apply what you read to your own circumstances. It is easier to do it now than to have to think of examples out of the blue in an exam.

2 Voice recognition is not yet advanced enough for any but the simplest applications ('say "one" if you want option 1') but as the technology develops it could be used to analyse responses made by customers during recorded telephone conversations with live staff and perhaps measure attitude from tone of voice. You may have thought of other answers.

3 The answer will be specific to your circumstances. Almost any kind of system you use that involves querying a database to find the answers to problems could be turned into an expert system.

4 Again the answer will be specific to your circumstances. At the very least you probably use e-mail and e-mail attachments to circulate documents or else have common access to documents via a computer network. You may use a program such as Outlook to manage appointments and meetings, and facilities in programs like Word or PowerPoint to add comments to others' drafts.

5 One strong danger is information overload – collecting or receiving more information from the system than you can possibly take in and make use of. Another is the danger that information will be inaccurate or out of date: you have no control over the reliability of external sources.

Now try Questions 2 and 3 at the end of the Study Text

Part B
Customer databases

Customer databases

Chapter topic list

1 Customer databases
2 Setting up a database
3 Database applications
4 Profiling customers and prospects
5 Data warehousing and data mining
6 Database marketing and marketing research

Syllabus content – knowledge and skill requirements

- 2.1 The application and role of customer relationship management (CRM) and the benefits of customer databases
- 2.2: The process for setting up a database
- 2.3: How organisations profile customers and prospects
- 2.4: The principles of data warehouses, data marts and data mining
- 2.5: The relationship between database marketing and marketing research

Introduction

All the topics that we have studied so far have assumed that useful marketing information is stored somewhere and that it can be retrieved, analysed and manipulated as and when required. We now need to look in detail at how this is done.

It is now very easy and relatively cheap to store vast amounts of data about customers using a computer **database** and appropriate software.

Database marketing holds that the whole point of finding out about a customer is to **attach information to a name and address** to which offers, product information and special deals can later be sent to develop a **relationship** that leads to **repeat purchasing**.

This rather long, but **very important chapter** deals with all of the syllabus requirements relating to customer databases.

Note that the relationship between **database marketing** and **marketing research** is outlined here, but this topic raises certain **ethical issues** which are reserved for Chapter 4, as are the legal and privacy issues surrounding the storage and use of customer data in the light of **Data Protection legislation**.

1 Customer databases

Pilot Paper, 12/03, 12/04, 12/05, 6/06, 6/07

FAST FORWARD

Customer databases can contain a wide variety of information about the customer such as **contact details**, **transaction history**, **personal details** and **preferences** and so on. Information may come from a variety of sources besides transaction processing systems, including specialist geodemographic data and lifestyle information.

Key concepts

A **customer database** is 'A manual or computerised source of data relevant to marketing decision making about an organisation's customers.' (Wilson 2002).

Database marketing has been defined as 'an interactive approach to marketing, which uses individually addressable marketing media and channels to extend help to a company's target audience, stimulate their demand and stay close to them by recording and keeping an electronic database memory of customer, prospect, and all communication and commercial contacts, to help them improve all future contacts and to ensure more realistic planning of all marketing.'

A marketing database can provide an organisation with much information about its customers and target groups. **Every purchase a customer makes has two functions**.

- Provision of **sales revenue**
- Provision of **information** as to future market opportunities

A typical customer database might include the following.

Element	Examples
Customer or company details	Account numbers, names, addresses and contact (telephone, fax, e-mail) details; basic 'mailing list' data, relationship to other customers. For business customers these fields might include sales contact, technical contact, parent company or subsidiaries, number of employees

Element	Examples
Professional details	Company; job title; responsibilities – especially for business-to-business marketing; industry type
Personal details	Sex, age, number of people at the same address, spouse's name, children, interests, and any other relevant data known, such as newspapers read, journals subscribed to
Transaction history	What products/services are ordered, date, how often, how much is spent (turnover), payment methods
Call/contact history	Sales or after sales service calls made, complaints/queries received, meetings at shows/exhibitions, mailings sent, etc
Credit/payment history	Credit rating, amounts outstanding, aged debts
Credit transaction details	Items currently on order, dates, prices, delivery arrangements
Special account details	Membership number, loyalty or incentive points earned, discount awarded), where customer loyalty or incentive schemes are used

The **sources** of information in a customer database and the **uses** to which it can be put are outlined in the diagram below.

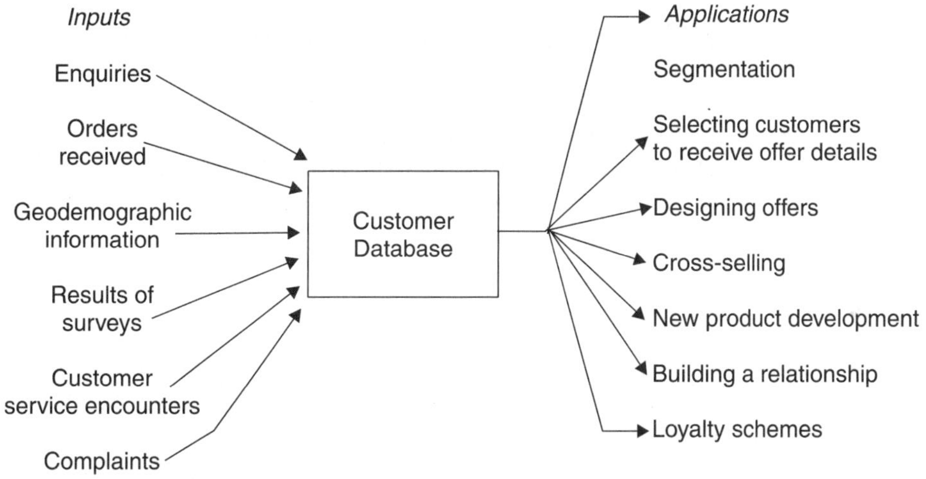

(a) The **majority** of customer information will be gleaned from the orders they place and the enquiries that they make. A relatively recent development in this area is the combination of cookies or user log-ins and server logging software, which enables **tracking and recording** of a customer's progress through a **website**, perhaps revealing interests that would otherwise have gone unnoticed.

(b) **Geodemographic** information relates to the characteristics of people living in different areas. Even simple post-code information can contain a lot of data about the customer.

(c) **Customer service** can be used to indicate particular concerns of customers. For example, in a DIY store, if customers have to ask service staff where items are stored, the volume of complaints might indicate poor signage and labelling.

(d) **Complaints** also indicate deficiencies in the product or the fact that customer expectations have been poorly communicated.

(e) The specific information held may **vary by type of market**. For example, an industrial database will hold data on key purchasers, influencers and decision makers, organisational structure, industry classification (SIC codes), and business size.

1.1 The benefits of customer databases

Databases can provide **valuable information** to marketing management.

(a) Computer databases make it easier to collect and store more **data/information**.

(b) Computer software allows the data to be **extracted** from the file and **processed** to provide whatever information management needs.

(c) In some cases businesses may have access to the databases of **external organisations**. Reuters, for example, provides an on-line information system about money market interest rates and foreign exchange rates to firms involved in money market and foreign exchange dealings, and to the treasury departments of a large number of companies.

Other benefits of database systems might include:

(a) Increased **sales and/or market share** (due to enhanced lead follow-up, cross-selling, customer contact)

(b) Increased **customer retention** (through better targeting)

(c) Better use of **resources** (targeting, less duplication of information handling)

Databases enable marketing managers to improve their **decision making**.

- **Understanding customers** and their preferences
- Managing **customer service** (helplines, complaints)
- Understanding the **market** (new products, channels etc)
- Understanding **competitors** (market share, prices)
- Managing **sales operations**
- Managing **marketing campaigns**
- **Communicating** with customers

A database built for marketing purposes will, like the marketing function itself, be **future orientated**. It will be possible to **exploit** the database to **drive future marketing programmes**, not just glory in what has happened in the past.

Exam tip

The type of information to be collected, the manner of its collection, and the benefits to be gained from it, are all part of regular exam questions. Ethical issues (such as the use of marketing research data) are also frequently examined.

1.2 Customer relationship management and databases

FAST FORWARD

Databases provide valuable **information** to assist with many marketing management tasks and decisions and can play a key part in **customer relationship management** because they permit **mass customisation**.

Key concept

Customer relationship management (CRM) describes the methodologies, software, and usually Internet capabilities that help an enterprise to manage customer relationships.

We mentioned 'CRM' in the previous chapter because it is now so commonly used as a label for marketing management software products. More precisely, however, customer relationship management consists of:

(a) Helping an enterprise to **identify** and **target** its **best customers**, manage marketing campaigns with clear goals and objectives, and generate quality leads

(b) **Allowing** the **formation of relationships** with **customers**, with the aim of **improving customer satisfaction** and **maximising profits**; identifying the most profitable customers and providing them with the highest level of service

(c) **Providing employees** with the **information** and **processes necessary** to know their customers, understand their needs, and effectively build relationships between the company, its customer base, and distribution partners

(d) Assisting the organisation to improve **sales**, **account**, and **sales management** by **optimising information shared**, and **streamlining existing processes** (for example, taking orders using mobile devices)

The **database** is clearly key to CRM. For example, an enterprise might build a database about its customers that describes relationships in enough detail to allow management, salespeople, service staff and maybe customers themselves to access information, match customer needs with product plans, remind customers of service requirements and know what other products a customer had purchased, and so on.

The result is something called **mass customisation**, in which a large number of customers can be reached, but simultaneously these customers can be treated **individually**. It has been remarked how the traditional values of the 'corner shop' are returning with the resurgence of relationship marketing and customer focus.

Marketing at Work

'Newcomers to database marketing have to make a mental leap from viewing the database as a collection of names to seeing it as an engine for driving truly personal marketing', says Melanie Howard, head of direct marketing studies at the Henley Centre. 'Companies must understand the database is not a way of marketing, but it facilitates the personal marketing approach. They must be careful. If they think they are doing personal marketing just because they have a name and address they have a problem.' They must understand what will win consumer loyalty.

'Analysing the data properly and using it effectively will separate the winners from the losers', argues Edwina Dunn of Dunn-Humby, the company involved in running Tesco ClubCard. 'Manufacturers have learned that data about purchasing is valuable and if they can link it to names and addresses that is even more valuable. Not many are grasping the deeper meaning of that. The few that do are forward-thinking and visionary,' she says.

She puts Tesco in that category. Its ClubCard collects purchasing information at the swipe of the card. The card can be used at any store, enabling marketers to build a picture of individual habits. Because the Tesco system is about collecting points then sending out vouchers, the retailer has a valid reason to write to customers.

'Being in the forefront of database marketing will take more than up-to-date technology and marketing skills', Dunn says. It will demand a third skill which she thinks has been left out of the database equation: statistical analysis. 'We are not bringing statisticians into the world of marketing. The bridge building is being done between marketing and IT. The big bridge that needs to be built now is between statisticians and marketing. That will separate out people who know what to do with the data.''

Marketing Business

2 Setting up a database 12/04

FAST FORWARD

Modern business databases are maintained on a central computer to enable **sharing of data** and avoid duplication. A typical relational database consists of a number of inter-related tables of records and fields.

A database need not be computerised. A paper address book that you keep in your briefcase is a form of database and so is a card index. However most modern business databases will be created and maintained **centrally on a computer**. This is obviously the most efficient method where **large amounts of data** are involved and for several important additional reasons.

(a) **Common data** for all users to share

(b) Avoidance of **data duplication** in files kept by different users

(c) **Consistency** in the organisation's use of data, and in the accuracy and up-to-dateness of data accessed by different users, because all records are centrally maintained and updated

(d) **Flexibility** in the way in which shared data can be queried, analysed and formatted by individual users for specific purposes, without altering the store of data itself

(e) **Speed** of data retrieval

The collection of computer programs that process data is more properly referred to as a **database management system (DBMS)**.

Basic features of database packages allow you to readily perform the following activities.

(a) **Find particular records**, using any data item you know

(b) **Sort records alphabetically**, numerically or by date, in ascending or descending order

(c) **Interrogate records**, generating the selection of records based on a complex set of criteria, from one or more linked tables. (For example, you might specify that you want all customer records where the field 'City' equals London or Birmingham and where the field 'Product' equals Widget and where the field 'Purchase Date' is between January 2005 and January 2006. The query would generate a table consisting of customers in London and Birmingham who purchased Widgets in 2005.)

(d) **Calculate and count** data entries. For example if you wanted to find out how many customers had purchased each product, you could run a query that asked the database to group the data by the field 'product' and then count by field 'customer ID': it would count the number of distinct customer ID numbers linked to each product. You could also ask to 'sum' or add up all the values in a field: total number of purchases, or total purchase value.

(e) **Format** selected data for a variety of uses, as reports, forms, mailing labels, charts and diagrams.

Action Programme 1

Find out what type(s) of database your organisation (or college) uses, and for what applications. If possible, get access to the database and browse through the index, directory or switchboard to see what databases/catalogues contain what database files or tables, queries, reports and forms, with what fields. If you can't get access to a database at work, try the local library, where you may find that the 'index card' system has been computerised as a database. Or use an Internet search engine or browser to interrogate some on-line databases. This is not really something you can learn from books – have a go!

2.1 Key components

There are two basic kinds of **computerised** database.

(a) A **flat file system** lumps all the data into single file. A single worksheet in a spreadsheet is an example.

(b) A **relational database system** allows greater flexibility and storage efficiency by splitting the data up into a number of tables, which are linked and can be integrated as necessary. For example, one table may contain customer names and another customers' payment histories. A linking field such as a customer ID number would allow the user to interrogate both tables and generate an integrated report on a particular customer's purchases and payments, or a list of customers who had made multiple purchases, or a list of those with a poor payment record.

Flat systems are easy to build and maintain, and are quite adequate for applications such as mailing lists, or membership databases. **Relational systems** integrate a wider range of business functions, for invoicing, accounting, inventory and marketing analysis: they are, however, complicated to develop and use properly. If your organisation already operates a relational system, learn how to use it. If you are required to set up or build a relational system, get help: use a 'wizard' or template (in the database package) or ask an expert, at least the first time.

All databases have some kind of structure, otherwise you would never be able to retrieve information from them. For instance a telephone directory stores entries in alphabetical order. Computer database packages store data as follows.

(a) **Fields** are the labels given to types of data. A simple customer database, for example, might include fields such as: Title, First name, Last name, Address fields, and other contact details. The fields are the **columns** in a tabular database.

(b) **Records** are the collection of fields relevant to one entry. So all the above data fields for a particular customer make up one customer record. The records are the **rows** in a tabular database.

ID	Title	First name	Last name	Address 1	Address 2	Address 3	City	County	Postcode	Country	Telephone	Fax	Email
1	Mr	Kieran	Davies	25 Dill Street	Merton		London		SW17 4QF	UK	020 7884 1122		kieran.davis@virgin.net
2	Mrs	Shagura	Jumal	37 Nelson Road	Trafford		Manchester		M41 2BD	UK	01584 452291		sjumal@freeserve.com

(c) **Tables** are collections of records that describe similar data. All the customer records for a particular region or product may be stored in one table.

(d) **Databases** are collections of all the tables relating to a particular set of information. So your customer database may include tables for various regions, products and customer contacts.

Action Programme 2

Why are records stored as rows rather than columns?

2.2 Data cleansing

FAST FORWARD

A key issue in setting up a database is **data cleansing**: ensuring that the information is correct, up-to-date and not duplicated. Much can be done at the data entry stage, but where data is imported from other systems a good deal of preparatory work may be needed to ensure that it is in the correct format.

Key concept

> **Data cleansing** is the process of amending or removing data in a database that is incorrect, out of date, incomplete, improperly formatted, or duplicated.

As mentioned in the previous chapter information systems are only valuable if they give **good** information, and that depends crucially on the accuracy of the data.

A typical organisation will have many years' worth of potentially valuable information and this will have got into the system in a variety of ways.

(a) It may have been typed in by hand – correctly or incorrectly

(b) It may have been scanned in from paper documents, but this depends on how good the scanning process is (accurate scanning of ordinary text has only been possible for a few years)

(c) It may have arisen from EPOS and EFTPOS systems

(d) It may have been imported from other systems in other parts of the organisation – perhaps in an incompatible format.

(e) It may have been purchased from another organisation (for instance a mailing list broker) or have arisen as a result of a merger between two organisations.

All of these methods are liable to lead to incorrect, out of date, incomplete, improperly formatted, or duplicated data that needs to be 'cleansed'.

Action Programme 3

Would data from EPOS/EFTPOS systems need to be cleansed?

2.3 Cleansing new data

2.3.1 Form elements

A great deal can be done to ensure that **new data is clean** at the time when it is initially entered into a system. For instance computerised forms for data entry can contain a variety of elements that help to avoid human error and bad data. These **pre-define the acceptable responses** and simply require the user to select the appropriate option rather than type anything.

(a) **Radio buttons** force the user to choose one and only one of a number of options.

Would you like to receive further information?

○ Yes

○ No

(b) **Check boxes** allow more than one choice, but still from a limited range of options

Which newspaper(s) do you read every day?

☐ Financial Times

☐ Guardian

☐ Telegraph

☐ Mirror

(c) **List boxes** operate in a similar way to either radio buttons or check boxes, but the selectable option or options drop down instead of being written out (this saves space on screen).

2.3.2 Validation

Validation is the application of pre-programmed tests and rules by the data entry program to make sure that **typed data input** is reasonable.

There are a number of different types of computer controls for validating a user's typed entries. Here are some examples.

(a) **Format checks** test the data in each input area against rules governing whether it should be numeric, alphabetic or a combination of the two and whether it should have a minimum or maximum number of characters. For example the software would not allow alphabetic characters to be entered in a box designated for a telephone number. It would check an e-mail address to ensure that it contained the @ symbol and at least one full stop.

(b) **Range checks** test that the data is within an appropriate range, for example no products are priced at less than £10 or more than £100. This will prevent somebody keying in the price of a customer purchase for £22.99 as £2,299 in error. These checks can also be applied to dates: for instance you should not be able to enter a date of birth of 31 February, or enter an 'account opened' date in 2007 if it is 2006.

(c) **Existence checks** compare the input data with some other piece of data in the system, to see if it is reasonable. For example a customer code might be compared with an existing list of customer records. If the code exists there will be no reason to duplicate data already entered. If the code does not exist the computer would give you the options of amending the code you entered (in case you typed it wrongly) or of creating a new customer account. Deliberately incorrect entries can also be prevented, or at least discouraged, by this means: for instance the system may query a customer name entered as 'Mickey Mouse', although some kind of override will be necessary, in case that really is the customer's name.

(d) **Completeness checks** ensure that all required data items have been entered. For example if the system requires a contact telephone number you will not be able to save a record until you provide one.

Action Programme 4

Checks like these are very common when filling in forms on websites. Watch out next time you fill in one of these. Ideally fill one in wrongly, deliberately, and try to work out how (or if) the computer knows you have made an error or given incorrect information. The amount of checking will vary from site to site.

2.3.3 Verification

Verification is the **comparison** of **input** data with the **source** document. Computers can't yet see in the way that humans can but they can encourage the person entering the data to check the accuracy of their inputs. For instance if the user enters a post code the computer may automatically display a street name and a range of house numbers. If the displayed information is not the same as the information that appears in the data source this should alert the user that either he or she has made a mistake or the source data is unreliable.

2.4 Cleansing data that is imported

2.4.1 Format and consistency

Suppose you **acquire an existing database** of customer addresses arranged with fields for:

Title, Last Name, First Name, House Number, Street Name, Town, City, Post Code

Your own database may have fields for:

Title, First Name, Last Name, Address1, Address2, Address 3, Post Code

On the face of it the information is the same in both databases but there are small differences that will make it **impossible to 'cut and paste'** the acquired data into your existing data without some cleansing work.

In this example the order of the fields is slightly different, and the acquired database has two fields for your 'Address1' field. Even if you succeed in importing the new data much of it will end up in the wrong field as far as your database is concerned and produce nonsense results when analysed.

Similar problems will arise if the data you want to import includes options that are **not allowed** in your database (a title of 'Prof.' or 'Lord', say), or if the **maximum size** of the Last Name field is 100 characters in one database and 50 characters in the other, or if **dates** are in US format (MM/DD/YYYY) in the new data but UK format (DD/MM/YYYY) in yours, or even if tiny things like **spacing** or **punctuation** (eg DD.MM.YYYY) are different or if **foreign characters** are used.

Computerised databases are sensitive to differences in format in a way that human beings are not because they need to **store** information as **efficiently** as possible for subsequent **high-speed analysis**. Before you can import data into your own database you need to ensure that it is in a format (the same order, the same field size and so on) that is consistent with your existing data. This can often involve a **considerable amount of preparatory work**.

A technology called **XML** is likely to alleviate many formatting problems, but most organisations have only just started down this path.

2.4.2 Deduplication

Duplication of entries in your database is one of the best ways of annoying your customers! Suppose your database contains a record for Mrs Jane Wordingham and another for Ms J. Wordingham. If you send 'both' of these people the same mailshot you may successfully reach two different customers ... or you may strongly irritate one.

Duplication can occur for a variety of reasons.

(a) The data may have been **acquired** from another part of the organisation, or from another organisation such as a list broker, and be recorded slightly differently. Different systems ask for different information (eg 'Initial' as opposed to 'First Name').

(b) **People are inconsistent** in the data they provide. For instance they may generally include their 'Town' when providing their address, but leave it out if they are in a hurry.

(c) Even if data is read in **automatically**, from a credit card, say, there is nothing to prevent someone using **more than one credit card** and having slightly different versions of their personal information on each.

Fortunately, it is usually a fairly simple matter to **identify duplicates**. The software should be able to **compare a common field** such as post code and either **delete** duplicates **automatically** or **generate a report** for further investigation. This may be more problematic in business-to-business marketing, where several different businesses may operate out of the same location, or the same business may operate out of multiple locations.

Action Programme 5

Some organisations deal with duplicates by deleting information relating to all but the most recent transaction ('overkill'). Others seem to rely on customers to tell them about duplicate entries but are otherwise happy to send mailshots to everyone on their database, even if some customers get two or more copies ('underkill').

What sort of organisations would be keen to avoid overkill?

2.5 Database maintenance

A customer database should be **regularly and systematically** maintained.

(a) **New fields** can be added to the database design as new types of information become available.

(b) Any **up-dated, altered or new information** should be entered in the database: changes of address, customer status, product interests.

(c) Names which have received **no response** after a certain period of time or number of contacts, should be **deleted**.

(d) If mailshots are **returned to the sender**, they will often be marked with the reason for non-delivery: no longer at this address, not known at this address. Whenever this happens addresses and names should be checked, and amended if possible (common errors include misspelt names, missing lines of the address, or the wrong company name).

(e) **Requests from customers** to have their **details erased** from the database should be honoured. This is a **legal requirement**: see Chapter 4.

3 Database applications

FAST FORWARD

The range of database applications include:

- focusing on **prime prospects**
- evaluating **new prospects**
- **cross-selling** related products
- **launching new products** to potential prospects
- identifying **new distribution channels**
- building **customer loyalty**
- **converting occasional users to regular users**
- generating **enquiries** and **follow-up sales**
- **targeting niche markets**.

The most valuable information in a customer-focused organisation is its knowledge of its customers. The customer database has two uses in such an organisation:

(a) **Operational support** (for example, when a telephone banking employee checks that the password given by a caller is correct before giving out details of the account)

(b) **Analytical uses** (the analysis by the same bank of the customers who receive a certain amount into their account each month and so may be targeted with personal loans or other offers)

The database may be applied to meet a variety of objectives with numerous advantages over traditional marketing methods.

- Focusing on prime prospects
- Evaluating new prospects
- Cross-selling related products
- Launching new products to potential prospects
- Identifying new distribution channels
- Building customer loyalty
- Converting occasional users to regular users
- Generating enquiries and follow-up sales
- Targeting niche markets

3.1 Identifying the most profitable customers

The Italian economist Vilfredo Pareto was the first to observe that in human affairs, 20% of the events result in 80% of the outcomes. This has become known as Pareto's law, or the 80/20 principle. It shows up quite often in marketing. For example, twenty percent of the effort you put into promotion may generate eighty percent of the sales revenue. Whatever the precise proportions, it is true that in general a small number of existing customers are 'heavy users' of a product or service and generate a high proportion of sales revenue, buying perhaps four times as much as a 'light user'.

A customer database which allows purchase frequency and value per customer to be calculated indicates to the marketer who the potential heavy users are, and therefore where the promotional budget can most profitably be spent.

3.2 Identifying buying trends

By tracking purchases per customer (or customer group) you may be able to identify:

(a) **Loyal repeat customers** who cost less to retain than new customers cost to find and attract

(b) **'Backsliding'** or lost customers, who have reduced or ceased the frequency or volume of their purchases. These may be a useful diagnostic sample for market research into declining sales or failing customer care.

(c) **Seasonal** or local purchase patterns (heavier consumption of soup in England in winter, for example).

(d) **Demographic purchase patterns**. These may be quite unexpected. Lower income consumers might buy top-of-the-range products, which they value and save for. Prestige and luxury goods, which marketers promote largely to affluent white-collar consumers, are also purchased by students, secretaries and young families, who have been dubbed 'Ultra Consumers' because they transcend demographic clusters.

(e) Purchase patterns in response to **promotional campaigns**. Increased sales volume or frequency following promotions is an important measurement of their effectiveness.

3.3 Identifying marketing opportunities

More detailed information (where available) on customer likes and dislikes, complaints, feedback and lifestyle values may offer useful information for:

(a) **Product** improvement

(b) **Customer care** and quality programmes

(c) New **product development**

(d) **Decision-making** across the marketing mix: on prices, product specifications, distribution channels, promotional messages.

Simple data fields such as 'contact type' will help to evaluate how contact is made with customers, of what types and in what numbers. Business leads may be generated most often by trade conferences and exhibitions, light users by promotional competitions and incentives, and loyal customers by personal contact through representatives.

Customers can be investigated using any data field included in the database: How many are on e-mail or the Internet? How many have spouses or children? Essentially, these parameters allow the marketer to **segment** the customer base for marketing purposes.

Marketing at Work

Hobbs, the UK fashion retailer, has 40 stores fitted with customer traffic monitoring systems, enabling senior management to see how individual stores are performing throughout each day.

(www.customercounting.com)

3.4 Using database information

The following is a summary of the main ways in which database information can be used.

(a) **Direct mail** used to:

- Maintain customer contact between (or instead of) sales calls
- Generate leads and 'warmed' prospects for sales calls
- Promote and/or sell products and services direct to customers
- Distribute product or service information

(b) **Transaction processing**. Databases can be linked to programmes which generate order confirmations, despatch notes, invoices, statements and receipts.

(c) **Marketing research and planning**. The database can be used to send out market surveys, and may itself be investigated to show purchasing patterns and trends.

(d) **Contacts planning**. The database can indicate what customers need to be contacted or given incentives to maintain their level of purchase and commitment. A separate database may similarly be used to track planned and on-going contacts at conferences and trade shows and invitation lists to marketing events.

(e) **Product development and improvement**. Product purchases can be tracked through the product life cycle, and weaknesses and opportunities identified from records of customer feedback, complaints and warranty/guarantee claims.

4 Profiling customers and prospects

FAST FORWARD

Building **accurate** and **up-to-date profiles** of customers enables the company to **extend help** to a company's **target audience**, to stimulate further demand, and to stay close to them. The company's own information can be enriched by collating it with geodemographic and lifestyle information from sources such as ACORN.

As we have seen, a database is a collection of available information on past and current customers together with future prospects, structured to allow for the implementation of effective marketing strategies.

Database marketing is a customer-oriented approach to marketing, and its special power lies in the techniques it uses to harness the capabilities of computer and telecommunications technology. Building **accurate and up-to-date profiles** of customers enables the company:

- to extend **help** to a company's target audience
- to **stimulate further demand**
- to **stay close** to them.

Keeping an electronic database of customers and prospects(and of all communications and commercial contacts) helps to improve all future contacts.

Marketing at Work

The explosion in personal text message usage has led to mutterings and ripples of excitement amongst researchers because of the new opportunities it represents. The growth in texting has been dramatic, reaching near saturation in some segments: 80% of 18-24 year olds use mobile phones, added to this, over 90% of this group use text messaging.

What started as a personal consumer-to-consumer pursuit, is increasingly moving towards a range of business-to-consumer activity. One rapidly emerging area is text-based advertising, whereby third parties communicate with their target market.

To achieve this, companies need to build large databases of mobile phone owning individuals, which ideally contain detailed profiling information to allow them to target their offerings precisely.

Research, 1 February 2002

4.1 Customer intelligence – why is it so important?

For years the rhetoric of marketing has been that of **warfare**: targets, campaigns, offensives. The approach has been one of trying to beat the 'enemy' into submission and 'win' new customers. Many organisations now realise that there is more to be gained from **alternative strategies**.

(a) Investing in activities which seek to **retain existing customers**, based on the argument that it costs more to attract new customers

(b) Encouraging existing customers to **spend more**

Retaining customers is the basis of such relationship marketing techniques. Customers are seen not only in terms of what they are buying today, but also in terms of their **potential for future purchases**.

Although it is clear that **added services** and **quality of service** are the key to retaining customers, this still begs questions: precisely what services to add, for instance?

Marketing at Work

In the red corner is Air Miles, the established brand with the support of the national flag-carrier (and its owner) British Airways and the UK's biggest retailer, Tesco. Other collection partners include Shell and NatWest, and it has around six million active members.

In the blue corner is Nectar, with the USP of being the first card-based multi-collector scheme in the UK and with rewards partners including McDonald's, Odeon Cinemas, Virgin Atlantic, Debenhams, Thresher and many others. It is the UK's largest rewards programme.

'Both Air Miles and Nectar have their merits, of course, but in actual fact their emphasis is subtly different, says the managing director of one consultancy which specialises in company loyalty schemes. 'Where Air Miles focuses on flights, Nectar sees everyday rewards as a more effective incentive to build consumer enthusiasm.'

Adapted from *Marketing Direct,* October 2002
(*www.nectar.com*)

To be effective at **retention marketing**, the organisation has to have a good database **profiling past, present and prospective customers**, with details of the nature of the relationship; it has to know about their attitudes, their perceptions of the organisation's products and service, and their expectations. Just as importantly, the organisation must know, from systematically-acquired **customer feedback**, precisely what it is doing wrong.

A well-developed customer database will use **postcodes** to overlay specialist **geodemographic data** from **ACORN** (see below) or other sources , or include **lifestyle information** allowing rich customer profiles to be developed.

Marketing at Work

CACI (www.caci.co.uk) is a company which provides market analysis, information systems and other data products to clients. It advertises itself as 'the winning combination of marketing and technology'.

As an illustration of the information available to the marketing manager for incorporation into corporate databases, here is an overview of some of their products.

Paycheck	This provides data about income levels for all the millions of individual post codes across the UK. This enables companies to see how mean income distribution varies from area to area.
People UK	This is a mix of geodemographics, life stage and lifestyle data. It is person rather than household specific and is designed for those companies requiring highly targeted campaigns.
eTypes	eTypes is a tool for understanding online consumer behaviour. It can tell organisations who their online customers are, and what they use the internet for – whether it's finding holidays, buying CDs, managing their stocks & shares or just chatting.
ACORN	This stands for A Classification of Residential Neighbourhoods, and has been used to profile residential neighbourhoods by post code since 1976. ACORN classifies people in any trading area or on any customer database into more than 50 different types.
Lifestyles UK	This database offers over 300 lifestyle selections on 44 million consumers in the UK. It helps with cross selling and customer retention strategies.

Monica	This can help a company to identify the age of people on its database by giving the likely age profile of their first names. It uses a combination of census data and real birth registrations.

4.2 Customer segmentation

Organisations with a large customer base, a wide range of products, a global market, and several discrete product/brand names may be tempted to treat customers as if they were all alike, all wanting much the same things, all applying similar criteria when judging the product, the service, or the organisation as a whole.

In practice, this is bound to be a misleading assumption. Customer A may want reliability of delivery on an hourly basis; Customer B may want an unusual range of financial options; Customer C may want the highest possible standards of after-sales support; Customer D is only interested in one product.

Research shows that there are differences in customers' expectations which can be exploited, if they are identified and recorded, by offering levels of service which match the needs of particular sectors, possibly withdrawing from some or increasing prices/charges to an economically-justified level.

Marketing at Work

Who wouldn't want loyal customers? Surely they should cost less to serve, they'd be willing to pay more than other customers, and they'd actively market your company by word of mouth, right? Maybe not.

Careful study of the relationship between customer loyalty and profits plumbed from 16,000 customers in four companies' databases tells a different story, with no evidence to support any of these claims. It was found that the link between customers and profitability was more complicated because customers fall into four groups, not two.

Not all loyal customers are profitable, and not all profitable customers are loyal. Traditional tools for segmenting customers do a poor job of identifying that latter group, causing companies to chase expensively after initially profitable customers who hold little promise of future profits.

The challenge in managing customers who are profitable but disloyal – the 'butterflies' – is to milk them for as much as you can while they're buying from you. A softly-softly approach is more appropriate for the profitable customers who are likely to stay loyal – your 'true friends.' As for highly loyal but not very profitable customers – the 'barnacles' – you need to find out whether they have the potential to spend more than they currently do.

And, of course, for the 'strangers' – those who generate no loyalty and no profits – the answer is simple: Identify early and don't invest anything.

5 Data warehousing and data mining

FAST FORWARD

Data warehousing involves extracting information from disparate organisational sources to build a coherent set of information available to be used across the organisation for management analysis and decision making. On-line analytical processing (OLAP) techniques allow the data to be viewed from many different perspectives.

Two techniques designed to utilise the **ever-increasing amounts of data** held by organisations are data warehousing and data mining.

5.1 Data warehousing

Key concept

Data warehousing involves a centrally stored source of data that has been extracted from various organisational databases and standardised and integrated for use throughout an organisation. Data warehouses contain a wide variety of data that present a coherent picture of business conditions at a single point in time.

A data warehouse contains data from a range of internal (eg sales order processing system, nominal ledger) and external sources. If necessary, the user can drill-down to access transaction level detail. Data is increasingly obtained from newer channels such as customer care systems, outside agencies or websites.

Components of a data warehouse

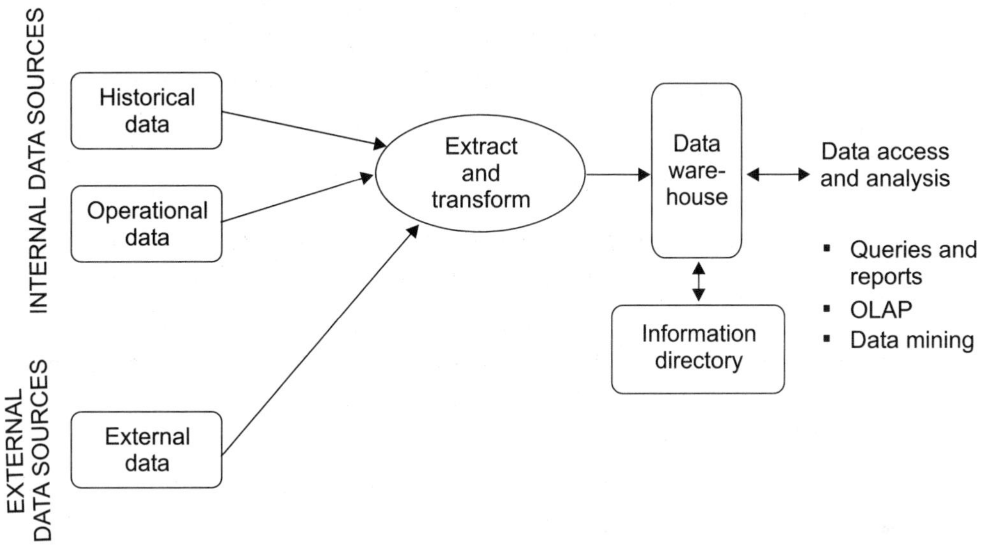

Data is copied to the data warehouse as often as required – usually either daily, weekly or monthly. The process of making any required changes to the format of data and copying it to the warehouse is usually automated.

The result should be a coherent set of information available to be used across the organisation for management analysis and decision making. The reporting and query tools available within the warehouse should facilitate management reporting and analysis.

The reporting and query tools should be flexible enough to allow multidimensional data analysis, also known as on-line analytical processing (**OLAP**). Each aspect of information (eg product, region, price, budgeted sales, actual sales, time period etc) represents a different dimension. OLAP enables data to be viewed from each dimension, allowing each aspect to be viewed and in relation to the other aspects.

5.1.1 Data marts

Organisations may build a single central data warehouse to serve the entire organisation or may create a series of smaller **data marts**. A data mart holds a selection of the organisation's data for a specific purpose.

A data mart can be constructed more quickly and cheaply than a data warehouse. However, if too many individual data marts are built, organisations may find it is more efficient to have a single data warehouse serving all areas.

5.1.2 Advantages of data warehouses and data marts

Advantages of setting up a data warehouse or data mart include the following.

(a) Decision makers can access data without affecting the use of operational systems.

(b) Having a wide range of data available to be queried easily encourages the taking of a wide perspective on organisational activities.

(c) Data warehouses have proved successful in some businesses for:

- Quantifying the effect of marketing initiatives
- Improving knowledge of customers
- Identifying and understanding an enterprise's most profitable revenues streams

Some organisations have found they have invested considerable resources implementing a data warehouse for little return. To benefit from the information a data warehouse can provide, organisations need to be flexible and prepared to act on what they find. If a warehouse system is implemented simply to follow current practice it will be of little value.

5.2 Data mining

FAST FORWARD

Data mining software examines the data in a database or data warehouse and discovers previously unknown relationships using complex statistical techniques. The hidden patterns and relationships the software identifies can be used to guide decision making and to predict future behaviour.

Key concept

Data mining is a class of database applications that look for hidden patterns in a group of data. For example, data mining software can help retail companies find customers with common interests. The term is commonly misused to describe software that presents data in new ways. True data mining software does not just change the presentation, but actually discovers previously unknown relationships among the data. This can be used to guide decision making and to **predict future behaviour**.

Marketing at Work

(1) The American retailer Wal-Mart discovered an unexpected relationship between the sale of nappies and beer! Wal-Mart found that both tended to sell at the same time, just after working hours, and concluded that men with small children stopped off to buy nappies on their way home, and bought beer at the same time. Logically therefore, if the two items were put in the same shopping aisle, sales of both should increase. Wal-Mart tried this and it worked.

(2) Some credit card companies have used data mining to predict which customers are likely to switch to a competitor in the next few months. Based on the data mining results, the bank can take action to retain these customers.

The types of relationships or patterns that data mining may uncover may be classified as follows.

Relationship\Discovery	Comment
Classification or cluster	These terms refer to the identification of patterns within the database between a range of data items. For example, data mining may find that unmarried males aged between 20 and 30, who have an income above £50,000 are more likely to purchase a high performance sports car than people from other demographic groups. This group could then be targeted when marketing material is produced/distributed.
Association	One event can be linked or correlated to another event – such as in the Wal-Mart example above.
Forecasting	Trends are identified within the data that can be extrapolated into the future.

Action Programme 6

Why might competitive pressures encourage data mining?

Most data mining models are either:

(a) **Predictive**: using known observations to predict future events (for example, predicting the probability that a recipient will opt out of an e-mail list)

(b) **Descriptive**: interrogating the database to identify patterns and relationships (for example, profiling the audience of a particular advertising campaign)

Some of the key statistical techniques used in data mining are described below.

(a) **Neural networks**: non-linear predictive models or formulas that adjust inputs and weightings through 'training'

(b) **Decision-trees**: paths are followed towards a solution or result, branching at decision points which are governed by rules (is gender male? Yes/No) giving a complex picture of possible outcomes

(c) **Classification techniques**: assigning people to predetermined classes based on their profile data (in complex combinations)

(d) **Clustering**: identifying occurrences in the database with similar characteristics and grouping them into clusters

Marketing at Work

Data mining software

The following is extracted from marketing material for a Data mining product called the NeoVista Decision Series.

Understand The Patterns In Your Business and Discover The Value In Your Data

Within your corporate database resides extremely valuable information – information that reflects how your business processes operate and how your customers behave. Every transaction your organisation makes is captured for accounting purposes, and with it, a wealth of potential knowledge.

When properly analysed, organised and presented, this information can be of enormous value. Conventional 'drill down' database query techniques may reveal some of these details, but much of the valuable **knowledge content will remain hidden**.

The NeoVista Decision Series is a suite of knowledge discovery software specifically designed to address this challenge. Analysing data without any preconceived notion of the patterns it contains, the Decision Series **seeks out relationships and trends**, and presents them in easy-to-understand form, enabling better business decisions.

The Decision Series is being used today by leading corporations to discover the hidden value in their data, providing them with major competitive advantages and organisational benefits.

- A Large Multi-National Retailer uses the Decision Series to **refine inventory stocking levels**, by store and by item, to dramatically reduce out-of-stock or overstocking situations and thereby improve revenues and reduce forced markdowns.
- A Health Maintenance Group uses the Decision Series to **predict which of its members are most at risk** from specific major illnesses. This presents opportunities for timely medical intervention and preventative treatment to promote the patient's well-being and reduce the healthcare provider's costs.
- An International Retail Sales Organisation uses the Decision Series to **optimise store and department layouts**, resulting in more accurate targeting of products to maximise sales within the scope of available resources.

NeoVista's unique software can be applied to a wide range of business problems, allowing you to:

- Determine the **relationships** that lie at the heart of your business.
- Make reliable **estimates of future behaviour** based on sophisticated analyses of past events.
- Make business **decisions** with a higher degree of understanding and confidence.

Data mining is renowned for exposing important facts and anomalies within data warehouses. The NeoVista Decision Series' knowledge discovery methodology has the proven ability to expose the patterns that are not merely interesting, but which are critical to your business. These patterns provide you with an advantage through insight and knowledge that your competition may never discover.

6 Database marketing and marketing research

Pilot Paper, 12/03, 12/04, 12/05, 6/06, 6/07

FAST FORWARD

Marketing managers must make a **distinction** between **information collected** in the **ordinary course of business** and **information collected via marketing research**. It is not acceptable to incorporate personal information derived from marketing research directly into a customer's record.

As we shall see in the next chapter when we discuss ethical and social responsibilities and codes of conduct, information collected by means of **marketing research** should **not be used** subsequently to create marketing databases that are used for **direct marketing**. Likewise direct marketing initiatives should not be disguised as marketing research, and customers should be given the opportunity to refuse to allow information they give you to be used for direct marketing purposes.

As a slightly frivolous example, let's say you discover, through the responses of willing participants in a **marketing research** study, that 87% of people who are over a certain weight prefer your company's Product A to Product B. That is probably useful information and it may legitimately be used for **general marketing purposes** such as designing advertising messages or choosing distribution outlets.

However, even though you may know that a particular customer of yours (who took part in the research) is not yet a purchaser of Product A, and you now know that he fits the weight criteria, it is considered **unethical** to add that specific data (the customer's weight) to that specific customer's record, and less ethical still to bombard him with brochures about Product A as a result of information that was not given to you with that purpose in mind.

It is only acceptable to enrich a customer database with marketing research information so long as **personal data** is represented in an **anonymous** form and is **partly aggregated**.

Exam tip

Pause for a moment and re-read the above if necessary to make sure you understand it. This distinction comes up regularly, so be careful about the solutions you propose. It is very tempting to use all the information you have, from any source, but you must respect the rights and the privacy of individuals.

Chapter Roundup

- **Customer databases** can contain a wide variety of information about the customer such as **contact details**, **transaction history**, **personal details** and **preferences** and so on. Information may come from a variety of sources besides transaction processing systems, including specialist geodemographic data and lifestyle information.
- Databases provide valuable **information** to assist with many marketing management tasks and decisions and can play a key part in **customer relationship management** because they permit **mass customisation**.
- Modern business databases are maintained on a central computer to enable **sharing of data** and avoid duplication. A typical relational database consists of a number of inter-related tables of records and fields.
- A key issue in setting up a database is **data cleansing**: ensuring that the information is correct, up-to-date, not duplicated and so on. Much can be done at the data entry stage, but where data is imported from other systems a good deal of preparatory work may be needed to ensure that it is in the correct format.
- The range of database applications include: focusing on **prime prospects**; evaluating **new prospects**; **cross-selling** related products; **launching new products** to potential prospects; identifying **new distribution channels**; building **customer loyalty**; **converting occasional users to regular users**; generating **enquiries** and **follow-up sales**; **targeting niche markets**.
- Building **accurate** and **up-to-date profiles** of customers enables the company to **extend help** to a company's **target audience**, to stimulate further demand, and to stay close to them. The company's own information can be enriched by collating it with geodemographic and lifestyle information from sources such as ACORN.
- **Data warehousing** involves extracting information from disparate organisational sources to build a coherent set of information available to be used across the organisation for management analysis and decision making. On-line analytical processing (OLAP) techniques allow the data to be viewed from many different perspectives.
- **Data mining software** examines the data in a database or data warehouse and discovers previously unknown relationships using complex statistical techniques. The hidden patterns and relationships the software identifies can be used to guide decision making and to predict future behaviour.
- Marketing managers must make a **distinction** between **information collected** in the **ordinary course of business** and **information collected via marketing research**. It is not acceptable to incorporate personal information derived from marketing research directly into a customer's record.

Quick Quiz

1 Draw a diagram indicating the sources of information in a customer databases and the possible uses to which it can be put.

2 List five ways in which a database can help to improve a marketing manager's decision making.

3 A database is key to customer relationship management because it facilitates:
M.................... C......................... Fill in the gaps.

4 Which of the following is true?

A A relational database is one that includes information about the customer's family
B 'Unclean' data is the fault of incompetent data entry staff
C Deduplication can usually be done automatically
D Computers are fast because they ignore things like spaces and punctuation in data

5 Give four examples of validation tests.

6 What kind of buying trends might be identified by an analysis of database information?

7 Give examples of the types of (externally-produced) profiling data that may enrich an organisation's customer database.

8 Data warehousing helps to avoid the problems caused by bad data entry. True or false? Explain your answer.

9 Data mining helps to uncover certain types of relationships summarised by the acronym CAF. What does CAF stand for?

10 Following a marketing research study your manager asks you to identify those respondents who are customers in your database and amend their profiles if they do not fit the standard ACORN profile for their post code. How should you respond?

Answers to Quick Quiz

1

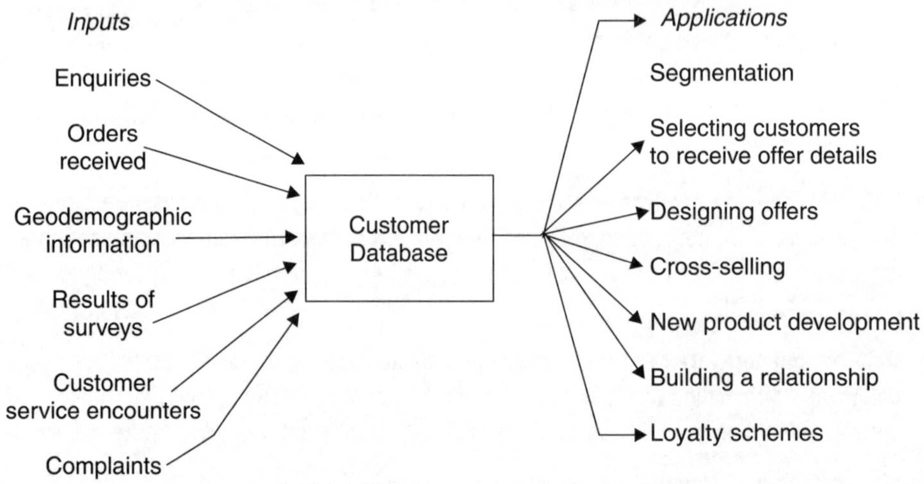

2 Here are the suggestions from earlier in the Text.

- Understanding customers and their preferences
- Managing customer service (helplines, complaints)
- Understanding the market (new products, channels etc)
- Understanding competitors (market share, prices)

- Managing sales operations
- Managing marketing campaigns
- Communicating with customers

3 Mass Customisation

4 C. Options A and D are quite untrue and option B is only one of many reasons.

5 Format checks
Range checks
Existence checks
Completeness checks

6
- Loyal repeat customers
- Backsliding customers
- Seasonal or local purchase patterns
- Demographic purchase patterns
- Purchase patterns in response to promotional campaigns

7 Examples include data about income levels, life stage and lifestyle data, age profiles, Internet browsing habits.

8 False. Data is not entered directly into a data warehouse, it is imported from other 'live' organisational sources as and when required.

9 Classification/Cluster, Association, Forecasting

10 You should point out to your manager that to do what he asks is considered unethical because the respondents did not give their information to the researchers for this purpose. It may be possible to make some changes in the database if you are very careful about aggregating personal data and keeping it anonymous.

Action Programme Review

1 You need to do this hands on.

2 Records are stored as rows as a convention, but it is much more practical than storing them in columns, because it is much easier (for humans) to **scroll down** through a list than to scroll **across** many columns.

3 EPOS and EFTPOS data is more likely to be reliable than many other sources of data and it is typically updated whenever a new transaction occurs. It could nevertheless be recorded in inconsistent formats, and the same customer could easily appear twice under two different card codes.

4 Again, you need to do this hands on.

5 Overkill is best avoided by organisations that are susceptible to fraud such as banks and credit card companies.

6 Data mining allows data to be used more productively through increased targeting and personalisation of the marketing mix. This assists with customer retention, which is crucially important in a highly competitive market.

Now try Questions 4 and 5 at the end of the Study Text

Part C
Marketing research in context

Marketing research in context

4

Chapter topic list

Syllabus content – knowledge and skill requirements

- 3.1: Nature and structure of the market research industry
- 3.2: Stages of the market research process
- 3.3: Procedures for selecting a market research supplier
- 3.6: Ethical and social responsibilities inherent in the market research task

Introduction

The remainder of this book is more or less focused on **marketing research**. We refer to 'market research' in some of the section headings in this chapter, but that is just because the syllabus does this.

In this chapter we are taking a high level view, looking at the **overall process** and the **key players** in the marketing research market. Most organisations will employ an agency to carry out research because it is too expensive to maintain an in-house department, but the marketing department will still need someone familiar with marketing research to liaise with the agency or agencies that are actually doing the research.

We'll be looking at the matters that an organisation will take into account when **selecting an agency** to carry out its research.

Last, but by no means least there is the very important matter of the **responsibilities** that a researcher has towards respondents (which is likely to be governed by **data protection** legislation) and towards clients. Many of the issues are anticipated in the ICC/ESOMAR **code of conduct** for professional market researchers: the rules are reproduced in full at the end of the chapter. These issues have a bearing on the previous chapter, too, especially with regard to maintaining the **distinction** between **marketing research** and **direct marketing**.

1 The stages of the market research process

FAST FORWARD

Although you will see variations there is general agreement that the marketing research process involves the following stages:

- **Definition**: identify and define the opportunity or threat
- **Objectives**: determine precisely what you need to know to deal with the opportunity or threat
- **Design** the research and the methods to be used (exploratory, descriptive, causal)
- **Collect** the data
- **Analyse** the data
- **Report** on the findings

If you read other books on marketing research you will find many slight variations on the suggested 'stages' of the market research process, partly depending on whether the book is written from the point of view of a client or a market research agency. There is fairly general agreement, however, that the process will entail the following stages, in this order (the process spells **DODCAR**, if you like mnemonics!).

Stage 1. **Definition**: identify and define the **opportunity or threat**

Stage 2. **Objectives**: determine precisely what you need to know to deal with the opportunity or threat

Stage 3. **Design** the research and the methods to be used

Stage 4. **Collect** the data

Stage 5. **Analyse** the data

Stage 6. **Report** on the findings

Where an organisation is using an agency or agencies to do the research it will send out a **research brief** at the end of Stage 2 and the various agencies that are asked to tender for the work will then submit **research proposals** (in outline, at least) covering Stage 3, explaining how they would do the work and why they should be chosen. Research proposals are discussed at more length in the next chapter.

The organisation will **select its preferred supplier(s)** based on the content and quality of their proposals (and on other factors such as cost, of course) and then Stage 3 will be done in detail.

1.1 Stage 1: Identify and define the opportunity or threat

We've phrased this so that it reminds you of SWOT analysis, since the identification of a need for market research will usually arise from strategic and marketing planning processes and reviews.

(a) An **opportunity** is something that occurs in the organisation's environment that could be advantageous – a **change in the law**, say, or a **new technology** that could be exploited

(b) A **threat** is an environmental development that could create problems and stop the organisation achieving its objectives – a **new competitor**, perhaps, or an adverse change in **buying behaviour**.

In either case the organisation will **want to know more**. How can it best take advantage? What action is most likely to stave off or reverse the problem? The answers will depend on **how the market reacts** to different possible solutions, and the organisation can be much more sure about this if it conducts **research**.

Bear in mind that marketing research, however well organised, is not a substitute for decision making. It can help to reduce the risks, but it will not make the decision. Professional marketing depends partially on sound judgement and reliable information, but it also needs flair and creativity.

1.2 Stage 2: Determine the objectives of the research

The objectives should set out the precise information needed, as clearly as possible: it is very wasteful of time and money to collect answers to questions that did not need to be asked. The objectives should relate only to the problem or opportunity.

Marketing research can sometimes be a waste of effort and resources.

(a) The research undertaken may be designed without reference to the decisions that will depend on, or be strongly influenced by, the results of the research.

(b) The research results may be ignored, misused, misunderstood, or misinterpreted. Sometimes this happens accidentally; more often it is deliberate because the results do not fit in with established beliefs.

(c) The research is poorly designed or carried out.

(d) The results of the research are themselves inconclusive, giving rise to different opinions about what the research signifies.

With issues like this in mind Wilson (2002) suggests **early consultation and involvement** of all the parties that will be involved in putting into action the decisions taken as a result of the proposed research, for example by setting up a project team. This has the advantage that those closest to the project will probably have the best idea of what **knowledge** the organisation **already possesses**, and does not need to be researched. It also means that the questions that **need** to be answered are more likely to get asked.

Action Programme 1

Your company manufactures cruelty-free bath products for a number of supermarket chains. You have been given responsibility for finding out about the market for a new line of cruelty-free cosmetics. List the likely research objectives.

Other matters that would be considered at this stage would be the available **budget** and the **timescale** for the work, and perhaps there would be outline thoughts about the **methods** to be used (for instance the scale of the research and the segments of the market to be included). All of this information, together with the requirements for the final **report**, would be included in the **research brief** (see the next chapter) if the work was now to be put out to tender.

1.3 Stage 3: Design the research and the methods to be used

The **category** of research must first be decided upon: the methods used will depend on that. Research may be **exploratory, descriptive** or **causal**.

1.3.1 Exploratory research

As the name suggests, **exploratory** research tends to **break new ground**. For instance if your organisation has a **completely new idea** for a product or service which consumers have never been offered before then exploratory research will be most appropriate in the first instance.

(a) Potential consumers may be totally uninterested, in which case exploratory research will quickly show that it is best to **abandon the idea** before any more money is spent on developing it.

(b) Consumers **may not understand** how the offer could benefit them, in which case exploratory research would show that it may be worth simplifying the product and introducing it to them in a different way, with different promotional techniques and messages.

(c) Consumers may not have responded because the **research methods used** were not appropriate, or because the wrong consumer group was chosen: exploratory research can help to define how more detailed research should be carried out.

Exploratory research may therefore be a **preliminary** to more detailed development of marketing ideas or a more detailed research project. It may even lead to abandonment of a product idea.

Research **methods** should involve as **little cost** and take as **little time** as possible. If use can be made of **existing research** by others then that is certainly desirable, as are methods that are not too labour and cost intensive such as **telephone** research or limited **Internet surveys**. (Research methods are covered in depth in Part D of this book.)

1.3.2 Descriptive research

Descriptive research aims to describe what is happening now (a single snapshot) or what has happened over a limited period of time (several snapshots).

(a) Now (a **'cross-sectional study'**): 'At present 45% of the target market are aware of our product whereas 95% are aware of Competitor A's product'.

(b) Over time (a **'longitudinal study'**): 'During the period of the in-store promotion (February to April) awareness of our product rose from 45% to 73%'.

In other words descriptive research is useful for answering 'where are we now?' questions, and it can also be used to summarise how things have changed over a period in time. Published market research reports are examples of descriptive research: if you subscribe today you will find out 'where you were' when the report was last published, and if you wait a while for the next edition you will find out how you have progressed.

The main problem (for researchers) with longitudinal descriptive research is to ensure that their respondents are either the same people each time or, if that is not possible, that answers from very similar respondents are aggregated. Research **methods** are likely to include **telephone** research, with the consumer's agreement, and specially invited **panels** of respondents.

1.3.3 Causal research

Although descriptive research is very common and is much used it may not really tell us the **cause** of the event or behaviour it describes. To paraphrase Wilson, virtually all marketing research projects fall somewhere along a continuum between purely **descriptive** and purely **causal**.

For example, the descriptive result 'During the period of the in-store promotion (February to April) awareness of our product rose from 45% to 73%' appears to suggest a reason for the change, but the only thing we know for certain is that two to three months have gone by. The change may be little or nothing to do with the in-store promotion. It may be due to a completely random factor such as temporary unavailability of a competitor's product, or uncontrolled and unmeasured actions taken by in-store staff, or to other promotional efforts such as TV ads.

The relationship between variables like this is not formally taken into account in descriptive research. **Causal** research attempts to identify and establish the relationship between all the variables, and determine whether one variable influences the value of others. **Experimental** research can be carried out, where one variable is deliberately changed to see the effect if any on other variables. The most obvious example is to see if lowering the price causes sales to rise.

Research **methods** might be similar to those for longitudinal descriptive research (panels of consumers for instance), but the information they are asked to provide will be more extensive and the time span may be longer. Research methods are covered in detail in Part D of this Text. In particular the researcher will need to consider the **sampling** method and parameters (how many people and of what type), where the people can be found, and the means of obtaining information (**interviews**, **questionnaires** etc).

1.4 Stage 4: Collect the data

Data can be collected from either primary or secondary data sources. We will look at data collection in much more detail in Part D.

(a) **Secondary data** is data collected for another purpose not specifically related to the proposed research, for instance all the **internal** information in the company's marketing information systems and databases, or information such as **published research** reports, **government** information, **newspapers** and trade journals.

(b) **Primary data** is information **collected specifically for the study** under consideration. Primary data may be **quantitative** (statistics), **qualitative** (attitudes etc) or **observational** videos of people browsing in a store, for instance).

1.5 Stage 5: Analyse the data

This stage will involve getting the data into analysable form by entering it into a computer and using statistics (for quantitative data) and other means of analysis and summary (qualitative data) to find out what it reveals.

1.6 Stage 6: Report on the findings

The final report is likely to take the form of a PowerPoint type **presentation** given to an audience of interested parties and a detailed **written report** explaining and summarising the findings, with appendices of figures and tables. Analysing and reporting data is covered in Part E of this book.

2 The nature and structure of the market research industry

FAST FORWARD

Some larger organisations have their own marketing research (or 'customer insight') departments, but for most this would be too expensive.

2.1 Internal marketing research departments

Most organisations will have somebody who is responsible for marketing research, even if that simply means liaising with external agencies who actually carry out the work.

Larger organisations that have a regular need for marketing research information (particularly FMCG organisations) are likely to set up their own **marketing research department**.

Marketing at Work

Catalyst, the left-wing think tank, has established its own pool of freelance research assistants, reflecting the growing number of policy areas that it covers (such as housing, transport and regional policy). This will enable it to start work on projects when they arrive at short notice, assisting it with its purpose of promoting 'policies for the redistribution of wealth, power and opportunity'.

(*www.research-live.com* (accessed 11 February 2004))

2.2 Specialist agencies

FAST FORWARD

Agencies include **specialist agencies** of various kinds (field agencies, data analysis agencies and so on), syndicated research agencies, list brokers, profilers, full service agencies and independent consultants.

As the name implies a specialist agency specialises in a particular type of work.

(a) Some agencies specialise in particular **markets** or market **sectors** or **regions**

(b) Others specialise in a particular **research services** such as questionnaire design, or collection and analysis of qualitative information.

(c) **Field agencies** have specialised skills in **conducting** personal or telephone interviews and **administering** postal or e-mail surveys.

(d) **Data analysis agencies** can be employed to code up, read in or input data collected (in questionnaires, say, or perhaps recorded in personal interviews) and analyse it using state-of-the-art hardware (for instance highly accurate scanners) and software (for instance highly specialised statistical packages).

(e) There are numerous **independent consultants** who will undertake a variety of tasks, usually on a **smaller scale**. Such people are typically ex-employees of larger research organisations or have gained their expertise in related disciplines such as IT or librarianship.

2.3 Syndicated research agencies

A syndicated service is one that is **not conducted for any specific client**. Regular research is conducted into areas that the agency knows for certain many organisations will be interested in (for instance newspaper and magazine readership) and is then sold to anyone willing to pay the price.

Marketing at Work

Well-known examples of syndicated research agencies include **Datamonitor** (with products like MarketWatch: Drinks and MarketWatch: Food), and **Mintel** (www.mintel.co.uk) which has a huge number of regularly updated reports available on a subscription basis (eg *Agricultural Machinery*, *Nail Color and Care*, *Disposable Nappies and Baby Wipes*, and hundreds of others). See *http:reportsmintel.com*

2.4 List brokers

A list broker **creates or acquires lists** of potential consumers **for the purpose of selling them on** to companies who are interested. Lists may be created from publicly available sources like the telephone book, yellow pages or the electoral roll but they will usually be **organised** for convenience, presented in **formats** that can be easily incorporated into client systems, and **checked** for accuracy and up-to-date-ness. The client could possibly do this in-house, but it would be very **time-consuming**. 'Names' are typically sold by the thousand at 10p to 20p each – it would almost certainly be more **expensive** for the client to find and record the information without help.

Lists that have arisen as a result of some other exercise such as responses to mailshots or entry into a 'free' draw may also be **acquired** by list brokers. You have probably noticed that you are often asked whether you object to your details being given to **third parties** when you enter into correspondence with an organisation, or even just register on a website. Now you know that those third parties are likely to be list brokers!

2.5 Profilers

We encountered the best-known UK profiler, CACI (www.caci.co.uk) with products like ACORN, in the previous chapter. A profiler is able to take an organisation's database and **superimpose profiling information** (demographics, lifestyle and life stage information) on the basis of post codes. This allows the organisation's database to be segmented according to the criteria that are most appropriate to that organisation.

A profiler may also have access to other lists and be able to offer these to its clients, much like a list broker, except that the profiler has closer knowledge of the characteristics of the clients' existing customers and so the list may have more appropriate prospects.

2.6 Full service agencies

As the name implies a full service agency **offers all of the above services** and so will be able to conduct a research project from start to finish. Well-known international examples are **BMRB** (www.bmrb.co.uk), **Taylor Nelson Sofres** (www.tns-global.com) and **Ipsos** (www.ipsos.com).

In addition many full service **adverting agencies** offer marketing research services, as do firms of **management consultants** like McKinsey (www.mckinsey.com).

Marketing at Work

This is an extract from the Ipsos website (*www.ipsos.com* – accessed 6 February 2004).

Research rooted in reality

'Welcome to Ipsos .... We explore, probe and challenge conventional wisdom. We assess market potential and interpret market trends. We test products and trends, and help our clients build long-term relationships with customers. We study audiences and their responses to various media. We measure public opinion around the globe.

We are an independent company whose sole focus is survey-based market research.'

Action Programme 2

An excellent way to get a flavour of the marketing research industry is to visit the websites mentioned above and click on 'Services' (or 'Solutions', or whatever) to see the range of work carried out by different types of organisation. Don't restrict your web survey to large multinational companies. See if you can find links to the websites of smaller organisations in your own country (try a directory such as *www.imriresearch.com.*)

2.7 Professional bodies

FAST FORWARD

The main professional bodies are the **Marketing Research Society** and **ESOMAR**.

Apart from the CIM, many of whose members are involved in marketing research in some capacity, most countries have an association of some sort for market researchers. The largest is the **Market Research Society** (www.marketresearch.org.uk) based in the UK, but with international membership.

Likewise the **World Association of Opinion and Marketing Research Professionals** (**ESOMAR**: the 'E' originally stood for European) (www.esomar.org) has members all over the world. MRS works closely with the ESOMAR in some respects: for instance later in this chapter we will look at the joint ESOMAR Code of Practice for research workers, to which the MRS subscribes.

3 Selecting a market research supplier **Pilot Paper**

FAST FORWARD

Selecting an agency will involve considerations such as the agency's **previous experience** and **expertise** in the area of research, and the **geographical area** to be covered.

Very few organisations can shoulder the cost of a large full-time staff of marketing research workers, especially a 'field force' of researchers spread around the country, or around every country in which the organisation does business.

3.1 Choosing and using consultants

Choosing the right agency or consultant to work with is a key element in a successful working relationship. The external expert must become a trusted part of the team.

It is equally important that the market researcher has the specialist knowledge and research service capabilities needed by the organisation. In the UK you would expect a research organisation to be associated to the professional body, the Market Research Society, and for those working on the account to have relevant qualifications.

It helps if the agency has some knowledge of the market or business in which the company operates. Therefore, it may be worthwhile to develop a long-standing relationship with the research organisation, because their understanding of the company's business and the marketplace will develop over time.

3.2 External agencies versus in-house programmes

There are a number of advantages and disadvantages to each alternative.

(a) **Using an external agency**

(i) **Advantages**

(1) External agencies **specialising** in research will have the necessary expertise in marketing research techniques. This should allow them to develop a cost-effective research programme to a **tighter timescale**.

(2) Skills in **monitoring and interpreting data** will allow the programme to be reviewed and modified as required.

(3) Nationwide or global agencies will be able to offer much **broader geographical coverage**.

(4) An external agency can provide an **objective input** without the bias which often results from a dependence on internal resources.

(5) **Costs** can be determined from the outset, allowing better **budgetary control**.

(6) When conducting **confidential research** into sensitive area, there is less risk of information being 'leaked' to competitors.

(ii) **Disadvantage**

Agency knowledge of the industry will be limited: a serious drawback if the agency needs a disproportionate amount of time to familiarise itself with the sector.

(b) **In-house programme**

(i) **Advantages**

(1) **Costs can be absorbed** into existing departmental overheads.
(2) It can **broaden the experience** and skills of existing staff.
(3) It might promote a **team spirit** and encourage a 'results-oriented' approach.

(ii) **Disadvantages**

(1) There is a danger of **overstretching current resources** and adversely affecting other projects.

(2) There is a risk of developing an **inappropriate programme**, yielding insufficient or poor quality data with inadequate analysis and control.

(3) If additional **training or recruitment** is required this could prove expensive and time consuming.

(4) **Bias** could result from using staff with pre-conceived views.

(5) **Company politics** may influence the results.

(6) Considerable **computing resources** with appropriate software packages would be required to analyse the data.

(7) There may be a lack of **appropriate facilities**. For example, focus group research is often conducted off premises during evenings or weekends.

In view of the shortcomings of a purely in-house or external agency approach, a **combination** of the two might be more appropriate. For example, it might be deemed preferable to design the programme in-house but contract out certain aspects.

3.3 Tenders and beauty parades

The selection process will generally involve the organisation sending out its research brief to a number of agencies and inviting each to submit a research proposal (see the next chapter). It is common for the agencies to give an oral presentation of their case: this part of the procedure is known as a 'beauty parade'.

4 Ethical and social responsibilities 12/04

Marketing research aims to collect data about people. It could not take place at all if people were not willing to provide data, and that means that it is as much in the interests of the marketing research industry as it is of respondents for researchers to behave responsibly with the information collected.

4.1 Data protection

FAST FORWARD

Marketing researchers depend on the trust of their respondents. Most developed countries have **specific legislation** to **protect the privacy of individuals**. In the UK there is the Data Protection Act 1998 which establishes eight data protection principles.

Most developed countries have specific legislation to protect the **privacy of individuals**. Many people feel unhappy about their personal details being retained by commercial organisations. Here are some of the concerns that people have.

(a) **Incorrect details** may be entered, causing anything from minor irritation to significant financial problems.

(b) A list or database may be **sold** to other organisations, who then try to sell various goods and services to the people on it.

(c) 'Personalised' mailings may be inappropriate – they might be generated for people who have died, for instance.

4.1.1 The Data Protection Act 1998

Data protection legislation was introduced in the UK in the early 1980s to try to prevent some of these abuses. The latest version is the **Data Protection Act 1998**.

The Act is concerned with **'personal data'**, which is information about **living, identifiable individuals**. This can be as little as a name and address: it need not be particularly sensitive information. If it is sensitive (explained later) then extra care is needed.

The Act gives individuals (**data subjects**) certain rights and it requires those who record and use personal information (**data controllers**) to be open about their use of that information and to follow 'sound and proper practices' (the Data Protection Principles).

4.1.2 The eight data protection principles

Data must be:

- Fairly and lawfully processed
- Processed for limited purposes
- Adequate, relevant and not excessive
- Accurate
- Not kept longer than necessary
- Processed in accordance with individual's rights
- Secure

- Not transferred to countries that do not have adequate data protection laws

If your organisation holds personal information about living individuals on computer or has such information processed on computer by others (for example, its accountants or auditors) your organisation probably needs to 'notify' under the Data Protection Act 1998.

'Notify' means that the organisation has to complete a form about the data it holds and how it is used and send it, with an annual registration fee, to the office of the Information Commissioner.

The Data Protection Act 1998 also covers some records held in **paper** form. These do not need to be notified to the Commissioner, but they should also be handled in accordance with the data protection principles. A set of **index cards** for a personnel system is a typical example of paper records that fall under the Data Protection Act 1998.

4.1.3 Fair processing for limited purposes

These two principles mean that when an organisation collects information from individuals it should be **honest and open** about why it wants the information and it should have a **legitimate reason** for processing the data. For instance organisations should explain:

- who they are
- what they intend to use the information for
- who, if anybody, they intend to give the personal data to.

4.1.4 Adequate, relevant and not excessive; accurate and no longer than necessary

Organisations should hold **neither too much nor too little** data about the individuals in their list. For instance, many companies collect date of birth or age range information from their customers, but in many cases all they actually need to know is that they are over eighteen.

Personal data should be **accurate and up-to-date** as far as possible. However, if an individual provides inaccurate information (for example lies about their age) the organisation would not normally be held to account for this.

There are only exceptional circumstances where personal data should be kept indefinitely. Data should be **removed when it is no longer required** for audit purposes or when a customer ceases to do business with you.

4.1.5 The rights of data subjects

Individuals have various rights including the following.

- The right to **be informed** of all the information held about them by an organisation
- The right to **prevent** the processing of their data for the purposes of direct marketing
- The right to **compensation** if they can show that they have been caused damage by any contravention of the Act
- The right to have any inaccurate data about them **removed** or corrected

Organisations have obligations if they receive a **written request** from an individual asking to see what data it holds about them, or to obtain a copy of it, or to be given an explanation of what it is used for, or who it is given to. The organisation must deal with the request promptly, and in any case within 40 days. The organisation is entitled, if it wishes, to ask for a fee of not more than £10 in which case the 40 days does not begin until this is received.

4.1.6 Security

Organisations should make sure that they provide **adequate security** for the data, taking into account the nature of the data, and the possible harm to the individual that could arise if the data is disclosed or lost.

(a) Measures to ensure that **access** to computer records **by staff** is authorised (for instance a system of passwords).

(b) Measures to control **access** to records by **people other than staff**. For instance care should be taken over the siting of computers to prevent casual callers to the organisation's premises being able to read personal data on screen. Also there should be procedures to verify the identity of callers (especially telephone callers) seeking information about an individual.

(c) Measures to prevent of the **accidental loss or theft** of personal data, for example backups and fire precautions.

4.1.7 Overseas transfers

If an organisation wishes to transfer personal data to a country **outside the European Economic Area (EEA)** it will either need to ensure there is adequate protection (e.g. a Data Protection Act) for the data in the receiving country, or obtain the consent of the individual.

All countries in the EEA already have suitable protection.

4.1.8 Sensitive data

The Act defines eight categories of sensitive personal data. If an organisation holds personal data falling into these categories it is likely that it will **need the explicit consent** of the individual concerned. It will also need to ensure that its security is adequate for the protection of sensitive data.

Here are the eight categories.

- The racial or ethnic origin of data subjects
- Their political opinions
- Their religious beliefs or other beliefs of a similar nature
- Whether they are a member of a trade union
- Their physical or mental health or condition
- Their sexual life
- The commission or alleged commission by them of any offence
- Any details of court proceedings or sentences against them

4.1.9 Enforcement

If an organisation is breaching the principles of the Act, the Commissioner has various powers to force it to comply, including issuing an enforcement notice, and the power to enter and search their premises, and examine equipment and documents. It is an offence to obstruct the Commissioner, and there are also fines and criminal penalties for holding data without being registered; for failing to comply with an enforcement notice; and for unauthorised disclosure of personal data.

4.2 Professional codes of practice

FAST FORWARD

The ICC/ESOMAR have issued a **code of practice** for marketing research professionals. Broadly, this covers The Rights of Respondents, The Professional Responsibilities of Researchers, and Mutual Rights and Responsibilities of Researchers and Clients.

In addition to adhering to legislation marketing researchers should act in the interests of the marketing research profession, and to help them do so a number of codes of practice have been developed by the various professional bodies. These do **not have legal status**, but breaches may result in **disciplinary action** by the professional body, including barring the transgressor from membership of the body.

The best known code is the ESOMAR code, the most important part of which is reproduced in full below with the permission of ESOMAR. The full document can be downloaded from the organisation's website: www.esomar.org.

Exam tip

The Pilot Paper focuses on 'the elements of the professional codes of marketing and social research practice that relate to the relationships between researchers and clients.'

4.3 ICC/ESOMAR code of marketing and social research practice

General	
B1	Marketing research must always be carried out objectively and in accordance with established scientific principles.
B2	Marketing research must always conform to the national and international legislation which applies in those countries involved in a given research project.
The Rights of Respondents	
B3	Respondents' co-operation in a marketing research project is entirely voluntary at all stages. They must not be misled when being asked for co-operation.
B4	Respondents' anonymity must be strictly preserved. If the respondent on request from the Researcher has given permission for data to be passed on in a form which allows that respondent to be identified personally: (a) the Respondent must first have been told to whom the information would be supplied and the purposes for which it will be used, and also (b) Researcher must ensure that the information will not be used for any non-research purpose and that the recipient of the information has agreed to conform to the requirements of the Code.
B5	The Researcher must take all reasonable precautions to ensure that Respondents are in no way directly harmed or adversely affected as a result of their participation in a marketing research project.
B6	The Researcher must take special care when interviewing children and young people. The informed consent of the parent or responsible adult must first be obtained for interviews with children.
B7	Respondents must be told (normally at the beginning of the interview) if observation techniques or recording equipment are used, except where these are used in a public place. If a respondent so wishes, the record or relevant section of it must be destroyed or deleted. Respondents' anonymity must not be infringed by the use of such methods.
B8	Respondents must be enabled to check without difficulty the identity and bona fides of the Researcher.
The Professional Responsibilities of Researchers	
B9	Researchers must not, whether knowingly or negligently, act in any way which could bring discredit on the marketing research profession or lead to a loss of public confidence in it.
B10	Researchers must not make false claims about their skills and experience or about those of their organisation.

The Professional Responsibilities of Researchers	
B11	Researchers must not unjustifiably criticise or disparage other Researchers.
B12	Researchers must always strive to design research which is cost-efficient and of adequate quality, and then to carry this out to the specification agreed with the Client.
B13	Researchers must ensure the security of all research records in their possession.
B14	Researchers must not knowingly allow the dissemination of conclusions from a marketing research project which are not adequately supported by the data. They must always be prepared to make available the technical information necessary to assess the validity of any published findings.
B15	When acting in their capacity as Researchers the latter must not undertake any non-research activities, for example database marketing involving data about individuals which will be used for direct marketing and promotional activities. Any such non-research activities must always, in the way they are organised and carried out, be clearly differentiated from marketing research activities.

Mutual Rights and Responsibilities of Researchers and Clients	
B16	These rights and responsibilities will normally be governed by a written Contract between the Researcher and the Client. The parties may amend the provisions of rules B19– B23 below if they have agreed this in writing beforehand; but the other requirements of this Code may not be altered in this way. Marketing research must also always be conducted according to the principles of fair competition, as generally understood and accepted.
B17	The Researcher must inform the Client if the work to be carried out for that Client is to be combined or syndicated in the same project with work for other Clients but must not disclose the identity of such clients without their permission.
B18	The Researcher must inform the Client as soon as possible in advance when any part of the work for that Client is to be subcontracted outside the Researcher's own organisation (including the use of any outside consultants). On request the Client must be told the identity of any such subcontractor.
B19	The Client does not have the right, without prior agreement between the parties involved, to exclusive use of the Researcher's services or those of his organisation, whether in whole or in part. In carrying out work for different clients, however, the Researcher must endeavour to avoid possible clashes of interest between the services provided to those clients.
B20	The following Records remain the property of the Client and must not be disclosed by the Researcher to any third party without the Client's permission: (a) marketing research briefs, specifications and other information provided by the Client; (b) research data and findings from a marketing research project (except in the case of syndicated or multi-client projects or services where the same data are available to more than one client). The Client has, however, no right to know the names or addresses of Respondents unless the latter's explicit permission for this has first been obtained by the Researcher (this particular requirement cannot be altered under Rule B16).

Mutual Rights and Responsibilities of Researchers and Clients	
B21	Unless it is specifically agreed to the contrary, the following Records remain the property of the Researcher: (a) marketing research proposals and cost quotations (unless these have been paid for by the Client). They must not be disclosed by the Client to any third party, other than to a consultant working for the Client on that project (with the exception of any consultant working also for a competitor of the Researcher). In particular, they must not be used by the Client to influence research proposals or cost quotations from other Researchers. (b) the contents of a report in the case of syndicated research and/or multi-client projects or services where the same data are available to more than one client and where it is clearly understood that the resulting reports are available for general purchase or subscription. The Client may not disclose the findings of such research to any third party (other than his own consultants and advisors for use in connection with his business) without the permission of the Researcher. (c) all other research Records prepared by the Researcher (with the exception in the case of non-syndicated projects of the report to the Client, and also the research design and questionnaire where the costs of developing these are covered by the charges paid by the Client).
B22	The Researcher must conform to current agreed professional practice relating to the keeping of such records for an appropriate period of time after the end of the project. On request the Researcher must supply the Client with duplicate copies of such records provided that such duplicates do not breach anonymity and confidentiality requirements (Rule B4); that the request is made within the agreed time limit for keeping the Records; and that the Client pays the reasonable costs of providing the duplicates.
B23	The Researcher must not disclose the identity of the Client (provided there is no legal obligation to do so) or any confidential information about the latter's business, to any third party without the Client's permission.
B24	The Researcher must, on request, allow the Client to arrange for checks on the quality of fieldwork and data preparation provided that the Client pays any additional costs involved in this. Any such checks must conform to the requirements of Rule B4.
B25	The Researcher must provide the Client with all appropriate technical details of any research project carried out for that Client.
B26	When reporting on the results of a marketing research project the Researcher must make a clear distinction between the findings as such, the Researcher's interpretation of these and any recommendations based on them.
B27	Where any of the findings of a research project are published by the Client, the latter has a responsibility to ensure that these are not misleading. The Researcher must be consulted and agree in advance the form and content of publication, and must take action to correct any misleading statements about the research and its findings.
B28	Researchers must not allow their names to be used in connection with any research project as an assurance that the latter has been carried out in conformity with this Code unless they are confident that the project has in all respects met the Code's requirements.
B29	Researchers must ensure that Clients are aware of the existence of this Code and of the need to comply with its requirements.

Chapter Roundup

- Although you will see variations there is general agreement that the marketing research process involves the following stages:
  - **Definition**: identify and define the opportunity or threat
  - **Objectives**: determine precisely what you need to know to deal with the opportunity or threat
  - **Design** the research and the methods to be used (exploratory, descriptive, causal)
  - **Collect** the data
  - **Analyse** the data
  - **Report** on the findings
- Some larger organisations have their own marketing research (or 'customer insight') departments, but for most this would be too expensive.
- Agencies include **specialist agencies** of various kinds (field agencies, data analysis agencies and so on), syndicated research agencies, list brokers, profilers, full service agencies and independent consultants.
- The main professional bodies are the **Marketing Research Society** and **ESOMAR**.
- **Selecting** an agency will involve considerations such as the agency's **previous experience** and **expertise** in the area of research, the **geographical area** to be covered.
- Marketing researchers depend on the trust of their respondents. Most developed countries have **specific legislation** to **protect the privacy of individuals**. In the UK there is the Data Protection Act 1998 which establishes eight data protection principles.
- The ICC/ESOMAR have issued a **code of practice** for marketing research professionals. Broadly, this covers The Rights of Respondents, The Professional Responsibilities of Researchers, and Mutual Rights and Responsibilities of Researchers and Clients.

Quick Quiz

1 What does DODCAR stand for?

2 The most elaborate kind of research is Causal/Descriptive/Exploratory. Delete as appropriate.

3 What is syndicated research?

4 Full service agencies do not have specialist research skills. True or false? Explain your answer.

5 What are five disadvantages of in-house market research departments?

6 List the eight data protection principles.

7 The ICC/ESOMAR code of conduct sets out six rights of respondents. Summarise them.

8 Which of the following is a requirement of the ICC/ESOMAR code?

A The Client has the right to exclusive use of the Researcher's services

B Researchers must not make false claims about their skills and experience

C The Researcher must make a clear distinction between the findings and any recommendations based on them

D The Researcher may refuse to allow the Client to check the quality of fieldwork

Answers to Quick Quiz

1 Definition, Objectives, Design, Collect, Analyse, Report. In other words the marketing research process.

2 Causal

3 Syndicated research is research undertaken on a regular basis, but not for any specific client. It is of sufficient interest to be saleable to many clients.

4 False, as a rule.

5 **Five from**

(1) There is a danger of **overstretching current resources** and adversely affecting other projects.

(2) There is a risk of developing an **inappropriate programme**, yielding insufficient or poor quality data with inadequate analysis and control.

(3) If additional **training or recruitment** is required this could prove expensive and time consuming.

(4) **Bias** could result from using staff with pre-conceived views.

(5) **Company politics** may influence the results.

(6) Considerable **computing resources** with appropriate software packages would be required to analyse the data.

6 Data must be:

- Fairly and lawfully processed
- Processed for limited purposes
- Adequate, relevant and not excessive
- Accurate
- Not kept longer than necessary
- Processed in accordance with individual's rights
- Secure
- Not transferred to countries that do not have adequate data protection laws

7

- Respondents' co-operation in a marketing research project is entirely voluntary
- Respondents' anonymity must be strictly preserved
- The Researcher must try to ensure that Respondents are not adversely affected as a result of taking part in research
- The Researcher must take special care when interviewing children and young people
- Respondents must be told if observation techniques or recording equipment are used
- Respondents must be enabled to check the identity and bona fides of the Researcher.

8 B and C are correct. (All the options are paraphrased to some extent.)

Action Programme Review

1 We've not given you enough information to enable you to be too precise. You would have much more information in real life of course.

To collect information about the market for a new line of cruelty-free cosmetics (lipsticks, eyeshadow and so on) with a view to drawing up and implementing a marketing plan.

(a) The size of market, value, number of items sold, number of customers

(b) The leading companies and their respective market share

(c) The breakdown of market by type of cosmetic (lipstick, eyeshadow etc)

(d) Current consumer trends in buying cruelty-free cosmetics (price, colour and so on)

(e) Consumer preferences in terms of packaging/presentation

(f) The importance to consumers of having a choice of colours within the range

(g) The influence on consumers of advertising and promotion that emphasises the cruelty-free nature of products.

Remember that objectives need to be SMART.

Research objectives	Discover re Action Programme above:
Specific	Size of market for *cruelty-free* cosmetics not cosmetics in general
Measurable	Respective market share in percentage terms of leading players
Actionable	Price range within which consumers will buy
Reasonable	A defined number of preferred colours
Timescaled	Information within 3 months so product can be marketed for Christmas

2 This is a hands-on exercise.

Now try Question 6 at the end of the Study Text

5

Briefs, proposals and information requirements

Chapter topic list

Syllabus content – knowledge and skill requirements

- 3.4: Information requirements to support a specific business decision in an organisation and development of a research brief to meet those requirements
- 3.5: Development of a research proposal to fulfil a given research brief

Introduction

The bulk of this chapter sets marketing research in the context of typical **marketing decisions** and the sort of **information** that may be required to make them. For the most part we have used the familiar **4Ps** framework, since this will hopefully help you to relate marketing research to your studies for other marketing papers.

Exam tip

Information requirements for particular marketing research proposals are likely to feature regularly in the exam. It is important to develop your thinking in this area, and to be able to identify where more information may be needed in any research planning.

We begin, however, with two topics that are highly likely to feature in your exam: the structure and contents of a **research brief** and a **research proposal**. You probably won't actually be able to write a decent proposal as yet, at least not in any depth, because you need to read more about marketing research methodologies, and evaluation and reporting techniques (Parts D and E of this book). But once you have read the remainder of the book this chapter is a key place to return to with revision and exam success in mind.

Action Programme 1

Since you know quite a lot about the 4Ps already, see if you can list the type of research information that might be sought under each of them.

1 The research brief

FAST FORWARD

A **research brief** is a document prepared by an organisation commissioning research. Typically it contains the following sections: Background, Rationale, Budget, Timescale, Objectives, Methods and Reports. The budget would typically not be revealed to agencies.

The key to good research information, whether collected by an in-house section or an external agency, lies in the quality of the research brief. A research brief is **prepared by the organisation commissioning the research**.

Exam tip

You need to be familiar with the content of a brief as you may well be called upon to produce one in the examination.

The research brief will normally cover the following.

(a) **Background**. This covers relevant information about the company, its products and services, its market place.

(b) **Rationale**. How the need for information arose and what the users intend to do with the information when they have it (what decisions will be taken).

(c) **Budget**. In general the benefits of collecting information should be greater than the costs of collecting it, but benefits in particular are not always easy to quantify. In any case the budget may be limited by other organisational factors such as availability of cash or a head office allocation of, say, £5,000 per annum for marketing research purposes. Clearly this will affect the scale and type of information search that can be carried out. This item will probably not be revealed to external suppliers however: see below.

(d) **Timescale**. Quite obviously, if the decisions have to be made by May then the information needs to be collected and analysed before then. Once again this will have an impact on the scale and type of information search that can be carried out.

(e) **Objectives**. The precise information needed, set out as clearly as possible. For instance 'To determine customer response to a price reduction of £250 in terms of repeat purchasing, word-of-mouth recommendations and willingness to purchase our other products and services". The objectives should relate **only** to the rationale: it might be 'nice to know' what type of car customers drive, but if this will make no difference to the decisions that will be taken once the information has been collected, there is no need to know about customers' cars in the first place.

(f) **Methods**. This need only be an outline, setting out, for instance, the scale of the search, the mix of quantitative and qualitative information needed, the segments of the market to be included.

(g) **Reports**. How the final information should be presented. Considerations here might include style of reports, degree of summarisation, use of charts and other graphics, format for quantitative information (eg in Excel spreadsheets, for ease of further analysis).

According to Wilson (2002) 'The **budget** available is rarely included within the brief' and that is most probably true of briefs that are **sent out to marketing research suppliers**, who will hopefully return research proposals that meet the organisation's needs, not just as much research as they are prepared to do for the price. However, the organisation obviously needs to have a clear idea of how much it is willing to spend on research.

2 Research proposals

Pilot Paper, 12/03, 6/04, 12/04, 6/05, 12/05, 6/06, 12/06, 6/07

FAST FORWARD

Research proposals are prepared and submitted to the client by agencies who receive the brief. Typical contents are as follows: Background, Objectives, Approach and Method, Reports, Timing, Fees and expenses, Personal CVs, Relevant experience, Contractual details.

Research proposals are **prepared by research agencies** who have been sent the brief and asked to put in a bid to do the job.

In structure a research proposal is similar to the research brief, but it will be much more detailed in certain parts.

Exam tip

In all probability, you will be asked to prepare a proposal, or at least the central parts of one, in the exam. Along with the identification of further information requirements, the question could be worth up to 50 marks.

(a) **Background**. This sets out the agency's understanding of the client company, its products and services and its market place, and its understanding of why the research is required. (If they've misunderstood the situation it will be clear to the client at the outset!)

(b) **Objectives**. These will probably be much the same as those in the brief, although the agency's understanding of research techniques may have helped to define them more precisely still.

(c) **Approach and Method**. How the agency proposes to carry out the research, what methods will be used, where the sample will be taken from. In other words this will cover the sort of topics that are dealt with in Part D of this Text, as appropriate to the situation.

(d) **Reports**. How the final information will be presented and whether interim reports will be made. Reporting is covered in Part E of this Text.

(e) **Timing**: how long the research will take and how it will be broken down into separate stages if appropriate.

(f) **Fees and expenses**: this is self-explanatory

(g) **Personal CVs** of the main agency personnel who will be involved in the project.

(h) **Relevant experience/references:** the agency will wish to assure the client that it is capable of carrying out the research, so it will include information about similar projects undertaken in the past, and possibly reference details (previous clients who are willing to testify to the competency of the agency).

(i) **Contractual details** will set out the agency's terms of trade and clarify matters about ownership of the data collected. See the relevant parts of the ESOMAR code of practice in the previous chapter for an indication of likely contents of this section.

3 Market research

FAST FORWARD

Marketing research typically embraces six major areas: **market research**; **product research**; **sales research**; **price research**; **distribution research**; and **advertising/communications research**.

Market research is one aspect of marketing research. Market research – that is, research into **markets** – is concerned with quantifying information to provide a forecast of sales and to assess potential sales. Market research is therefore based on the use of **mathematical and statistical techniques** to reduce uncertainty.

3.1 Market forecasts and sales forecasts

Market forecasts and sales forecasts complement each other. They should not be undertaken separately. The market forecast should be carried out first of all and should cover a longer period of time.

(a) **Market forecast**. This is a forecast for the market as a whole. It is mainly involved in the assessment of environmental factors, outside the organisation's control, which will affect the demand for its products/services. Often it consists of three components.

  (i) **The economic review** (national economy, government policy, covering forecasts on investment, population, gross national product)

  (ii) **Specific market research** (to obtain data about specific markets and forecasts concerning total market demand)

  (iii) **Evaluation of total market demand for the firm's and similar products** (covering profitability, market potential)

(b) **Sales forecasts**. These are estimates of sales of a product in a future period at a given price and using a stated method(s) of sales promotion which will cost a given amount of money.

Unlike the market forecast, a sales forecast concerns the firm's activity directly. It takes into account such aspects as sales to certain categories of customer, sales promotion activities, the extent of competition, product life cycle, performance of major products. Sales forecasts are expressed in volume, value and profit.

3.2 Research into potential sales

FAST FORWARD

Market research tries to **quantify** information to provide sales forecasts and assess potential sales.

Sales potential is an estimate of the part of the market which is within the possible reach of a product. The potential will vary according to the price of the product and the amount of money spent on sales promotion, and market research should attempt to quantify these variations. Sales potential also depends on:

- How essential the product is to consumers
- Whether it is a durable commodity whose purchase is postponable
- The overall size of the possible market
- Competition

Whether sales potential is worth exploiting will depend on the cost of sales promotion and selling which must be incurred to realise the potential. Consider a company which has done market research which indicates that the sales potential of product X is as follows.

	Sales value	*Contribution earned before selling costs deducted*	*Cost of selling*
either	£100,000	£40,000	£10,000
or	£110,000	£44,000	£15,000

In this example, it would not be worth spending an extra £5,000 on selling in order to realise an extra sales potential of £10,000, because the net effect would be a loss of £(5,000 – 4,000) = £1,000.

Sales potential will influence the decisions by a company on how much of each product to make. The market situation is dynamic, and market research should reveal changing situations. A company might decide that maximum profits will be earned by concentrating all its production and sales promotion efforts on one segment of a market. Action by competitors might then adversely affect sales and market research might reveal that another market segment has become relatively more profitable. The company might therefore decide to divert some production capacity and sales promotion spending to the new segment in order to revive its profits.

3.3 Other aspects of market research

Market research, to be comprehensive, must show an awareness of the various environmental influences which may affect supply and demand for a product.

Market research also involves investigation of the following.

- The expansion or decline of demand within a particular **market segment**
- The expansion or decline of demand within a particular **geographical area**
- The **timing of demand** (Is there a cyclical or seasonal pattern of demand?)

3.4 Concentration ratios

One way of expressing concentration ratios is to assess the percentage of the market that is held by the top firms. For example, an industry might have the following concentration ratios.

	% of market
Top three firms	60
Top five firms	68
Top ten firms	85

4 Product research

FAST FORWARD

Product research seeks to achieve a **marketing orientation** to the organisation's research-and-development focus.

Key concept

Product research is concerned with the product itself, whether new, improved or already on the market, and customer reactions to it.

This aspect of marketing research attempts to make product **research and development** customer orientated.

New product ideas may come from anywhere – from research and development personnel, marketing and sales personnel, competitors, customers, outside scientific or technological discoveries, individual employees or executives. Research and development is carried out by company scientists, engineers or designers; much wasted effort can be saved for them, however, if new ideas are first tested in the market, in other words if product research is carried out.

4.1 The process of product research

New ideas are first screened by a range of specialists (market researchers, designers, research and development staff) and are rejected if they have any of the following characteristics.

- They have a low profit potential or insufficient market potential.
- They have a high cost and involve high risk.
- They do not conform to company objectives.
- They cannot be produced and distributed with the available resources.

Ideas which survive the screening process should be product tested and possibly test marketed. Test marketing in selected areas will give a better indication of how well the product will sell if produced for a wider market, but it also gives competitors an early warning of what is happening.

Product research also includes the need to keep the product range of a company's goods under review for the following reasons.

(a) **Variety reduction** may be desirable to reduce production costs, or when there are insufficient sales of certain items in the product range to justify continued production. In practice, there is often strong resistance, both from within a company and from customers, to the elimination of products from the market.

(b) **Product diversification** increases a product range by introducing new items, and a wide range of products can often improve a company's market image.

(c) **Segmentation** is a policy which aims at securing a new class of customer for an existing range of products, perhaps by making some adjustments to the products to appeal to the new segments.

Product research also involves finding **new uses for existing products**, and this could be considered a means of extending a product range. The uses for plastics and nylon, for example, have been extended rapidly in the past as a result of effective research.

4.2 Product life cycle research

FAST FORWARD

The **product life cycle** is a useful model for marketing planning and control, although there are difficulties in predicting the precise shape of the PLC curve for any given product/service.

4.2.1 The product life cycle

The profitability and sales of a product can be expected to change over time. The **product life cycle** (PLC) is an attempt to recognise distinct stages in a product's sales history. Although you will have encountered the PLC before, a brief recap is provided below.

Marketing managers distinguish between the following.

(a) **Product class**: this is a broad category of product, such as cars, washing machines, newspapers, also referred to as the generic product.

(b) **Product form**: within a product class there are different forms that the product can take, for example five-door hatchback cars or two-seater sports cars; twin tub or front loading automatic washing machines; national daily newspapers or weekly local papers.

(c) The particular **brand or make** of the product form (for example Ford Escort, Vauxhall Astra; **Financial Times**, **Daily Mail** and **Sun**).

The product life cycle applies in differing degrees to each of the three cases. A product-class may have a long maturity stage, and a particular make or brand might have an erratic life cycle. Product forms however tend to conform to the 'classic' life cycle pattern, commonly described by a curve as follows. You will be familiar with each of the stages.

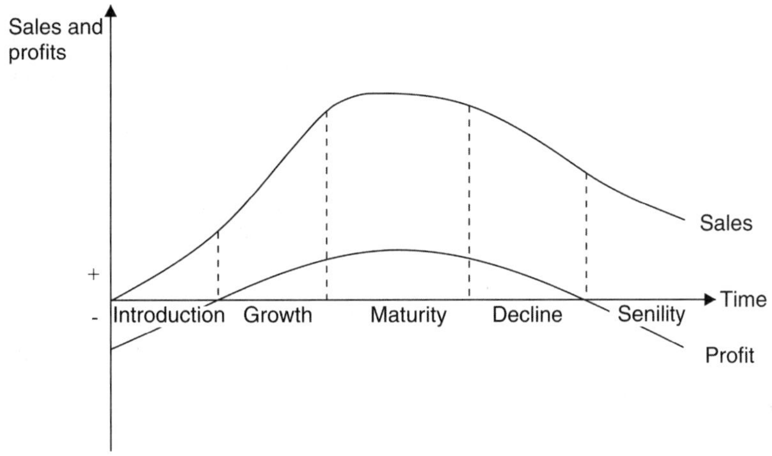

4.2.2 The relevance of the product life cycle to planning and control

A company selling a range of products must try to look into the longer term, beyond the immediate budget period, and estimate how much each of its products is likely to contribute towards sales revenue and profitability. It is therefore necessary to make an assessment of the following.

(a) The stage of its life cycle that any product has reached

(b) For how much longer the product will be able to contribute significantly to profits and sales, allowing for price changes, other marketing strategies, cost control and product modifications

Another aspect of product life cycle analysis is new product development, and strategic planners must consider the following.

(a) How urgent is the need to innovate, and how much will have to be spent on R & D to develop new products in time?

(b) New products cost money to introduce. Not only are there R & D costs, but there is also capital expenditure on plant and equipment, and probably heavy expenditure on advertising and sales promotion. A new product will use up substantial amounts of cash in its early life, and it will not be until its growth phase is well under way, or even the maturity phase reached, that a product will pay back the initial outlays of capital and marketing expenditure.

It is essential that firms plan their portfolio of products to ensure that new products are generating positive cash flow before existing 'earners' enter the decline stage. In this situation the company is likely to experience cash flow problems:

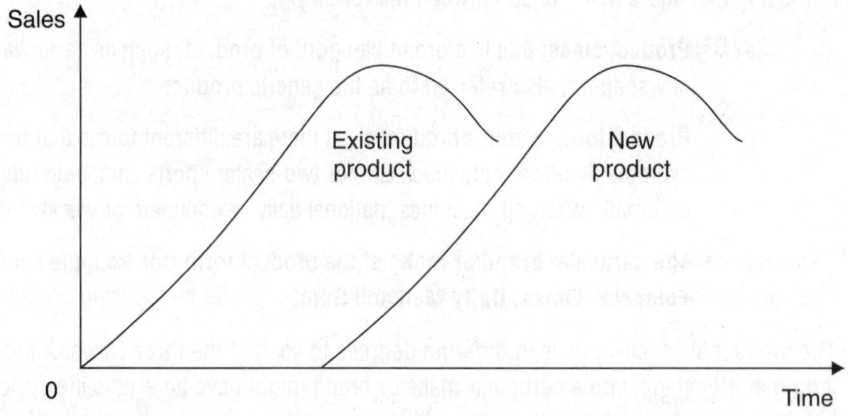

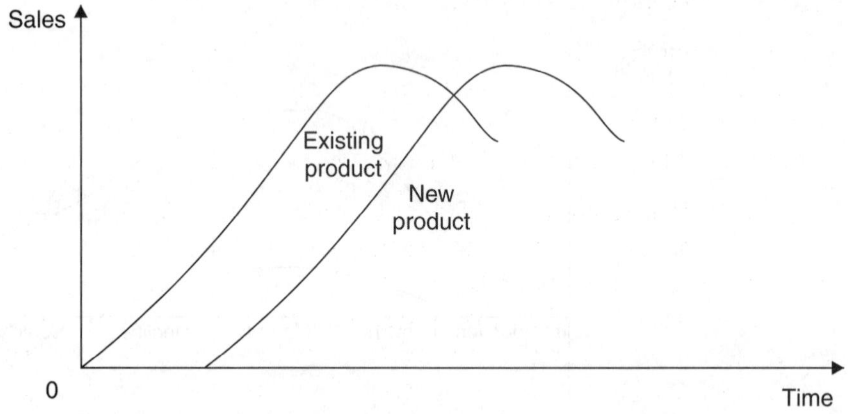

By considering the product life cycle of the existing product, when planning the timing for launch of a new product, cash flow problems can be avoided.

It is perhaps easy enough to accept that products have a life cycle, but it is not so easy to sort out how far through its life a product is, and what its expected future life might be. Information about the stage a product has reached in its life cycle may be an important indication of how long its market will continue and how soon new product developments must be introduced to replace it.

(a) There ought to be a **regular review** of existing products, as a part of marketing management responsibilities.

(b) Information should be obtained about the likely future of each product and sources of such information might be as follows.

- An analysis of past sales and profit trends
- The history of other products
- Market research
- If possible, an analysis of competitors

The future of each product should be estimated in terms of both sales revenue and profits.

Once the assessments have been made, decisions must be taken about what to do with each product. The choices are as follows.

(a) To **continue selling** the product, with no foreseeable intention yet of stopping production

(b) To initiate action to **prolong a product's life**, perhaps by product modification, advertising more, by trying to cut costs or raise prices, by improving distribution, or packaging or sales promotion methods, or by putting in more direct selling effort

(c) To plan to **stop producing the product** and either to replace it with new ones in the same line or to diversify into new product-market areas

4.3 Category management

FAST FORWARD

Effective category management requires analysis of accurate data from consumers, EPOS and market research.

Key concept

Category management has been defined as 'the distributor/supplier process of managing categories as strategic business units, producing enhanced business results by focusing on delivering consumer value' (Joint Industry Project on Efficient Consumer Response).

Category management is a comparatively new theme in retailing and emphasises decision making based upon analysis of consumer data, EPOS data and market research data. The aim of the new discipline is to reduce costs and inventories while improving the consumer's choice.

A category is defined as a distinct, manageable group of products or services that customers perceive to be related and/or substitutable in meeting a consumer need. Thus tinned vegetables (tomatoes, baked beans, sweetcorn) might form a category, or frozen desserts or household paper products. The retailer manages each category as a **strategic business unit**.

Each category is managed according to its own particular strategy. Typical strategies might include traffic building (increasing the number of customers passing through the category shelfspace), profit contribution or cash penetration. Category management is therefore intensely data-driven, and needs accurate data at store level. For example, a store might want to rank profit or volume sales of a particular product and compare that with national or regional figures. The scanned data from the store can be combined with market sales data and consumer information to identify where, for example, sales are below what would be expected. The category or product may become the focus for enhanced promotion to boost sales, or re-pricing to improve its contribution margin.

4.4 Product testing 12/06

Key concept

Product testing is 'the evaluation and development of the products themselves from a marketing point of view'.

The following circumstances should be taken into account when establishing the most appropriate product test design.

(a) **Management information required**. For example, is information required on the best shape/colour mix, or on whether it is worth investing more time and money in the product, or which is the best of a group of similar products.

(b) **The market in which the product will be sold**. If the market consists of children, for example, their inability to perform certain tasks must be taken into account. Industrial and consumer markets obviously differ and a highly-branded market means that the product will need to be well branded.

(c) **The type of product being tested**. The following product characteristics are likely to affect the design of product tests.

- How new the product is to users (a new product cannot be compared to another)

- How easily the product can be assessed by users
- How much information consumers gather before selecting a product

(d) **The availability of time and finance**.

(e) **The need for standardisation of the procedures across a wide range of products**. Standardised tests mean that researchers gain more experience of the procedures, the procedure can be refined and results of different tests are more likely to be comparable.

The essential differences between product tests centre around the following.

(a) **Sample size** (cost and data reliability must be weighed up)

(b) **The type of people used as testers** (current users of the brand, current users in the product field, users in the product field plus potential users or a general cross section of the population?)

(c) **The type of test given to the testers**

(i) **Monadic**. Each person is given just one product (either a new product or a line extension) to evaluate.

(ii) **Comparative**. Each person is given two or more products to compare on the same occasion. Such tests are typically used for new product formulation.

(iii) **Sequential**. Each person tries one product, waits a specific time period, tries a second and then gives an opinion.

(iv) **Conjoint**. Such tests focus on product features rather than identifying the best product.

Other choices face the researcher in terms of what testers are asked to do.

- Whether the products should be branded or blind
- Whether competitors' brands should be included among the products tested
- Which order the products should be presented in comparative tests
- Whether the test should be on the spot or in use (at home)
- Which attributes are to be tested
- The time given to testers

(d) The **analysis techniques** used on the collected data will vary.

4.5 Attitude measurement 6/06

Key concept

An **attitude** is a predisposition to act in a particular way. A knowledge of attitudes may therefore enable predictions about likely behaviour patterns. A significant proportion of marketing research is aimed at finding out about consumer attitudes.

A favourable pre-disposition towards a product may lead to a purchase. However, such causal relationships are very seldom this direct.

There are three components to 'attitude'.

(a) A **cognitive component** which is what the individual knows or believes about an object or act

(b) An **affective component** which is what the individual feels emotionally about an object or act

(c) A **conative component** which is how the individual is disposed to behave towards an object or act

Attitude is multi-dimensional and any attempt to measure attitudes needs to recognise this. For example, a number of different attitudes could affect a particular buying decision. 'I like the coat, it's red' but 'red reminds me of blood and danger' and 'it's not a bad price, I can afford it' but 'my parents would never have spent so much on a coat' and yet 'it does feel good on' and 'the shop assistant said it looks good on' but 'it has a real fur collar and an animal has been killed to make this coat' and yet 'animal skins have been a source of clothing for thousands of years' but 'I'm a vegetarian' and so on. Eventually, a decision to buy or not to buy may be made on the basis of the buyer's various attitudes and which attitudes are the most powerful, but these attitudes may also be balanced by social pressures.

It is therefore important that attitudes are incorporated into marketing research. Two scaling techniques which attempt to measure attitude are **Likert scales** and **semantic differential scales**.

4.5.1 Buyer motivation

It is in an organisation's interests to know the **reasons or motives** behind people's behaviour. The reasons why people seek a product or product category, and how they go about obtaining it, are of vital importance to the marketer.

Patronage motives (price, service, location, honesty, product variety) influence where a person purchases products on a regular basis.

To analyse the major motives that influence consumers to buy or not buy their products, markets conduct motivation research using **in-depth interviews**, **focus groups** and **projective techniques**.

5 Price research

FAST FORWARD

Price sensitivity is influenced by five major factors, including the extent to which customers use the **'just price' concept**, the **nature of the purchase** involved, and **perceptions of price versus 'value'**.

5.1 Reasons for conducting price research

Reasons for conducting price research are as follows.

(i) Where a firm is aware of competitive pricing and offers, it can use the data as a **reference point** for its own pricing.

(ii) Once the firm has established the market prices, it can, through market research, calculate the **price elasticity of demand** and hence derive anticipated sales volume based on proposed price levels.

(iii) Given the market price, the firm can benchmark its level of **product / service quality**

(iv) Pricing research can help identify more profitable customers and market segments as well as compare costs with a view to **maximising profitability**.

5.2 Price sensitivity

Price sensitivity will vary amongst purchasers. Those who can pass on the cost of purchases will be least sensitive and will respond more to other elements of the marketing mix.

(a) Provided that it fits the corporate budget, the business traveller will be more concerned about the level of service and quality of food when looking for an hotel than price. In contrast, a family on holiday are likely to be very price sensitive when choosing an overnight stay.

(b) In industrial marketing the purchasing manager is likely to be more price sensitive than the engineer who might be the actual user of new equipment that is being sourced. The engineer and purchasing manager are using different criteria in making the choice. The engineer places product characteristics as first priority, the purchasing manager is more price oriented.

Price decisions are often seen as highly sensitive and as such may involve top management more clearly than other marketing decisions. Price has a very obvious and direct relationship with profit. Ethical considerations, such as whether or not to exploit short-term shortages through higher prices, are a further factor.

5.3 Finding out about price sensitivity

Research on price sensitivity of customers has demonstrated the following.

(a) Customers have a concept of a **'just price'** – a feel for what is about the right price to pay for a commodity.

(b) Unless a regular purchase is involved, customers search for price information before buying, becoming price aware when wanting to buy but forgetting soon afterwards.

(c) Customers will buy at what they consider to be a bargain price without full regard for need and actual price.

Marketing at Work

Bell Telephones in the US were concerned about the lack of sales of extension telephones. When, as part of a market research survey, customers were asked to name the actual price of an extension telephone, most overestimated it. By keeping the existing price but running an advertising campaign featuring it, Bell were able to increase sales as customers became aware of the lower than anticipated price.

5.4 Finding out about price perception

Price perception is important as it determines ways customers react to prices. The economist's downward sloping demand curve may not in fact hold, at least in the short term. For example, customers may react to a price increase by buying for one or more of a number of reasons.

- They expect further price increases to follow. (They are 'stocking up'.)
- They assume the quality has increased.
- The brand takes on a 'snob appeal' because of the high price.

5.5 Factors affecting pricing decisions

Several factors complicate the pricing decisions which an organisation has to make.

5.5.1 Intermediaries' objectives

If an organisation distributes products or services to the market through independent intermediaries, the objectives of these intermediaries have an effect on the pricing decision. Thus conflict over price can arise between suppliers and intermediaries which may be difficult to resolve.

5.5.2 Competitors' actions and reactions

An organisation, in setting prices, sends out signals to **rivals**. These rivals are likely to react in some way. In some industries (such as petrol retailing) pricing moves in unison; in others, price changes by one supplier may initiate a price war, with each supplier undercutting the others.

5.5.3 Suppliers

If an organisation's **suppliers** notice that the prices for an organisation's products are rising, they may seek a rise in the price for their supplies to the organisation.

5.5.4 Inflation

In periods of inflation the organisation's prices may need to change in order to reflect increases in the prices of supplies, labour, rent and so on. Such changes may be needed to keep relative (real) prices unchanged (this is the process of prices being adjusted for the rate of inflation).

5.5.5 Quality connotations

In the absence of other information, customers tend to judge quality by price. Thus a price change may send signals to customers concerning the quality of the product. A rise may be taken to indicate improvements, a reduction may signal reduced quality.

5.5.6 New product pricing

Most pricing decisions for existing products relate to price changes. Such changes have a reference point from which to move (the existing price). But when a new product is introduced for the first time there may be no such reference points; pricing decisions are most difficult to make in such circumstances. It may be possible to seek alternative reference points, such as the price in another market where the new product has already been launched, or the price set by a competitor.

5.5.7 Income effects

In times of rising incomes, price may become a less important marketing variable than, for instance, product quality or convenience of access. When income levels are falling and/or unemployment levels rising, price will become a much more important marketing variable.

Marketing at Work

Accenture, the global consulting firm, has developed a tool called 'Personalised Pricing Tool' to enable firms to set prices that will boost prices and increase customer satisfaction.

It does this by helping the retailer to understand the purchasing behaviour of individual customers, providing clues about future buying decisions.

As a customer enters a store, he or she receives coupons from a kiosk, using a loyalty card. These coupons are tailored to their product preferences and price sensitivities.

(*www.accenture.com*)

5.5.8 Multiple products

Most organisations market not just one product but a range of products. These products are commonly interrelated, perhaps being **complements** or **substitutes**. Take, for example, the use of **loss leaders**: a very low price for one product is intended to make consumers buy other products in the range which carry higher profit margins: razors are sold at very low prices whilst blades for them are sold at a higher profit margin. Loss leaders also attract customers into retail stores where they will usually buy normally priced products as well as the loss leaders. This is the rationale behind the leading supermarkets' own-label and price-conscious ranges.

6 Distribution research

FAST FORWARD

Distribution research addresses such issues as **timeliness** of distribution channels, the distribution **options** available (and whether traditions can be challenged) and the **profitability** of various distribution methods.

Place as an element in the marketing mix is largely concerned with the selection of distribution channels and with the physical distribution of goods.

In selecting an **appropriate marketing channel** for a product, a firm has the following options.

(a) **Selling direct to the customer**. Consumer goods can be sold direct with mail order catalogues, telephone selling, door-to-door selling of consumer goods, or selling 'off the page' with magazine advertisements. Industrial goods are commonly sold direct by sales representatives, visiting industrial buyers.

(b) **Selling through agents or recognised distributors**, who specialise in the firm's products. For example, a chain of garden centres might act as specialist stockists and distributors for the products of just one garden shed manufacturer.

(c) **Selling through wholesalers** or to retailers who stock and sell the goods and brands of several rival manufacturers.

Some organisations might use channels of distribution for their goods which are unprofitable to use, and which should either be abandoned in favour of more profitable channels, or made profitable by giving some attention to cutting costs or increasing minimum order sizes.

As well as **cost and profitability analyses**, distribution research can embrace the following.

(a) To what extent is the distribution channel **actually working**? In other words, how effective is the distributor at delivering products to customers?

(b) To what extent is the distributor favouring its own brand or competitors' products over your own, in terms of shelf space and positioning and in-store promotions?

This latter point is important as own-brand products are becoming increasingly competitive with branded goods. Supermarket chains promote their own brand extensively.

Normal **market research techniques** can be used to assess the effectiveness of distribution channels. Questions in market research questionnaires can ask how easy it is for customers to obtain products and information, and where they are obtained. An example might be a newspaper readership questionnaire, which will ask where the customer acquires the newspaper (eg delivered at home, or bought on way to work).

7 Marketing communications research

FAST FORWARD

Advertising is normally measured against four specific criteria: **impact**, **persuasion**, **message delivery** and **liking**.

Advertising may be judged to have been effective if it has met the objectives or tasks previously set for it. The following table gives some examples.

Advertising task/objectives	Example of measure of effect
Support increase in sales For example a local plumber's advert in a regional newspaper	Orders; levels of enquiries
Inform consumers For example an Amnesty International advert about political prisoners	Donations Number of new members clipping appeal coupon
Remind For example a Yellow Pages television commercial	Awareness levels
Create/reinforce image For example Halifax's 'people' commercials	Awareness levels Image created
Change attitude For example British Nuclear Fuel Ltd's Sellafield open door poster campaign	Attitude

Although there may well be a number of short-term effects resulting fairly soon after an advertising campaign has appeared, a brand will probably reap positive long-term effects from advertising effort stretching over a number of years. All advertising, whatever the objectives for any individual campaign, will contribute to the overall perception of that brand by the consumer.

7.1 Creative development research

This is research carried out early in the advertising process, using **qualitative techniques** to guide and help develop the advertising for a product or service. It can be used to help feed into initial creative ideas or, alternatively, to check whether a rough idea is understood by consumers. Storyboards, outline scripts or rough layouts of mocked up adverts may be shown to groups of consumers to monitor their response.

7.2 Pre-testing

Advertising pre-testing is research for **predictive** purposes. Advertisements are tested quantitatively, at a much more highly finished stage than in creative development research, against set criteria. Recently, quantitative pre testing has seen a resurgence in popularity. As advertising budgets are made to work harder, advertisers have felt the need to build in more checks to ensure that their advertising is on target.

Quantitative testing can be administered via **hall or studio tests**. Specialist research agencies can cater for all kinds of media executions. Respondents are shown clusters of TV commercials either on their own or within television programmes; print executions are shown in folders amongst other adverts; poster executions may be shown in a simulated road drive scene via 35mm slides.

Advertisements are measured against specific criteria such as those listed below.

(a) **Impact**. Does the advert stand out against others?

(b) **Persuasion**. Does the advert create favourable predisposition towards the brand?

(c) **Message delivery**. Does the advert deliver the message in terms of understanding and credibility?

(d) **Liking**. This attribute is deemed to mean not only that the advert is enjoyable and interesting, but is also personally meaningful to the consumer, relevant and believable. Thus, an RSPCA advert depicting a maltreated animal might not be likeable in the conventional sense, but may be rated highly by a respondent on this attribute because it draws attention to an issue which is important to the consumer.

The specialist research agencies that carry out this form of research have developed a set of normal values or scores, which act as **benchmarks** against which to measure quantitative results.

7.3 Tracking studies

Advertising effects may be measured over time via tracking studies which monitor **pre– and post-advertising variables**. Clients will normally buy into a series of **omnibus surveys** to monitor criteria such as:

- Brand/product awareness (unprompted *versus* prompted recall)
- Attitudinal change
- Imagery associations

Panel research is another form of tracking study. For instance, Taylor Nelson's Superpanel monitors changes in grocery shopping behaviour of 8,500 households. The research company have placed portable bar code scanners in homes and families undertake to use the device to record purchases made. The data is collated every week and gives diagnostic information. For instance, if the panel buy less of a particular brand, it is possible to identify what brand they have switched to instead.

With tracking studies, it is important to try to examine **all possible reasons** for any changes in audience behaviour. An increase in level of sales as tracked over time by panel-based research may be ascribed in part to the effect of the advertising. However, sales increases are equally likely to have come about due to changes in price levels, seasonality, competitive activity or a change in product quality levels.

Marketing at Work

QualiQuant International (QiQ) specialises in the measurement of consumer emotions. The interactive computer interview has many uses here, as consumers feel more honest and spontaneous than they would in a more conventional interview situation. QiQ uses qualitative in-depth techniques such as word and picture associations, collages, guided dreams, bubble pictures and so on.

(*www.QiQInternational.com*)

7.4 Communications research

Advertising research as described above is but one aspect of communications research. As a marketing manager you will be concerned with the following aspects of your decision making.

(a) **Economy** – The need to minimise the cost of inputs

(b) **Efficiency** – The process of maximising the productivity of inputs

(c) **Effectiveness** – The extent to which the output generated meets the objectives set for the organisation

You will therefore be continuously assessing the effectiveness as well as the relative costs of each element of the promotional mix using research methods.

(a) **Sales research**

- What are the selling costs for different customers?
- How can we improve sales presentations so as to obtain more orders?
- Should we have fewer personal visits and more telephone calls?
- Is personal selling more effective than direct marketing?

(b) **Sales promotion research**

- What extra sales resulted from the extra costs for these promotions?
- What level of retention of extra sales was there post promotion?
- What proportion of the budget should go on consumer incentives as opposed to dealer incentives or salesforce incentives?

(c) **PR/publicity research**

- How effective is PR relative to other forms of promotion?
- How can changes in image and attitudes be measured?
- How much notice do potential customers take of editorials?

Chapter Roundup

- A **research brief** is a document prepared by an organisation commissioning research. Typically it contains the following sections: Background, Rationale, Budget, Timescale, Objectives, Methods and Reports. The budget would typically not be revealed to agencies.
- **Research proposals** are prepared and submitted to the client by agencies who receive the brief. Typical contents are as follows: Background, Objectives, Approach and Method, Reports, Timing, Fees and expenses, Personal CVs, Relevant experience, Contractual details.
- Marketing research typically embraces six major areas: **market research**; **product research**; **sales research**; **price research**; **distribution research**; and **advertising/communications research**.
- Market research tries to **quantify** information to provide sales forecasts and assess potential sales.
- Product research seeks to achieve a **marketing orientation** to the organisation's research-and-development focus.
- The **product life cycle** is a useful model for marketing planning and control, although there are difficulties in predicting the precise shape of the PLC curve for any given product/service.
- **Effective category management** requires analysis of accurate data from consumers, EPOS and market research.
- **Price sensitivity** is influenced by the extent to which customers use the **'just price' concept**, the **nature of the purchase** involved, and **perceptions of price versus 'value'**.
- **Distribution research** addresses such issues as **timeliness** of distribution channels, the distribution **options** available (and whether traditions can be challenged) and the **profitability** of various distribution methods.
- **Advertising** is normally measured against four specific criteria: **impact**, **persuasion**, **message delivery** and **liking**.

Quick Quiz

1 Why should an agency tell a client about the client's background in a research proposal?

2 What are three common components of a market forecast?

3 Why might a new product idea be rejected?

4 Why does product research include the need to keep the product range of a company's goods under review?

5 What is category management?

6 What circumstances should be taken into account when establishing the most appropriate product test design?

7 What is meant by the term 'attitude'?

8 Why conduct price research?

9 List five possible objectives or aims associated with advertising.

10 What are the four criteria used to assess the effectiveness of advertising?

Answers to Quick Quiz

1 To set out the agency's understanding in order to avoid costly mistakes.

2 Economic review; specific market research; evaluation of total market demand.

3 Low profit or insufficient market potential; high cost or low risk; do not conform to company's objectives; cannot be produced and distributed within the available resources.

4 Variety reduction (cost control); product diversification opportunities; segmentation; (appeal to new types of customer).

5 Decision making based upon analysis of market data, EPOS data and market research data.

6 Management information required; market in which they are sold; type of product being tested; available time and finance; need for standardisation.

7 A pre-disposition to act in a certain way.

8 To establish an organisation's position in relation to its competitors; price elasticity of demand; for benchmarking; to identify more profitable target markets and customers.

9 Support increase in sales; inform consumers; remind; create/reinforce image; change attitudes.

10 Impact; persuasion; message delivery; liking.

Action Programme Review

1

Type	*Application*
Product research (Product) Analysis of substitute products Comparison of competition products Test marketing Product extension Brand name generation and testing Product testing of existing products Packaging design studies	Likely acceptance of new products
Price research (Price) Cost analysis Profit analysis Market potential Sales potential Sales forecast (volume) Customer perception of price Effect of price change on demand (elasticity of demand) Discounting Credit terms	Competitor prices (analysis)
Distribution research (Place) Design and location of distribution centres In-house versus outsource logistics Export/international studies Channel coverage studies	Planning channel decisions
Advertising and communications research (Promotion) Product satisfaction Brand awareness studies Segmentation studies Buying intentions Monitor and evaluate buyer behaviour Buying habit/pattern studies	Brand preferences Brand attitude

Now try Question 7 at the end of the Study Text

Part D
Research methodologies

6

Secondary data

Chapter topic list

Syllabus content – knowledge and skill requirements

- 4.1: The uses, benefits and limitations of secondary data
- 4.2: The key sources of primary and secondary data
- 4.4: The various methods for collecting qualitative and quantitative data

Introduction

Secondary data is data that already exists in some form. Collection of secondary data is known as 'desk research'. Originally this was to distinguish it from research that involves getting out and about in the world, talking to people and watching them. In fact a great deal of research can now be **done from your desk** in a literal sense, using your desktop computer and the Internet.

Key concepts

Secondary data is data (including internal data) not created specifically for the purpose at hand but used and analysed to provide marketing information where primary data is not (yet) available or not sufficient.

Desk research is the term used to describe a proactive search for existing data, usually as an initial, exploratory research task.

It may seem odd that we deal with 'secondary' data **before we look at primary data**, but it would very silly to embark on substantial amounts of **primary** research without seeing what secondary data already exists. **Checking what is known already** is also likely to give insights into how and what to investigate further.

Typical desk research activities

Desk research typically involves **knowing where and how to look for** existing information. That is not necessarily as easy as it sounds, but there are clear principles. Here are some typical activities.

(a) Accessing the **organisation's own information systems** records and databases. As we've seen, internal information gathered by other departments for a different purpose to the research in hand would include:

- (i) Production data about quantities produced, materials and labour used etc
- (ii) Data about inventory/stock
- (iii) Data from the sales system about sales volumes, analysed by sales area, salesman, quantity, profitability, distribution outlet, customer etc
- (iv) Data about marketing itself – promotion and brand data, current marketing plans, previous marketing audits.

(b) Tapping into the **Internet** and subscription-based **on-line databases**.

(c) Making use of **library sources**, such as journals, periodicals, recent academic books etc.

(d) **Buying in data and reports** prepared externally, either as secondary data likely to be of interest to many users or as primary data collected for another organisation but then syndicated.

Action Programme 1

Can you think of any limitations to desk research?

1 Secondary data 12/06

FAST FORWARD

The **collection of secondary data** is often referred to as **desk research**, since it does not involve the collection of raw data from the market direct. Desk research includes using library sources, the organisation's information system, databases and internal reports.

As consumers ourselves (as well as marketers) we are continually using secondary data for our own purchasing decisions. If a movie is recommended by a friend you may well go and see it, too, even though your friend did not see it for your benefit. Secondary data is **data neither collected by, nor specifically for, the user**, and is often collected under conditions not known by the user.

Secondary data **cannot replace the experience itself** nor the more rigorous enquiries we might decide to make ourselves. If you know that your friend usually likes the same sort of movies as you there is a good chance that you will like your friend's latest recommendation. But the movie may contain violent scenes that you cannot stomach, or you may hate musicals because they are unreal, or whatever. Likewise you might see a dress or suit that is recommended in a fashion magazine: you would still go out and look at the garment 'in the flesh', feel it, try it on and so forth, before you decided to buy it.

Action Programme 2

How true do you think it is that people want to look at their purchases in the flesh before buying? Consider a variety of different purchases, such as clothes, food, electrical goods and cars.

1.1 The use of secondary data

Secondary information is now **available** in every form and on a **huge scale**. The problem is how to decide what information is required. The use of secondary data will generally come **early** in the process of **marketing research**. In some cases, secondary data may be sufficient in itself, but not always.

Secondary data:

- Can provide a backdrop to primary research
- Can act as a substitute for field research
- Can be used as a technique in itself

1.1.1 Backdrop to primary research

In **unfamiliar territory**, it is natural that the marketer will carry out some **basic research** in the area, using journals, existing market reports, the press and any contacts with relevant knowledge. Such investigations will aid the marketer by providing guidance on a number of areas.

- Possible data sources
- Methods of data collection (relevant populations, sampling methods)
- The general state of the market (demand, competition and the like)

1.1.2 Substitute for primary research

The often substantial **cost** of primary research **might be avoided** if existing secondary data is sufficient. This data might not be perfect for the needs of the business, though and to judge whether it *is* enough, or whether primary research ought to be undertaken, a cost-benefit analysis should be implemented weighing up the advantages of each method.

There are some situations in which secondary data is bound to be **insufficient**. For instance if your brand new version of an existing product is hugely superior to your competitors' versions because of your unique use of new technology, you have changed the entire market. Primary research will be a necessity to find out the impact of your product.

1.1.3 A technique in itself

Some types of information **can only be acquired** by examining secondary data, in particular **trends over time**. Historical data cannot realistically be replaced by a one-off study and an organisation's internal data would only give a limited picture.

Marketing at Work

In a technology-driven market, forecasting is a vital skill. Companies such as Teligen, Gartner, Forrester, IDC and Ovum, largely unknown to readers of market research league tables, have a presence in IT and telecom companies based primarily on their forecasting and technical capabilities. Sizing markets and forecasting market and technology trends is their bread and butter, with dedicated teams of people in separate technology groups steeped in specialist secondary research activity.

Research: 1st February 2002

Exam tip

The December 2006 exam contained a question on secondary data, covering why it should be gathered before undertaking primary research, and its limitations.

2 The Internet

FAST FORWARD

The **Internet** is the richest secondary source of information of all, on practically any subject you can think of. Not all of it is good information, however, and although in theory it is easy to search the Internet, in practice it often takes longer to find exactly what you want than another method would have taken. Knowing which search tool to use and how to use it is a key skill for a researcher.

There are a number of ways to access information on the Internet.

- Go directly to a site, if you have the address
- Browse or surf
- Explore a subject directory or portal
- Conduct a search using a search engine
- Explore information stored in live databases on the Web, known as the 'invisible web or the 'deep web'

The distinctions between directories, search engines and so on are becoming increasingly blurred, as each type of search tool picks up and adopts ideas from its competitors.

2.1 Going directly to an Internet address (URLs)

You may know the precise address of an Internet site that you wish to visit. TV and radio programs and advertisements frequently give you a web address to visit to find more information. You will also see addresses in newspapers, magazines and books. You may be sent a link in an e-mail.

Typically the format is something like 'www.bbc.co.uk'. This is also known as a **Uniform Resource Locator** or **URL** for short.

All you need to do is type the URL into the Address box of your browser.

Action Programme 3

Up-to-date versions of Microsoft Internet Explorer and Netscape Navigator can sometimes find the precise site you are looking for if you just type a guess directly in the address box.

Try this with four or five well-known organisations and see what results you get. Can you see any drawbacks to this method of finding sites?

2.2 Browsing or surfing

Random browsing of pages on the Web is another haphazard way of collecting information, although it can be very interesting if you are not pressed for time.

For instance you may visit a particular news site regularly and find that an article contains links to other pages, either within that site or on an external site that contain more information about the topic. To see this in action find an article of interest to you at www.bbc.co.uk and follow up some of the external links.

2.3 Directories and portals

A directory is a service that offers links to web pages organized into subject categories. Directory services supposedly contain links only to pages that have been evaluated by human beings, using various selection criteria, though the selectivity varies among services.

The best known example of a directory is Yahoo! (www.yahoo.com), although Yahoo! does not evaluate sites as carefully as some other directories and it is aimed more at the leisure interests of home computer users than at the serious academic or business researcher.

Most directories also include some kind of search facility, which either searches the directory only or (confusingly) searches the web in general, perhaps using another type of search tool. Yahoo searches, for instance, are powered by the Google search engine (described below), so Yahoo is actually a mixture between a directory and a search engine.

The best subject directories include notes about sites written by independent reviewers, describing and evaluating site content. For instance you would probably find a site such as the Social Science Information Gateway (SOSIG) (www.sosig.ac.uk) far more informative about useful business-related sites than Yahoo.

A **portal** is similar to a directory (and the terms are often used interchangeably) but many portals are much narrower in scope, restricting their links to specific subjects. Examples include www.thisislondon.co.uk and www.fool.com (for investors) or, more generally, the home pages of most of the leading ISPs.

Yet another term you may see used is **vortal** (vertical industry portal) which is a portal providing information and resources for a particular industry. Examples include www.accountingweb.co.uk and www.privatehealth.co.uk amongst thousands of others.

Typical services offered by portal or vortal sites include a directory of related websites, a facility to search for other sites, news, and community services such as discussion boards and suppliers directories.

2.4 Search engines

Search engines such as AltaVista or Google retrieve links to, and brief descriptions of, websites containing a word or phrase entered by the user. The descriptions are derived from the webpage itself: there is no human judgement involved other than the judgement of the original author of the page.

Search engines are fairly indiscriminate. Some of the results they give may come from reputable sources and provide you with valuable up to date information, but others may be out of date, inaccurate or incomplete.

With a **'first generation'** search engine such as the original **AltaVista** (www.altavista.com) the results of a search are usually presented in 'term ranked' order. This means that a document appears higher in the list of results if your search terms occur very frequently in the document, or in the document title, or near the beginning of the document, or close together in the document.

Many, if not all, first generation search engines have transformed themselves into portals and/or have some 'second-generation' features, because basic term-ranked searching is indiscriminate and gives far too many results.

Marketing at Work

'Second generation' search engines such as **Google** (www.google.com) order search results by links or popularity, by concept, by keyword, or by type of site. These search engines generally give better quality results because there is at least some human element in determining what is relevant.

For example, one of the ways that **Google** ranks pages is according to the number of other pages that link to it. The more web authors there are who have decided that it is worth including a link to a page the more likely it is that the page is useful and relevant to the topic you are searching for.

Ixquick (www.ixquick.com) is a **metasearch engine**, which means that it uses multiple other search engines simultaneously and returns the results in a single list with duplicate files removed.

Ixquick only returns the top ten results from the source search services, so in theory you can harness the collective judgement of many search tools about the relevancy and usefulness of sites on a topic all in a single search.

By default the sources Ixquick uses are country specific. In other words it checks where you are dialling in from and then uses search tools that mainly return results from that country. You can of course override this, if you wish to look at sites from other countries.

2.5 Internet databases (the 'deep web')

Many websites consist of pages that are generated 'dynamically' using content stored in a database. In other words the contents that you see are only assembled—and put into a web page that your browser can read—on request. The page does not actually exist in the form of a saved file and therefore it can't be found by a search engine or listed in a directory.

Typical sites that use databases will be those that have often-changing data such as airline information sites, and news-related sites with up to the minute current stories and archived stories and articles going back several years.

Such content is called the 'invisible' web or the 'deep' web and estimates suggest that there is now at least 500 times more material in this form than there is on the conventional web. The reason is because it is more efficient to store data in this way. Most web pages consist of standard elements like logos and navigation menus and tables defining layout, so it is more efficient to create a single template for all the elements that do not change and simply 'plug' the required information into a space in the template.

Clearly you cannot afford to ignore such a large source of information, but how do you find it? The only way you can do so is to search the database itself. This is not as complicated as it sounds: from the point of view of the user you either just click on what appears to be an ordinary link or you type a few words in the 'Search' box on the site itself.

For example if you were using www.dictionary.com and wanted to find definitions for the term 'dynamic' you would simply type 'dynamic' into the search box and click on the 'Look it up' button. This takes you to the URL dictionary.reference.com/search?q=dynamic: the part of the URL after the question mark is actually an instruction to extract relevant material from the site's database about the term 'dynamic' and present it in a web page.

2.6 Refining a search

Many people—especially new users—find searching the web extremely frustrating because they cannot find what they are looking for quickly enough. In this section we describe some of the things you can do to make your searches more productive.

2.6.1 Use your initial search proactively

If you are researching a new topic the chances are that you will not be very familiar with the concepts and terminology of that subject.

In this case, when you do an initial search spend a few moments skim reading the first few results pages. They probably won't tell you what you want to know, but they may well include words and phrases that you could add to your search terms to give more useful results, or words and phrases that you could exclude from your search (we'll explain how to do this in a moment).

Some search engines display words such as More Like This or Similar pages next to each entry. For instance if you searched for 'management tips' you would find that one of the first few results was to do with time management. If time management happened to be your specific interest you could get a new list of sites specifically on that subject simply by clicking on the Similar Pages or More Like This link.

2.6.2 Restrict the search area

Some search engines have options to restrict the number of sites searched, for instance to UK sites only, or to English language sites only. Even if that option is not available you will generally find that if you simply add UK to your search term the results will be closer to the ones you need.

2.6.3 Advanced search techniques

On many (though not all) sites the search facility allows you to use **symbols** and/or what are known as **Boolean operators** to help refine what should and should not be searched for. These so-called 'advanced' searching techniques are extremely useful.

Different search engines have slightly different rules for formulating queries, so it is always a good idea to **read the help files** at the site before you start a search.

(a) **Plus signs (+)** If you put a plus sign (+) directly in front of a word (with no space) this tells the search engine that the word **must** be present in all the pages that are found. So if you type **+management +tips**, you will only get pages that contain both words (though not necessarily together or in the order you specify).

(b) **Minus signs (–)** As you might expect, the – sign works in the opposite way to +. If you put a minus sign directly in front of a word the search engine will **ignore** any documents that contain that word. So, if you type **+management +tips –racing** you will avoid pages that have tips on the horses! However intuitive you are at using the minus sign you are still likely to get links that you are not interested in. You probably would not think of typing, say, **+management +tips –pest,** for example, because the idea of pest management in gardening would probably not occur to you when you were thinking about managing your workteam.

(c) **Quotation marks (")** To find **only** pages that contain the phrase **management tips,** with the words together in that order, you enclose them in double quotation marks: **"management tips"**. This is very useful so long as your phrase is only two or three words long or if you know exactly how the phrase should be worded (because it is a famous quotation, say).

(d) **OR** There is a good chance that some of the pages relevant to your search will use alternative words to the ones you first think of. If you can guess what the alternatives might be you can use OR to make the search engine look for pages that contain at least one of them: for instance **management +tips OR hints OR advice**.

Action Programme 4

Try all of these techniques in a search engine such as Google and observe the different results that you get. You can either use our example 'management tips' or some other phrase of your own, if you prefer.

3 Published secondary data

FAST FORWARD

Many **useful reports** and statistics are published by **government** and **non-government sources**.

By published we mean **published in any form** – on the web, in book form, on CD. Much published data is now available in several forms.

3.1 Directories

Directories can make a good starting point for research. The information provided is usually on industries and markets, manufacturers (size, location), products, sales and profits. Examples of business directories include the following (although there are many others).

(a) Kompass Register (Kompass)
(www.kompass.co.uk)

(b) Who owns Whom (Dun and Bradstreet)
(www.dnb.com)

(c) Key British Enterprises (Dun and Bradstreet)
(www.dnb.com/UK)

3.2 Computerised databases

These include the following.

- ACORN (consumption indices by class of neighbourhood) (www.caci.co.uk)
- Marketing Surveys Index (CIM) (www.cim.co.uk)
- MRS Yearbook (Market Research Agencies and their specialisms) (www.mrs.org.uk)
- TGI and other syndicated omnibus surveys (www.tgisurveys.com)
- Kompass Online (www.kompass.co.uk)
- Financial Times Company Information (www.ft.com) and many other newspapers
- Hoppenstedt Austria/Germany/Netherlands (www.hoppenstedt.de)
- Jordanwatch (www.jordans.co.uk)
- Reuters (www.reuters.com)
- LexisNexis (www.lexisnexis.com)

Such databases are generally **subscription-based**. Subscriptions are not cheap, but it is usually much less expensive than collecting the information oneself. A trained operator should be used to begin with, to avoid expensive waste of the resources.

3.3 Associations

There are associations in almost every field of business and leisure activity. All these bodies collect and publish data for their members which can be of great interest to other users. Examples of such bodies include the Road Haulage Association (RHA), the British Association of Ski Instructors and ... you name it, there will almost certainly be an association for it.

3.4 Government agencies

There is a wealth of published statistics which can be used in marketing research. There are two prime sources – government and non-government.

Governments are a major source of economic information and information about industry and population trends. To find material from the UK on the web the best place to start is **www.statistics.gov.uk**. Other countries have similar government sites.

Official statistics are also published by other government bodies such as the European Union, the United Nations and local authorities.

3.4.1 Non-government sources of information

There are numerous other sources.

(a) Companies and other organisations specialising in the provision of economic and financial data (eg the Financial Times Business Information Service, the Data Research Institute, LexisNexis, Reuters, the Extel Group).

(b) Directories and yearbooks, such as Kompass or Kelly's Directory (online as www.kellysearch.com)

(c) Professional institutions (eg Chartered Institute of Marketing, Industrial Marketing Research Association, Institute of Management, Institute of Practitioners in Advertising)

(d) Specialist libraries, such as the City Business Library in London, collect published information from a wide variety of sources

(e) Trade associations, trade unions and Chambers of Commerce

(f) Trade journals

(g) Commercial organisations such as banks and TV networks

(h) Market research agencies

3.5 Environmental scanning

FAST FORWARD

Environmental scanning is an informal process resulting in the possession of market intelligence. Sources include newspapers, journals and attending conferences.

Environmental scanning means **keeping your eyes and ears open to** what is going on generally in **the market place**, especially with respect to competitors, and more widely in the technological, social, economic and political environment. Much of the data will be qualitative but could be systematically logged and backed up by quantitative data if possible.

The result of environmental scanning is market intelligence. Excellent sources are as follows.

(a) Business and financial newspapers, especially the *Financial Times* and the *Wall Street Journal*

(b) General business magazines, such as the *Economist*, *Business Week* and *Marketing Business* (published ten times a year by the Chartered Institute of Marketing (CIM) and sent to CIM students)

(c) Trade journals, such as *Research*, for marketing research or *The Grocer* for retailers or a huge host of others for all sorts of businesses

(d) Academic journals, such as *Harvard Business Review*

(e) Attending conferences, exhibitions, courses and trade fairs

(f) Making use of salesforce feedback

(g) Developing and making use of a network of personal contacts in the trade

(h) Watching competitors (extremely important)

With regard to watching competitors, a **competitor intelligence system** needs to be set up to cope with a vast amount of data from:

- Financial statements
- Common customers and suppliers
- Inspection of a competitor's products
- The competitor's former employees
- Job advertisements

In other words there is a combination of published data and 'field data', which need to be compiled (eg clipping services on- or offline, standard monthly reports on competitors' activities), catalogued, and analysed (summarised, ranked by reliability, extrapolated data from financial reports).

The object of what is usually an informal but constant process is to ensure that the organisation is not caught by surprise by developments which could have and should have been picked up. The organisation needs to be able to adapt to changing circumstances.

3.6 Other published sources

This group includes all other publications. The following is just a tiny selection to indicate the type of data available.

(a) Some **digests** and **pocket books**

- Lifestyle Pocket Book (annual by the Advertising Association) (www.adassoc.org.uk)
- Retail Pocket Book (annual by Nielsen) (www.acnielsen.com)
- A to Z of UK Marketing Data (Euromonitor) (www.euromonitor.com)
- UK in figures (annual, free from Office for National Statistics) (www.ons.gov.uk)

(b) Some important **periodicals** (often available in the public libraries)

- *Economist* (general) (www.economist.com)
- *Campaign* (advertising) (www.campaignlive.com)
- World Advertising Research Center (www.warc.com), publishers of ADMAP (advertising)
- Mintel (consumer market reports) (www.mintel.com)
- BRAD (all media selling advertising space in the UK including TV, radio, newspapers and magazines) (www.intellagencia.com)

4 Panels and indexes

FAST FORWARD

Data and reports can be **bought in** from **marketing research organisations**. Often these are the result of continuous research using consumer and retail panels.

The sources of secondary data we have looked at so far have generally been **free** because they are **in the public domain**. Inexpensiveness is an advantage which can be offset by the fact that the information is unspecific and needs considerable analysis before being useable.

A middle step between adapting secondary data and commissioning primary research is the **purchase of data collected by market research companies** or business publishing houses. The data tend to be expensive but less costly than primary research.

There are a great many commercial sources of secondary data, and a number of guides to these sources are available.

- *The Source Book*, Key Note Publications
- *Guide to Official Statistics*, HMSO
- *Published Data of European Markets*, Industrial Aids Ltd
- *Compendium of Marketing Information Sources*, Euromonitor
- *Market-Search*, British Overseas Trade Board

Commonly used sources of data on particular industries and markets are:

- Key Note Publications
- *Retail Business*, Economist Intelligence Unit
- Mintel publications
- *Market Research GB*, Euromonitor

4.1 Consumer panels

A form of continuous research which results in secondary data is that generated by **consumer panels**. These constitute a representative sample of individuals and households whose buying activity in a defined area is monitored either continuously (every day, with results aggregated) or at regular intervals, **over a period of time**. There are panels set up to monitor purchases of groceries, consumer durables, cars, baby products and many others.

Marketing at Work

Translucis has a constant need to keep in touch with fast-changing young opinions in order to keep its offering relevant to its audience. MR is seen as an investment, a tool for both adding value to the service the company provides to advertisers and demonstrating its understanding of the youth sector.

The main vehicle for this is a continuous qualitative programme conducted exclusively by specialist youth agency 2cv:research (2cv) under the name Grapevine. At its core is a schedule of two focus groups a month, rotating between London, Manchester and Glasgow.

There are 16 panellists in each city, selected for being 'interesting mainstream' – articulate, with compelling things to say about themselves and their lifestyles, but not necessarily style leaders.

To keep the dialogue fresh, panellists serve on two rounds of research before being replaced by new recruits. Included in the total are three male and three female 'trend scouts', chosen because they show a particular interest in emerging fashions.

Topics typically range from what ads they've seen recently and their views on various media, to how they would categorise a cross-section of consumer brands.

Research, 1st February 2002

Most consumer panels consisting of a **representative cross-section of consumers** who have agreed to give information about their attitudes or buying habits (through personal visits or postal questionnaires) at regular intervals of time. Consumer panels with personal visits are called **home audit panels**.

There are some problems with such panels:

(a) It is **difficult** to select a panel which is a **representative** sample. The panel must be representative of:

  (i) All the customers in the target market.

  (ii) The decision making units who will make the purchase decision (eg male as well as female partners).

(b) Panel members **tend to become sophisticated** in interviewing techniques and responses and so the panel becomes 'corrupt'.

(c) It is **difficult to maintain a stable personnel**; turnover of members may be high and this will affect results as new members are enlisted.

Consumer panels generate a vast amount of data which need to be sorted if they are to be digestible. Analyses available include:

(a) **Standard trend analysis**, showing how the market and its major brands have fared since the last analysis, grossed up to reflect the entire population or a particular region.

(b) **Special analyses** depending on industrial preferences. Common ones are:

  (i) Source of purchase analysis

  (ii) Frequency of purchase analysis

  (iii) **Demographic analysis** (in terms of household age, number of children, ACORN classification)

  (iv) Tracking of individuals, to show their degree of brand loyalty, how and when they change brands.

4.2 Retail panels

Trade audits are carried out among panels of wholesalers and retailers, and the term 'retail audits' refers to panels of retailers only. A research firm sends 'auditors' to selected outlets at regular intervals to count stock and deliveries, thus enabling an estimate of throughput to be made. Sometimes it is possible to do a universal audit of all retail outlets. EPOS makes the process easier.

The audits provide details of the following.

(a) Retail sales for selected products and brands, sales by different types of retail outlet, market shares and brand shares.

(b) Retail stocks of products and brands (enabling a firm subscribing to the audit to compare stocks of its own goods with those of competitors).

(c) Selling prices in retail outlets, including information about discounts.

4.3 The Nielsen Retail Index

Nielsen was the first market research organisation to establish continuous retail tracking operations in the UK. The Nielsen Index refers to a **range of continuous sales and distribution measurements**, embracing ten separate product fields.

- Grocery
- Health and beauty
- Confectionery
- Home improvements
- Cash and carry outlets
- Sportswear
- Liquor
- Toys
- Tobacco
- Electrical

These indexes together measure a large number of sales and distribution variables for over 600 different product categories and over 120,000 brands and associated brand variants.

Data are collected from the **major multiples** (like Tesco and Sainsbury) through their EPOS systems. For other types of shop where EPOS data are not available, a monthly audit of stocks is undertaken and, using data from deliveries, the level of what sales must have been since the last audit is determined.

Increasingly, **Nielsen clients receive their data electronically** on databases, Nielsen having developed a range of data management and analysis software. A Nielsen service called Inf*Act Workstation offers a powerful yet flexible personal, computer-based decision support system.

4.4 Taylor Nelson Sofres Superpanel

The Superpanel (www.tnsofres.com/superpanel) consists of 8,500 households, covering the **purchases of some 28,000 individuals** aged between 5 and 79, who are resident in **domestic households** across Great Britain.

Data collection is through **personal data terminals** equipped with a laser light pen. The terminal is designed to resemble a digital phone and is kept in a modem linked to the domestic power supply and the telephone socket. Data capture is via overnight polling (which means that AGB's central computer dials each panel number in turn and accesses the data stored in the modem).

All that is required from informants is that when they unpack their shopping, they pass the laser light pen over the barcode for each item, and also enter standardised data about the date, shop(s) visited and prices paid. The process incorporates procedures for entering details of products either without barcodes or which have a bar-code that is difficult to read.

Recruitment to the AGB Superpanel uses a multi-stage procedure. A large sample of households are screened to identify those in each sampling point eligible for the service and with known demographics. For this purpose, AGB uses personal home interviews, some 200,000 annually, within 270 parliamentary constituencies (about half the total number).

The households with the relevant target demographics are then selected and the 'housewife' (who may be male or female) for each household is contacted by phone. If the initial contact proves positive, the household as a whole is briefed and the equipment installed.

4.5 Taylor Nelson Sofres Omnimas

Omnimas (www.tnsofres.com/consumeromnibus/omnimas) is one of the largest single **random omnibus surveys** in the world, with some **2,100 adults being interviewed face-to-face** every week.

A random sampling approach is employed, using the **electoral registers** from 233 parliamentary constituencies selected in proportion to size within each of the ten standard regions of the UK.

Each interviewer has a minimum of 13 interviews to do a week. Because the only quota set is that the interviewer should obtain either six men and seven women, or vice versa, there is a control on sex, but everything else depends on the randomness of the sample.

The Omnimas questionnaire is divided into three sections.

(a) A **continuous section**, including questions asked on every survey and inserted on behalf of a particular client.

(b) An **ad-hoc section** of questions included on a one-off basis.

(c) A **classification section** that includes all the demographic questions.

Given an average completion time of 25 minutes per respondent and the 20-30 seconds needed to administer an average question, the total number of Omnimas questions will not be more than about 60-70. Most questions are fixed-choice, with a predetermined number of possible responses, but some clients require open-ended questions and the Omnimas approach allows for a few of these to be included.

4.6 Target Group Index (TGI)

TGI is owned by BMRB (www.bmrb.co.uk) but has its own website (www.tgisurveys.com). The purpose of TGI (www.tgisurveys.com) is to increase the efficiency of marketing operations by identifying and describing **target groups** of consumers and their **exposure to the media** (newspapers, magazines, television and radio) and the extent to which they see or hear other media.

In design, TGI is a regular interval survey and is also 'single source', in that it covers both **product usage data** and **media exposure data**.

Respondents are questioned on a number of areas; **purchase behaviour and media use are cross-tabulated** to enable more accurate media audience targeting.

- Their use of 400 different products covering 3,500 brands
- Their readership of over 170 magazines and newspapers
- Cinema attendance
- ITV television watching
- Listening patterns for commercial radio stations
- Their lifestyles, based on nearly 200 attitude questions

The major **product fields** covered are foods, household goods, medicaments, toiletries and cosmetics, drink, confectionery, tobacco, motoring, clothing, leisure, holidays, financial services and consumer durables. It is worth noting that respondents are only asked about the use, ownership and consumption of the products identified, not about purchases made or prices paid.

The **lifestyle questions** are in the form of Likert-type attitude statements with which people are asked to agree or disagree on a five-point scale from 'definitely agree' to 'definitely disagree'. These attitude statements cover the main areas of food, drink, shopping, diet/health, personal appearance, DIY, holidays, finance, travel, media, motivation/self-perception, plus questions on some specific products and attitudes to sponsorship.

Each questionnaire runs to more than 90 pages and can take four hours to complete. However, the document is totally pre-coded and adapted for optical mark reading, with respondents being able to indicate their replies by pencil strokes. There are three versions of the questionnaire, for men, for housewives, and for other women.

TGI results supply enormous amounts of information, both within categories and cross-tabulated against other relevant categories. There are about 25,000 responses per annum.

(a) **Total numbers of product users** for each demographic category.

(b) **Percentages of product users** in each demographic category.

(c) Information on **heavy/medium/light** and **non-users** for each product or product category.

(d) For **brands and product fields** with more than one million claimed users, consumption can be **cross-tabulated** against a range of **demographic variables** including sex, age, social class, area, number of children, and media usage.

(e) Brand usage tables, listing the following.

- **Solus users** – users of the product group who use the brand exclusively.
- **Most-often users** – those who prefer it, but use another brand as well.
- **Minor users** – those who do not discriminate between brands.

TGI appears in 34 volumes, published annually in July and August, but subscribers have **on-line access** to datasets for which they have subscribed, and they can analyse the data on their own PCs.

5 Benefits, risks and dangers of reliance on secondary data 12/06

FAST FORWARD

Secondary sources of data are of **limited use** because of the **scope for compounding errors** arising from why and how the data were collected in the first place, who collected them and how long ago.

When considering the quality of the secondary data it is a good idea to consider the following characteristics of it:

(a) The **producers** of the data (they may have an axe to grind; trade associations may not include data which runs counter to the interest of its members).

(b) The **reason for the data** being collected in the first place.

(c) The **collection method** (random samples with a poor response rate are particularly questionable).

(d) How **old** the data is (government statistics and information based on them are often relatively dated, though information technology has speeded up the process).

(e) **How parameters were defined**. For instance, the definition of family used by some researchers could be different to that used by others.

5.1 Advantages and disadvantages of secondary data

FAST FORWARD

Secondary data can be **immensely cost-effective**, but have to be **used with care**.

The **advantages** arising from the use of secondary data include the following.

(a) Secondary data may solve the problem without the need for any primary research: **time and money is thereby saved**.

(b) Cost savings can be substantial because secondary data sources are a great deal **cheaper** than those for primary research.

(c) Secondary data, while not necessarily fulfilling all the needs of the business, can be of great use by:

(i) **Setting the parameters**, defining a hypothesis, highlighting variables, in other words, helping to focus on the central problem.

(ii) **Providing guidance**, by showing past methods of research, for primary data collection.

(iii) **Helping to assimilate the primary research** with past research, highlighting trends and the like.

(iv) **Defining sampling parameter**, (target populations, variables).

There are, of course, plenty of **disadvantages** to the use of secondary data.

(a) **Relevance**. The data may not be relevant to the research objectives in terms of the data content itself, classifications used or units of measurement.

(b) **Cost**. Although secondary data is usually cheaper than primary data, some specialist reports can cost large amounts of money. A cost-benefit analysis will determine whether such secondary data should be used or whether primary research would be more economical.

(c) **Availability**. Secondary data may not exist in the specific product or market area.

(d) **Bias**. The secondary data may be biased, depending on who originally carried it out and for what purpose. Attempts should be made to obtain the most original source of the data, to assess it for such bias.

(e) **Accuracy**. The accuracy of the data should be questioned. Here is a possible checklist.

- Was the sample representative?
- Was the questionnaire or other measurement instrument(s) properly constructed?
- Were possible biases in response or in non-response corrected and accounted for?
- Was the data properly analysed using appropriate statistical techniques?
- Was a sufficiently large sample used?
- Does the report include the raw data?
- To what degree were the field-workers supervised?

In addition, was any raw data omitted from the final report, and why?

(f) **Sufficiency**. Even after fulfilling all the above criteria, the secondary data may be insufficient and primary research would therefore be necessary.

Action Programme 5

How can secondary data help when a firm is considering an international advertising campaign?

The golden rule when using secondary data is **use only meaningful data**. It is obviously sensible to begin with internal sources and a firm with a good management information system should be able to provide a great deal of data. External information should be consulted in order of ease and speed of access: directories, catalogues and indexes before books, abstracts and periodicals. A good librarian should be a great help.

Chapter Roundup

- The **collection of secondary data** is often referred to as **desk research**, since it does not involve the collection of raw data from the market direct. Desk research includes using library sources, the organisation's information system, databases and internal reports.
- The **Internet** is the richest secondary source of information of all, on practically any subject you can think of. Not all of it is good information, however, and although in theory it is easy to search the Internet, in practice it often takes longer to find exactly what you want than another method would have taken. Knowing which search tool to use and how to use it is a key skill for a researcher.
- Many **useful reports** and statistics are published by **government** and **non-government sources**.
- **Environmental scanning** is an informal process resulting in the possession of market intelligence. Sources include newspapers, journals and attending conferences.
- **Data and reports** can be **bought in** from **marketing research organisations**. Often these are the result of continuous research using consumer and retail panels.
- Secondary sources of data are of **limited use** because of the **scope for compounding errors** arising from why and how the data were collected in the first place, who collected them and how long ago.
- Secondary data can be **immensely cost-effective**, but have to be **used with care**.

Quick Quiz

1 Secondary data is external data. True or false? Explain your answer.

2 Secondary data can perform three roles: what are they?

3 Why might a directory be a better source of useful information than a general purpose search engine?

4 Why might this search produced unexpected results?

5 What are three difficulties with consumer panels?

6 BARCAS is a possible mnemonic for some of the limitations of secondary data. What does it stand for?

Answers to Quick Quiz

1 False. Secondary data may be any information not created specifically for the research task including internal data such as sales transaction data.

2 It can provide a backdrop to primary research; it can act as a substitute for field research; and it can be used as a technique in itself.

3 Good directories are compiled by human experts who can review the quality and usefulness of links, whereas a general purpose search engine is fairly indiscriminate about the quality of the pages it turns up in a search.

4 The results will be (probably millions of) pages that contain the words secondary and data, but not necessarily the phrase "secondary data". The phrase should be enclosed in inverted commas.

5 It is difficult to select a panel which is a representative sample; panel members tend to become sophisticated in interviewing techniques and responses and so the panel becomes 'corrupt'; and it is difficult to maintain a stable personnel.

6 Bias, Availability, Relevance, Cost, Accuracy, Sufficiency. Make sure you could expand upon each of these terms.

Action Programme Review

1 The limitations of desk research are as follows.

(a) The data gathered is by definition not specific to the matter under analysis. It was gathered and prepared for another purpose and so is unlikely to be ideal.

(b) Because it was gathered for another purpose, the data are likely to require a fair amount of adaptation and analysis before they can be used.

(c) The data gathered are historical and may be some time out of date.

2 It is worthwhile having a discussion with colleagues about this because people vary considerably in their views. For example the writer of this book would not dream of buying a car online, but would happily buy any of the other items mentioned in the question. You may feel quite differently.

3 This approach is too haphazard, as you have probably discovered, having tried this activity. The main drawback is that you usually need to guess the second part of the address (.com, .co.uk, .org, .net): it may take several goes before you get it right, in which case it would have been quicker to use a proper search tool.

4 This is a 'hands-on' exercise.

5 Secondary data sources can be used to investigate the advertising regulations in different countries. In certain countries there may be restrictions on advertising directed at children, on advertising tobacco or alcohol. Some countries may insist on pre-broadcast screening. The secondary data could also provide information on the advertising authorities in each country (if any).

Now try Question 8 at the end of the Study Text

7

Collecting qualitative data

Chapter topic list

Syllabus content – knowledge and skill requirements

- 4.2: The key sources of primary and secondary data
- 4.3: Procedures for observing behaviour
- 4.4: The various methods for collecting qualitative and quantitative data

Introduction

Qualitative research is a process which aims to collect primary data. Its main methods are the open-ended interview, whether this be a **depth interview** (one-to-one) or a **group discussion** (focus group), and **projective techniques**. The form of the data collected is narrative, rather than isolated statements reducible to numbers. The main purpose is to **understand** consumer behaviour and perceptions rather than to measure them.

Key concept

Qualitative research is 'research which is undertaken using an unstructured research approach with a small number of carefully selected individuals to produce non-quantifiable insights into behaviour, motivation and attitudes.' (Wilson, 2002).

We'll begin this chapter by considering when it might be **appropriate** to conduct qualitative research. Then we go on to consider each of the main methods.

The **analysis** of qualitative data is considered in Part E of this book.

Marketing at Work

Consensus Global is a company specialising in speaking to 'decision makers' and 'opinion leaders'. This aids researchers in organising interviews or focus groups with people who are usually very difficult to reach.

(*www.research-live.com*)

1 Using qualitative research

FAST FORWARD

Qualitative research is particularly useful for new product research, marketing communications development and preliminary (exploratory) research prior to a more detailed, probably quantitative study.

1.0.1 New products or services

New products and services (and also proposed improvements to existing products and services) have the disadvantage that there is **no existing data** to measure and perhaps **nothing more tangible than an idea** to present to people.

Qualitative research can help at the initial stages of development to help the company decide whether or not to continue with development at all, and later on, once there is a prototype of some kind, to find out what **further development** is necessary – what **other benefits** customers would like to see that could be included.

It may also help the company to decide **what part of the market** to target: the idea may be very warmly received by some groups but generate no interest whatever amongst others.

1.0.2 Advertising and promotion

Qualitative research is fairly widely used in the **development** of marketing communications messages to assess how consumers feel about a product or service and what sort of message they are most likely to respond to.

Qualitative methods can also be used to **pre-test** marketing communications messages to make sure the message is understood and that no unintended messages are conveyed.

1.0.3 Other exploratory research

For existing products and services qualitative research may be used to find the answers to a variety of questions about customer attitudes and perceptions, segmentation and buying behaviour, often as a **preliminary** to help define the direction of **more detailed research**. For instance if ultimately you want statistical data about the decision-making process amongst different buyer segments you need to know what the different decision-making processes are in the first place, so you know what to measure.

2 Interviews

FAST FORWARD

The main method of qualitative research is the **interview**.

The key to qualitative research is to allow the respondents to say what they feel and think in response to flexible, 'prompting' questioning, rather than to give their responses to set questions and often set answers in a questionnaire.

2.1 Unstructured interviews

Neither interviewer or respondent is bound by the structure of a questionnaire in an unstructured interview. Interviewers may have a checklist of topics to cover in questioning, but they are free to word such questions as they wish. The order in which questions are covered may also be varied. This will allow the respondent to control the data flow and for the interviewer to explore more thoroughly particular views of the respondent and why they are held. Unstructured interviews are a very useful way of capturing data which is qualitative in nature. Such interviews may also provide the researcher with relevant questions which could be put to a wider audience of respondents using structured or semi-structured interview techniques, especially if quantitative data is required.

2.2 Depth interviews

Motivational research often uses the psychoanalytic method of **depth interviews**. The pattern of questioning should assist the respondent to explore deeper levels of thought. Motives and explanations of behaviour often lie well **below the surface**. It is a **time-consuming** and **expensive** process. Taped interviews and analysis of transcripts are often used. A single individual or a small team may conduct depth interviewing. Depth interviews may have fewer than ten respondents.

The **strengths of depth interviews** include the following.

(a) **Longitudinal information** (such as information on decision-making processes) can be gathered from one respondent at a time, thereby aiding clarity of interpretation and analysis.

(b) Intimate and **personal material** can be more easily accessed and discussed.

(c) Respondents are **less likely to confine themselves** simply to reiterating socially acceptable attitudes.

There are, however, **disadvantages** of depth interviews.

(a) They are **time consuming** to conduct and to analyse. If each interview lasts between one and two hours, a maximum of three or four per day is often all that is possible.

(b) They are more **costly** than group discussions.

(c) There is a temptation to begin treating depth interviews as if they were simply another form of questionnaire survey, thinking in terms of quantitative questions like 'how many' rather than qualitative issues like 'how', 'why' or 'what'.

In a depth interview the key line of communication is between the interviewer and the respondent. They have an **open-ended conversation**, not constrained by a formal questionnaire, and the qualitative data are captured as narrative by means of an audio or video tape.

Action Programme 1

Which do you think is preferable: audio or video tape?

The factors to consider when planning a depth interview are as follows.

(a) **Who should the respondent be?**

(i) The kind of person depends on the subject being discussed. It may be a consumer interview for discussion of consumer goods or an executive interview for discussing industrial buying.

(ii) The number of people undergoing depth interviews in the course of the research should be considered in the light of the time they take. 10-15 is usually more than enough.

(iii) Respondents for consumer interviews are pre-recruited and asked to agree to the interview.

(b) **What type of interview?** Although depth interviews are usually one-to-one, there may be more than one respondent and there may also be an informant, there to give information about tangible things (eg how big the organisation's purchase budget is) but not about his own attitudes.

(c) **How long should it be?** Genuine depth interviews interpret the meanings and implications of what is said and can therefore take some time. By contrast, a mini-depth interview may take only 15 minutes, because it can focus on one, predefined topic like a pack design.

(d) **How structured should it be?** It can be totally open-ended, ranging over whatever topics come up, or it can be semi-structured with an interview guide and perhaps the use of show material.

(e) **What material should be used?** The type of material that is commonly used includes mock-ups or prototypes, storyboards or concept boards, narrative tapes and animatics, a form of cartoon.

(f) **Where should the interview take place?** Usually at home or in the workplace.

3 Projective techniques 12/03, 12/04, 6/05, 12/05, 6/06, 12/06

FAST FORWARD

Projective techniques attempt to draw out attitudes, opinions and motives by a variety of methods.

Many interview techniques rely on the assumption that you need only to ask people and they will tell you what you want to know. This is not always the case. People may respond differently to how they would act. People may tell you what they think you want to hear or give a different answer because their true answer may reflect badly on them or because they consider it too personal.

Alternatively, people may find difficulty in articulating their motives which lie buried deep within the sub-conscious mind. So as to overcome problems associated with articulating complex or sub-conscious motives, researchers have borrowed techniques developed by psychologists in their studies of mentally disturbed people who have difficulty explaining why they do things.

These techniques are referred to as **projective techniques**. Attitudes, opinions and motives are drawn out from the individual in response to given stimuli.

A number of techniques might be employed.

(a) **Third person**, or 'friendly Martian' as it is sometimes called, is designed to get the respondent talking about issues which do not interest them. The researcher asks the respondent to describe what someone else might do (a friendly Martian). For example, if someone wanted to buy a house, what do they need to do? Can you describe the steps they would need to take?

(b) **Word association** is based on an assumption that if a question is answered quickly, it is spontaneous and sub-conscious thoughts are therefore revealed. The person's conscious mind does not have time to think up an alternative response.

(c) **Sentence completion** is a useful way to get people to respond quickly so that underlying attitudes and opinions are revealed.

- Men who watch football are ....?
- Women wear red to ....?
- People who Morris dance are ....?

(d) In **thematic apperception tests** (TAT tests), people are shown a picture and asked to describe what is happening in the picture. They may be asked what happened just before or just after the picture. It is hoped that the descriptions reveal information about deeply held attitudes, beliefs, motives and opinions stored in the sub-conscious mind.

(e) **Story completion** allows the respondent to say what they think happens next and why.

(f) **Cartoon completion** is often used in competitions. There are usually speech balloons which need to be completed. A comment may be present in one and another left blank for the respondent to fill in.

(g) **Psychodrama** consists of fantasy situations. Respondents are often asked to imagine themselves as a product and describe their feelings about being used. Sometimes respondents are asked to imagine themselves as a brand and to describe particular attributes.

Marketing at Work

Household goods maker Reckitt Benckiser uses face to face interviewing for its brand tracking. The company believes that this allows it far more flexibility with the stimulus material that it can use to test brand responses. *(www.research-live.com)*

3.1 Problems and value of projective research methods

There are a few problems associated with projective techniques.

(a) Hard evidence of their validity is lacking. Highly exotic motives can be imputed to quite ordinary buying decisions. (One study concluded that women preferred spray to pellets when it came to killing cockroaches because being able to spray the cockroaches directly and watch them die was an expression of hostility towards, and control over, men!)

(b) As with other forms of intensive qualitative research, the samples of the population can only be very small, and it may not be possible to generalise findings to the market as a whole.

(c) Analysis of projective test findings – as with depth interviews – is highly **subjective** and prone to bias. Different analysts can produce different explanations for a single set of test results.

(d) Many of the tests were not developed for the study of marketing or consumer behaviour, and **may not therefore be considered scientifically valid** as methods of enquiry in those areas.

(e) There are **ethical problems** with 'invasion' of an individual's subconscious mind in conditions where he is often not made aware that he is exposing himself to such probing. (On the other hand, one of the flaws in projective testing is that subjects may be all too well aware of the nature of the test. The identification of sexual images in inkblots has become a standard joke.)

The major drawback with projective techniques is that answers given by respondents require considerable and **skilled analysis and interpretation**. The techniques are most valuable in providing **insights** rather than **answers** to specific research questions.

However, motivational research is still in use. Emotion and subconscious motivation is still believed to be vitally important in consumer choice, and qualitative techniques can give marketers a deeper insight into those areas than conventional, quantitative marketing research.

Since motivational research often **reveals hidden motives** for product/brand purchase and usage, its main value lies in the following.

(a) Developing **new promotional messages** which will appeal to deep, often unrecognised, needs and associations

(b) Allowing the **testing of brand names**, symbols and advertising copy, to check for positive, negative and/or irrelevant associations and interpretations

(c) Providing **hypotheses which can be tested** on larger, more representative samples of the population, using more structured quantitative techniques (questionnaires, surveys).

4 Focus groups 6/05, 12/05, 6/06, 12/06

FAST FORWARD

Focus groups concentrate on discussion of chosen topics in an attempt to find out attitudes. They do have limitations despite advantages such as the ability to observe a whole range of responses at the same time.

These are useful in providing the researcher with qualitative data.

Key concept

Focus groups usually consist of 8 to 10 respondents and an interviewer taking the role of group moderator. The group moderator introduces topics for discussion and intervenes as necessary to encourage respondents or to direct discussions if they threaten to wander too far off the point. The moderator will also need to control any powerful personalities and prevent them from dominating the group.

The researcher must be careful not to generalise too much from such small scale qualitative research. Group discussion is very dependent on the skill of the group moderator. It is inexpensive to conduct, it can be done quickly and it can provide useful, timely, qualitative data.

Focus groups are often used at the early stage of research to get a feel for the subject matter under discussion and to create possibilities for more structured research. Four to eight groups may be assembled and each group interviewed for one, two or three hours.

When planning qualitative research using focus groups, a number of factors need to be considered.

(a) **Type of group**. A standard group is of 7-9 respondents, but other types may also be used.

(b) **Membership**. Who takes part in the discussion depends on who the researcher wants to talk to (users or non-users, for instance) and whether they all need to be similar (homogenous).

(c) **Number of groups**. Having more than twelve groups in a research project would be very unusual, mainly because nothing new would come out of a thirteenth one!

(d) **Recruitment**. Usually on the basis of a quota sample: respondents are screened by a short questionnaire to see whether they are suitable. In order to persuade them to join in, the members are usually given an incentive plus expenses.

(e) **Discussion topics**. These will be decided by the researcher with regard to the purpose of the group discussion, that is the data that are required. There should be a number of topics since the interviewer needs to be able to restart discussion once a topic has been fully discussed.

4.1 Discussion guide

A discussion guide (also known as a topic guide) is the guide prepared by a depth interviewer or focus group moderator to guide the topics under discussion. Topic guides can take many different forms, according to clients' preferences and the needs of the research, from looser lists of subject areas to be covered to more strictly structured lists of specific question areas.

The general format is to have three phases.

(a) **Introduction**, welcoming the group, explaining the purpose of the meeting and outlining the topics that will be discussed, and introducing the participants or getting them to do so themselves.

(b) **Discussion**, which may have several themed sub-phases and involve product trial

(c) **Summary** and thanks

Exam tip

The use of discussion guides and projective techniques for group discussions have been the subject of questions in recent sittings.

Marketing at Work

SAMPLE DISCUSSION GUIDE: HIGH FIBRE MICROWAVE PIZZA

Introduction

Introduce self, note ground rules and mention taping.

Warm up: Go around the table and state name and what types of pizzas you buy (briefly).

Discussion

Discuss pizza category: What's out there? What is most popular? What's changed in your pizza eating habits in the last five years?

When cooking pizza at home, what kinds do you make? (frozen, chilled, baked, microwaved, etc.) Any related products?

Probe issues: Convenience, costs, variations, family likes and dislikes

Probe issues: Any nutritional concerns?

Present Concept: Better nutritional content from whole wheat and bran crust, high in dietary fibre. Strong convenience position due to microwavability. Competitive price. Several flavours available. Get reactions.

Probe: Is fibre a concern? Target opportunity for some consumers?

Probe: Is microwave preparation appealing? Concerns about browning/sogginess/crispness?

Taste and discuss representative prototypes. Discuss pros and cons. Probe important sensory attributes. Reasons for likes and/or dislikes.

Review concepts and issues. Ask for clarification.

Ask for new product suggestions or variations on the theme.

Last chance for suggestions. False close (go behind mirror).

If further discussion or probes from clients, pick up thread and restart discussion.

Summary

Close, thanks, distribute incentives, dismissal.

4.2 Moderator

Key to the success of a focus group will be the skill of the person running it, usually called the **moderator**.

(a) The moderator needs to be able to **build a rapport** between a group of people who have never met before.

(b) He or she needs to make sure that **everyone gets an opportunity** to speak.

(c) The moderator needs to ensure that the discussion **stays focused** on the topics at hand.

(d) The moderator must be **sensitive to the mood** of the group throughout the discussion. It is likely to change a number of times even during a relatively short meeting.

Action Programme 2

Next time you are in a meeting see if you can sense the changes in mood. You are most likely to notice a change when the meeting has gone on a bit too long and people start to want to leave! Look for tell-tale signs like body language and tone of voice, as well as changes in the quality of discussion.

Wilson (2002) draws attention to the typical thinking process of a focus group.

(a) Initially there will be **anxieties and doubts**: participants won't know exactly why they are there and what is expected of them. The moderator needs to be aware of this and set their minds at rest: perhaps even ask them to share their doubts.

(b) Participants will **wish to feel included** so it is important to get contributions from each member early on.

(c) Especially because they are strangers, the group members are likely to want to **establish their own status**: what their experience of the matter under discussion is, why they should be listened to. This tends to die down after a while and participants are more interested in sharing and **relating to each other**. Depending on the individuals, however, intervention from the moderator may be required to prevent one or two people dominating the discussion.

(d) People are keen to feel that their **opinions are valued**: the moderator needs good listening skills (good eye contact, asking for points made to be developed).

(e) Sooner or later people will start to **wish to leave**, so the moderator needs to give indications of how much ground has been covered and what is left to be covered at regular intervals.

4.2.1 Advantages and disadvantages of focus groups

The **key advantages** of focus groups include the following.

(a) The group environment with 'everybody in the same boat' can be **less intimidating** than other techniques of research which rely on one-to-one contact (such as depth interviews).

(b) What respondents say in a group often **sparks off experiences** or ideas on the part of others.

(c) **Differences between consumers** are highlighted, making it possible to understand a range of attitudes in a short space of time.

(d) It is **easier to observe groups** and there is more to observe simply because of the intricate behaviour patterns within a collection of people.

(e) **Social and cultural influences** are highlighted.

(f) Groups provide a **social context** that is a 'hot-house' reflection of the real world.

(g) Groups are **cheaper and faster** than depth interviews.

(h) **Technology** may help to facilitate and add value to the process.

   (i) Group discussions can be **video tape recorded** for later analysis and interpretation, or they may even be **shown 'live'** to the client via CCTV or webcam.

   (ii) In business-to-business situations it may be possible to use **video-conferencing**, enabling opinions to be sought from a wider variety of locations.

   (iii) **Forums** and **chat rooms** on the web can be used.

The principal **disadvantages** of groups are as follows.

(a) Group processes may **inhibit some people from making a full contribution** and may encourage others to become exhibitionistic.

(b) Group processes **may stall** to the point where they cannot be retrieved by the moderator.

(c) Some groups may **take a life of their own**, so that what is said has validity only in the short-lived context of the group.

(d) It is not usually possible to identify **which group members said what**, unless the proceedings have been video recorded.

Action Programme 3

What are the advantages and disadvantages of group discussions and depth interviews?

Chapter Roundup

- **Qualitative research** is particularly useful for new product research, marketing communications development and preliminary (exploratory) research prior to a more detailed, probably quantitative study.
- The main method of qualitative research is the **interview**.
- **Projective techniques** attempt to draw out attitudes, opinions and motives by a variety of methods.
- **Focus groups** concentrate on discussion of chosen topics in an attempt to find out attitudes. They do have limitations despite advantages such as the ability to observe a whole range of responses at the same time.

Quick Quiz

1 Qualitative research is particularly appropriate in three cases. What are they?

2 If you are stopped in the street and asked a series of questions by someone with a clipboard you have taken part in qualitative research. True or false? Explain your answer.

3 Which of the following is most likely to be a question asked in a depth interview?

A How often do you buy this product?
B Which product do you prefer?
C Why do you like this product?

4 What projective technique is being described in each case?

.... Fantasy situations

.... Get someone talking about issues which do not interest them

.... Sub-conscious thoughts may be revealed

.... Underlying attitudes and opinions may be revealed

.... What happens next

.... What is happening in the picture

.... What people think as opposed to what they say

5 List five factors that need to be considered when planning qualitative research using focus groups.

Answers to Quick Quiz

1 New product or service research, advertising and promotion research and exploratory research.

2 Probably not: the person with the clipboard will most likely be asking a series of pre-defined questions and asking you to choose between pre-defined options. Qualitative research is supposed to allow the respondents to say whatever they feel and think in response to flexible, 'prompting' questioning.

3 C. The other questions would be better asked as part of a questionnaire with pre-defined options, since there are only a limited number of possible answers.

4

Psychodrama	Fantasy situations
Third person or 'Friendly Martian	Get someone talking about issues which do not interest them
Word association	Sub-conscious thoughts may be revealed
Sentence completion	Underlying attitudes and opinions may be revealed
Story completion	What happens next
Thematic apperception tests	What is happening in the picture
Cartoon completion	What people think as opposed to what they say

5 We only asked for a list, but see if you can add a comment to each item.

(a) Type of group
(b) Membership
(c) Number of groups
(d) Recruitment
(e) Discussion topics

Action Programme Review

1 There is no definite answer, but people are more likely to be self-conscious about being captured on video than they are on tape and may even refuse to allow you to video them. If they are not comfortable it is less likely that you will get the information you require.

2 Don't forget to take part in the meeting, too!

3

Group discussions	Depth interview
Advantages	
Less intimidating Easily observed Range of attitudes can be measured Social aspect reflects real world Dynamic and creative Cheaper	Decision making *processes* can be analysed Majority *and* minority opinion can be captured Sensitive topics more easily discussed 'Unusual' behaviour can be discussed
Disadvantages	
Participants may not express what they really think – they may be inhibited or they may be showing off Views may be unrealistic – meaningful in a group context but not for the individual	Time consuming Less creative More expensive

8

Questionnaires and quantitative data

Chapter topic list

1 Questionnaires and questionnaire design
2 Interviews, surveys and tests
3 Observation

Syllabus content – knowledge and skill requirements

- 4.2: The key sources of primary and secondary data
- 4.3: Procedures for observing behaviour
- 4.4: The various methods for collecting qualitative and quantitative data
- 4.5: Design a questionnaire and discussion guide to meet a project's research objectives

Introduction

The questionnaire is the most important means of collecting primary quantitative data, aside from information collected in the ordinary course of business.

Key concept

Quantitative research is structured to collect specific data regarding a specific set of circumstances.

As you probably know from personal experience many questionnaires are extremely **badly designed**. We begin this chapter by recommending a methodical approach and explaining and illustrating the **issues** that arise, and the **mistakes to avoid**.

Exam tip

You may have to design a questionnaire in your exam, or else comment on questionnaire design issues.

Surveys may be **administered** face-to-face, by telephone, by post, or even on the web and each of these methods raises certain issues. Some forms of primary data collection will involve the customer trying out the product or service, as well as giving responses to questions.

Observation is another method of collecting primary data, although it is only possible for certain kinds of research where the behaviour you are interested in can actually be determined without direct interaction with the customer.

The **analysis** of quantitative data (statistics) is covered in Part E.

1 Questionnaires and questionnaire design

Pilot paper, 6/04, 6/07

FAST FORWARD

Questionnaire design should be done methodically: **develop question topics**; **select question and response formats** and take care with **wording**; **determine the sequence**; **design the layout** and **pilot test**.

In the majority of research projects, the most critical technical issue is likely to be the **quality of the research techniques that have been used**. Where research findings are suspect, this is most commonly because there are fundamental **flaws in the design of the questionnaire**. In this section, therefore, we will spend some time looking at some of the key issues involved in designing an effective questionnaire.

Wilson (2002) recommends a methodical approach to designing questionnaires, with the following steps.

- Develop **question topics**: these will derive from the research **objectives** and may be refined by initial **qualitative research**. We have covered these topics in earlier chapters.
- Select question and response **formats and wording**
- Determine **sequence**
- Design **layout**
- **Pilot test**

Marketing at Work

The lack of experienced field researchers, misplaced attitudes of agencies and clients, and the perceived low profile of market research are all affecting response rates in business-to-business research. One researcher claimed that in one year the response rate for a particular survey dropped from one in 20 to one in 40.

... there was criticism of research executives who have unrealistic expectations about the time needed for specific questionnaires and the quality of the samples they provide for the field researchers. There were calls for all executives to have a more hands on role in the piloting of questionnaires to establish their usability as well as a more honest and open relationship with clients.

Adapted from *Research,* 1st June 2001

Exam tip

The December 2003 paper contained a question addressing falling response rates in marketing research, and the action that could be taken. 'Better questionnaire design' is one good example. The June 2007 paper contained a question linking questionnaire design to research objectives.

1.1 Question and response formats and wording

FAST FORWARD

Questions need to be **worded with precision**, avoiding ambiguity and lack of clarity, not conflating multiple issues, not making unjustified assumptions, making it easy and clear for respondents to answer.

1.1.1 Precision

Even though most marketing research questionnaires explore comparatively straightforward issues, **precision** should always be a primary concern.

The principles set out in the following paragraphs may sound so obvious as to be **hardly worth stating** and yet, in many questionnaires, these apparently self-evident points are **routinely disregarded**. All too often, there is little clarity about the information that is required, there is woolliness and imprecision in the framing of questions and there are confusions both about the meaning of the question and about the interpretation of the response.

The potential causes of this imprecision are numerous, but there are a number of common pitfalls that are worth highlighting.

(a) **Ambiguity and uncertainty about language or terminology**. In framing a question, managers will often assume a common understanding of words or phrases, where no such commonality actually exists.

(b) **Lack of clarity about the information required**. Questionnaires are frequently weakened by a lack of clarity about the nature and detail of the information they are intended to collect. You should always stop and ask yourself some fundamental questions.

- Why am I asking this question?
- What is it intended to find out?
- What exactly do I want to know?
- Will this question give me the information I need?

These questions are often not explicitly addressed, with the result that the wrong question (or only part of the right question) is asked. In one employee survey, for example, the questionnaire asked:

Which of the following do you feel are barriers to your undertaking further training or development in your own time?

- Lack of spare time
- Lack of motivation
- Personal/domestic commitments
- Cost

Not surprisingly, many respondents ticked most if not all of these options. The questionnaire designer really wanted to ask not **whether** these factors were seen as barriers, but **which** were the most significant barriers and **how** significant they were.

(c) **Conflation of multiple questions into one**. In one survey, for example, respondents were asked, 'How often does your workgroup meet to discuss performance, quality and safety issues?' The assumption behind this question – which was part of the evaluation of a team development programme – was that managers called workgroups together to discuss all three of these issues, as they were required to do. In fact, practice varied considerably across the organisation. Some workgroups did not meet at all, some met infrequently and many met relatively often but only discussed performance issues. However, this fact, which was crucial to evaluating the effectiveness of the programme, only emerged during subsequent focus group.

(d) **Making unjustified assumptions**. Similar problems can arise when the phrasing of the question implies an assumption of a preconception that is not justified by the evidence available to you. It is not uncommon, for instance, to encounter questions such as, 'In reviewing your performance, which of the following methods does your manager use?' The assumption here, of course, is that the manager reviews the respondent's performance at all.

1.1.2 Open and closed questions

Closed questions give people a choice of predetermined answers or can simply be answered with a 'Yes' or 'No' or a tick in a box or a very short factual answer. In conversation and information gathering they help to establish the basic facts.

Title	Mr	☐	Mrs	☐	Miss	☐	Ms	☐	Dr	☐	Other	☐
Would you like a sales representative to call you?									Yes	☐	No	☐

- The advantage is that you will get short, relevant answers that are easy to analyse.
- The disadvantage is that the choices may be too restrictive to cover every possibility.

Open questions let people respond in their own words. Typically an open question begins with 'Why ...?' or 'How ...?' or a phrase like 'Could you describe...' or 'Tell me more about ..'.

(a) The advantage of this type of question is that it is less likely to lead people into giving the answer they think you want.

(b) The disadvantage is that you may end up collecting a large amount of subjective data. This may or may not be relevant, and you will need to spend time reading and interpreting it to find out.

For instance, suppose you design a questionnaire with the following (open) question and put a large blank box underneath for the answer.

What method(s) of communication did you use the last time you arranged to meet someone or a group of other people?

Some people would simply respond 'PHONE & E-MAIL', but (depending on the size of the blank box) others may be tempted to scribble you a little story about what the event was, who was there, how the initial idea for the event was a spontaneous conversation in the kitchen at work, how the news spread like wildfire by phone and e-mail - all of which you would have to decipher, read and interpret, but almost all of which you do not need to know!

A much better way to get the information you want is to offer a limited range of possible responses to the question, something along these lines.

Please indicate what methods of communication you used the last time you arranged to meet someone or a group of other people (✓ *Tick all boxes that apply)*			
E-mail	☐	I do not meet other people	☐
Telephone conversation	☐	Message pinned on notice board	☐
Post	☐	Website/chat-room	☐
Text message	☐	Face-to-face	☐
Other (please give brief details)			

The answers to this (almost closed) question will be much easier to analyse, and it will be much quicker for people to answer the question if they do not have to think up their own words.

(a) So far as possible you should avoid putting the choices in the order that you think reflects their popularity: note the two column layout, which tries to avoid this.

(b) Note that the text and the associated boxes to tick are closely aligned and shaded so that it is clear which box belongs to which option.

(c) It is also clear in this example that you want a tick, not a cross. Actually it probably doesn't matter what mark people use, but remember that lots of people are scared of forms: save them from worrying and make it clear for them.

(d) If the answer is 'Other' it is clear from the wording and the limited space for the answer that you do not want much detail.

1.1.3 Leading questions

Even when the question has been very carefully and precisely planned, it may still provide misleading or inaccurate data if it appears to be **leading the respondent towards a particular answer**. People may still feel **uncertain** about its outcomes and they may still feel **suspicious of your motives** for conducting it. In such cases, some may feel very keen to give the 'right' answer – the answer that they believe the organisation wants to hear. Regardless of your care in drafting the questionnaire, you may not be able to avoid this problem entirely.

This problem occurs most commonly when respondents are asked to **indicate their level of agreement or disagreement** with a particular statement. The preferences or prejudices of the questionnaire designer can appear too obvious to the respondent. It is prudent, therefore, to include a **mixture of positive and negative statements**, which do not suggest any intrinsic preference.

In some cases, the choice of statement can **significantly undermine the value of the information obtained**. In one questionnaire, for instance, respondents were asked to indicate their agreement or disagreement with the statement, 'The quality of work in my department is generally excellent'. If the respondent agreed with this statement the meaning was clear – that he or she thought the quality of work in the department was generally excellent. However, if the respondent **disagreed** with the statement, the meaning was less clear. Did they think the quality was moderate or even poor? From the information provided by the question, there was no way of telling.

1.1.4 Formats

FAST FORWARD

Question types include **Yes/No**, **multiple choice**, **ratings** and **scales**: the primary purpose is to facilitate statistical analysis. Two of the best known scales are the Likert scale and the Semantic Differential scale.

Apart from a simple **'Yes/No'** format, there are various **other ways** of structuring questions. In general, the questions in a written questionnaire should be of the **multiple choice** type, so providing the basis for quantitative analysis. The primary purpose of a written questionnaire is to facilitate **precise statistical analysis**. If the questionnaire includes too many narrative or open questions, analysis becomes very difficult.

Questions can be divided into two broad categories; those **exploring attitudes** or opinions and those **seeking some form of factual information**. In the former category would generally fall, for example, the 'agree/disagree' format, such as 'Safety is always a paramount concern for the organisation. Do you agree strongly/agree slightly/disagree slightly/disagree strongly'. In the latter category might fall questions about, say, the frequency of workgroup meetings or about recent experience of training.

Action Programme 1

You will often receive questionnaires, perhaps in the post, perhaps as door drops, perhaps when you purchase a new product. Don't throw them away, start collecting a file of them and make careful note of the styles of question used, use of graphics and symbols, layout. Some will be much better than others, of course, but it is worth keeping the bad examples too.

Within these two broad categories, a number of formats can be applied. Questions on attitude or opinion generally ask the respondent to indicate both the direction and the strength of feeling – say, 'strongly agree' to 'strongly disagree'. Alternatively, you might ask for the range of opinion relating to a given topic with a question like 'Do you think the quality of work in your department is generally excellent/good/fair/poor?' In such cases, where you are effectively asking respondents to commit themselves to a specific opinion, you need to be aware of what is sometimes called, in an experimental content, the 'error of the central tendency'.

In other words, **respondents are commonly reluctant to give extreme responses** and prefer to hover around the middle ground. If you have an odd number of items in your scale, you may find that respondents disproportionately opt for the neutral option. There are benefits in forcing respondents off the fence by **offering only an even number of options**, so that the respondent has to choose between, say, 'agree slightly' and 'disagree slightly'. In this way, you gain a clearer perspective on the **true direction of opinion**.

Where you are asking to identify preferences from among a number of options, you may ask respondents to **rank the options against a given criterion**, such as 'Which of the following do you think are the most important contributors to high workgroup performance? (Please rank in order of importance.)'

(a) If you use this format, you should remember to indicate **how the ranking should be applied**. Is number 1 the **most** or the **least** important factor? Ranking questions can seem **confusing** to respondents and are best used sparingly. In any cases, it is rarely worth asking respondents to rank more than the first three or four items. Beyond that, rankings usually become fairly arbitrary.

(b) A more straightforward approach is to ask respondents simply to **select one item** – 'Which of the following do you think is the single most important contributor to high workgroup performance? (Please tick one only.)' Although slightly less detailed, this question is easier both to complete and to analyse.

In collecting **factual** information, you may again wish to **use scales** where the required information lies on a continuum. For example, 'How many days have you spent training in the past twelve months? Fewer than 3 days/4 – 6 days/6 – 10 days/more than 10 days.'

Where you are exploring more discrete items of information, you may simply ask respondents to **select the most relevant items**. For example, you might ask, 'Which of the following types of training have you undertaken in the last year? (Please tick any that apply.)' In this case, you are not asking respondents to evaluate the options against one another, but simply to make a choice between those that are and those that are not significant. This format can also be applied in cases of **opinions and attitudes**.

Marketing at Work

snap Professional Edition is a software product that incorporates paper and phone surveys. Design and publish your questionnaire, collect replies and analyse the results to produce tables, charts and statistics.

Questionnaire design

- Survey Constructor wizard
- WYSIWYG questionnaire design
- Questionnaire templates
- Set response types
- Access to SurveyPak question libraries
- Question routing
- Add images and logos

Data entry

- Four data entry modes
- Browsing of selected cases
- Verification of entered data
- Editing and cleaning

Results analysis

- Easy to read summary report
- Crosstabulations
- Frequency, grid and holecount tables
- 2D and 3D charts
- Statistical analysis
- Filtering / subsets
- Weighting
- Derived / recode variables
- Analysis of literals
- Templates for tables and charts
- Printed and electronic reports
- Volume batch reporting
- Exporting results

(www.mercator.co.uk)

The Likert scale

This approach can be summarised in three steps.

Step 1. A list of statements is prepared about the topic being researched, and a test group of respondents is asked to rate each statement on a scale from strong agreement to strong disagreement.

Step 2. A numerical value is given to each response:

5 Strongly agree
4 Agree
3 Don't know
2 Disagree
1 Strongly disagree

Name	*Description*	*Example*
		CLOSED-END QUESTIONS
Dichotomous	A question with two possible answers.	'In arranging this trip, did you personally phone British Airways?' Yes ☐ No ☐
Multiple choice	A question with three or more answers.	'With whom are you travelling on this flight?' No one ☐ Children only ☐ Spouse ☐ Business associates/ friends/relatives ☐ Spouse and children ☐ An organised tour group ☐
Likert scale	A statement with which the respondent shows the amount of agreement/	'Small airlines generally give better service Strongly disagree 1 ☐ Disagree 2 ☐ Neither agree nor disagree 3 ☐ Agree 4 ☐ Strongly agree 5 ☐
Semantic differential	A scale connecting two bipolar words, where the respondent selects the point	*British Airways* Large ------------------- Small Experienced -------------- Inexperienced Modern Old-fashioned
Importance scale	A scale that rates the importance of some attribute.	Extremely important 1 ☐ Very important 2 ☐ Somewhat important 3 ☐ Not very important 4 ☐ Not at all important 5 ☐
Rating scale	A scale that rates some attribute from 'poor' to 'excellent'.	Excellent Very good Good Fair Poor
Intention-to-buy scale	A scale that describes the respondent's intention to buy.	'If an inflight telephone was available on a long flight, I would' Definitely buy 1 ☐ Probably buy 2 ☐ Not sure 3 ☐ Probably not buy 4 ☐ Definitely not buy 5 ☐
		OPEN-END QUESTIONS
Completely unstructured	A question that respondents can answer in an almost unlimited number of ways.	'What is your opinion of British Airways?'
Word association	Words are presented, one at a time, and respondents mention the first word that comes to mind.	'What is the first word that comes to mind when you hear the following' Airline ______ British ______ Travel ______
Sentence completion	An incomplete sentence is presented and respondents complete the sentence.	'When I choose an airline, the most important consideration in my decision is ______ .
Story completion	An incomplete story is presented, and respondents are asked to complete it.	'I flew B.A. a few days ago. I noticed that the exterior and interior of the plane had bright colours. This aroused in me the following thoughts and feelings.' Now complete the story.
Picture completion	A picture of two characters is presented, with one making a statement. Respondents are asked to identify with the other and fill in the empty balloon.	
Thematic Apperception Test (TAT)	A picture is presented and respondents are asked to make up a story about what they think is happening or may happen in the picture.	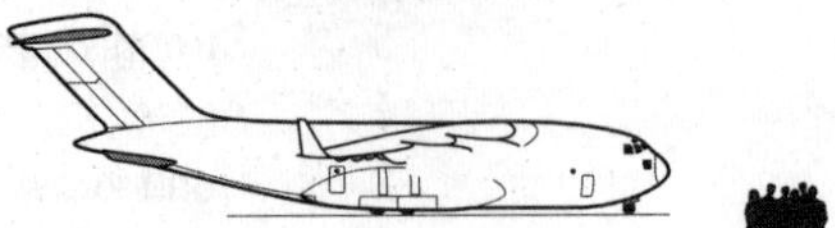

Step 3. Each respondent's scores for all the statements are added up to give a total score for the topic, which may reflect overall positive or negative attitudes: responses to individual statements can also be analysed to get more meaningful information about the pattern of responses.

Likert scales are simple to prepare and administer. You may have been asked to complete such an inventory test over the telephone, or seen one in a magazine. However, again you should be aware that scale values have no absolute meaning, and are limited in their statistical uses, on an 'interval' scale.

1.1.5 The Semantic Differential scale

(a) Scales are constructed on a number of **'dimensions'** – pairs of opposite attributes or qualities, expressed as adjectives – valued on a continuum from +3 to –3.

Profile of Car Model X

	+3	*+2*	*+1*	*0*	*–1*	*–2*	*–3*	
Modern								Old-fashioned
Fast								Slow
Attractive								Unattractive
Powerful								Weak
Responsive								Unresponsive
Glamorous								Ordinary

(b) Respondents are asked to **select the position of the object** being researched (in this case the car) on each continuum, according to the degree to which they think the adjective describes the object. (If the car is very powerful but not terribly responsive, say, it might rate +3 on the powerful-weak dimension, and +1 on the responsive-unresponsive scale.)

(c) A **'profile'** is thus built up by each respondent.

The main problem with Semantic Differential scales is the **subjectivity attached to language**. Words mean different things to different people. (The word 'old-fashioned' in our car profile above may mean 'old-hat' to some and 'classic' to others.)

The other problem of measuring responses to, and perceptions of, different attributes of the same thing is that **one attribute can influence our perception of other attributes** and some attributes bring clusters of other assumed attributes with them (stereotypes). Think, for example, about our model X car: if it looks sleek and attractive, we may perceive it as a fast car – whether it is or not – and if we think of old-fashioned cars as glamorous (because of stereotypes of 'classic' cars and the people who drive them) we might distort our glamour rating.

1.2 Sequence

The overall structure of the questionnaire can take a number of forms, depending on the purpose and nature of the research. As a general rule, when you are exploring a given topic, you should aim to be as systematic as possible in **progressing from the general to the specific**. Typically, your initial aim should be to gain an understanding of the **broad context** within which opinions are held. You can then progress to gaining an understanding of the **nature and strength of opinion** in a given area. Finally, you can move, step by step, towards identifying the **detail that underpins these**.

To illustrate this, let us take a specific example – and one where you can easily put yourself in the position of the customer, assuming you enjoy being paid by your organisation! This is a staff questionnaire (staff are **internal customers**, of course) designed to explore attitudes to reward and recognition. The questionnaire might begin, for example, by asking a question about perceptions of reward and recognition in the organisation generally.

> How satisfied are you with the level of recognition and reward you receive for your achievements at work?
> Very satisfied
> Fairly satisfied
> Fairly unsatisfied
> Very dissatisfied?

The **responses** to this question will help provide you with a **context** within which you can interpret the more detailed information you will obtain from subsequent questions.

Having defined the broad organisational context, you can begin to focus more precisely on the detail of the specific topic. The next question might be:

> If you feel that your work achievements are recognised, what form does this recognition generally take? (Please tick any that apply.)
>
> Increased basic pay
>
> Bonus payment
>
> Other financial reward
>
> Promotion
>
> Verbal congratulations
>
> Non-financial reward
>
> Other (please specify)

This will provide you with an understanding of the **current perceptions of the topic** – what respondents' perceptions of the rewards they typically receive for work achievements are. It is important not to make assumptions (in this case it would be all too easy to assume that **your** perceptions and perspective reflect those of the wider workforce, but that may not be the case). The broad rule, as in most aspects of research, is **do not make assumptions**. If you have any doubts at all about people's views or perceptions, test them out.

Having identified people's perceptions of the current state of play in the specific area, you can then move to the next level of detail and begin to explore, for example, internal customers' **preferences** for reward and recognition. You might ask:

> Which of the following forms of recognition for work achievements do you find most motivating? (Please tick one only.)
>
> Increased basic pay
>
> Bonus payment
>
> Other financial reward
>
> Promotion
>
> Verbal congratulations
>
> Non-financial reward
>
> Other (please specify)

FAST FORWARD

As a general rule a questionnaire should **progress from the general to the particular** (funnelling). It may be helpful to avoid a pattern of negative responses by distributing questions about respective topics throughout the questionnaire rather than bunching them together.

Mapping these expressed preferences against the current perceived position should indicate very clearly **if or where there is gap between the current and the desired positions**. This, in turn, will enable the organisation to focus its future activities very precisely on these areas, where they are likely to bring maximum pay-back. Having identified the most important issues in this way, you can then, of course, move on to look in detail at specific aspects of the topic.

This process of moving from the general to the specific is sometimes known as **'funnelling'**. Clearly, it is an important device for **ensuring precision in interpretation**. In addition, it may also help you to provide a meaningful interpretation of responses that may be influenced by extraneous factors, such as **self-interest**. The use of broad, contextual questions, however, will help you to interpret such responses against a range of other issues and concerns. You might, for instance, ask respondents, initially, to rank areas of potential dissatisfaction in order of significance. This will then provide you with a basis on which to evaluate any specific expression of dissatisfaction with the really important issue.

Other questionnaire structures can also be used, to **minimise the influence of external factors**. If you are exploring a range of issues, for example, it can be helpful to distribute questions about each respective issue throughout the questionnaire, rather than bunching them in discrete sections. This can help reduce what is sometimes known as the **'halo effect'**, which is when overall positive or negative feelings about a given issue influence responses to individual questions. For example, if customers generally feel unhappy about delivery times, they may feel inclined to give negative responses to **all** questions relating to delivery, even though they may actually be highly satisfied with, say, quality of packaging. Distributing questions about delivery throughout the questionnaire may help to prevent such respondents establishing a **pattern of negative responses**.

1.3 Questionnaire length and layout

FAST FORWARD

Questionnaire **length** will depend on the circumstances, but **short is better than long**. Clear instructions and layout are vital.

One of the most common questions asked by those conducting or commissioning research is, 'What length of questionnaire is acceptable?' As with sampling, there is **no straightforward answer**. It depends on the nature and complexity of the **questions** being asked. It depends on the **population** being researched, and their familiarity and confidence with questionnaires. It depends on the **methods being used** to administer the questionnaire. It is also true that the appliance and format of the questionnaire may be just as important as its length. Everything else being equal, a well-designed and clearly laid out questionnaire can afford to be longer than a poorly constructed equivalent.

Above all, of course, there is generally a trade-off between questionnaire length and the level of response. The **longer and more detailed** the questionnaire, the **more likely** you are to encounter **resistance** from potential respondents. Ultimately, you will need to balance these two factors. In some cases, for instance, you may feel that a smaller response is justified by the need to obtain a higher level of detail from the questionnaire.

Despite these caveats, the following crude guidelines for different forms of questionnaire administration may be helpful.

(a) **Cold surveys**. Where the questionnaire is being sent out with no preparation and where respondents have no particular incentive to respond, you should aim for an absolute maximum of 4 sides of paper and no more than 15 to 20 questions (including sub-questions), but in many cases, it will be preferable to aim for just 1 or 2 sides of paper and even fewer questions. The key issue here is likely to be one of presentation. You will want to suggest that the questionnaire is easy to complete and will involve comparatively little of the respondent's time. Therefore, simple, 'user-friendly' layout is likely to be an even more significant issue than the overall length.

(b) **Postal questionnaires**. Where respondents have been briefed and prepared, but are nevertheless expected to complete the questionnaire entirely in their own time, you should generally aim for a questionnaire of some 6 to 8 sides of paper, ideally with no more than 30 to 40 questions. You will still need to ensure that the form is not unduly intimidating or off-putting and, ideally, respondents should feel encouraged to complete it immediately rather than delaying. If potential respondents put the questionnaire to one side, the chances are that a substantial proportion will not get around to completing it at all.

Some other general points about questionnaire design are also worth stressing. First, make sure that you provide **clear instructions** throughout, indicating precisely how the questionnaire should be completed. These should be simply phrased and as concise as possible. It is also a good idea to **provide some examples** of specific question types and how they should be completed. As always, one good example is worth several dozen words of explanation.

Try to **avoid over-complicated instructions**. In some cases, a degree of complexity may be inevitable – particularly where, for example, some respondents are required to skip a number of the questions. Nevertheless, the most effective questionnaires, in terms of ease of response, are those where all respondents are able to proceed straightforwardly through the questionnaire from the first question to the last.

1.3.1 Laying out the questionnaire

(a) If respondents have to complete the questionnaire themselves, it must be approachable and as short as possible. Consider the use of **lines, boxes, different type faces and print sizes and small pictures**. Use plenty of space.

(b) Consider the use of **tick boxes**. Is it clear where ticks go or how to respond in each case? For analysis, will it be easy to transfer responses from the forms to a summary sheet or a computer? Consider pre-coding the answers.

(c) Explain the **purpose of the research** at the beginning of the questionnaire and where possible guarantee confidentiality. Emphasise the date by which it must be returned.

(d) At the end of the questionnaire, **thank the respondent** and make it clear what they should do with the completed questionnaire.

Exam tip

The question on the Pilot paper on questionnaire design asks you to demonstrate your knowledge of:

- Sequencing
- Question wording
- Question/response format

This is also required in a question on the June 2007 paper.

1.4 Pilot tests

Finally, it is **vital** to pilot test questionnaires since mistakes, ambiguities and embarrassments in a questionnaire can be extremely expensive once the main data collection phase has been entered. The **conditions** for the test should be the **same as**, or as close as possible to, the intended conditions for **the real thing**: respondents of the type you really want to test, using interviewers or self-administered questionnaires.

2 Interviews, surveys and tests 6/05

FAST FORWARD

Interviews are **classified according to where they occur** (in the street, in a shop, in the home). Despite possible interviewer bias interviews can improve the quality and rate of responses.

Postal surveys are less costly and time consuming. Telephone surveys have some advantages, especially the ability to cover a wider geographical area, but have the disadvantage of lack of rapport and confusion with telesales.

Many surveys in UK market research take place as **face-to-face** interviews. The interviewers are often freelancers but can be employees of a market research organisation. An interview is a social encounter, where the personal interface between interviewee(s) and interviewer is crucial.

There are five main styles of interview, classified according to where they occur.

(a) **Street surveys** take place typically in busy town centres, with the interviewer approaching individuals as they pass by. They need to be brief (5 minutes is too long for most people in their lunch break or going to or from work) and should not require too much concentration from the interviewees, so getting them to consider show material should be avoided. A survey taking place in a shopping centre requires the centre's manager's permission, and a fee may be payable.

(b) **Shop surveys** take place inside or just outside a particular shop, obviously with the shop's permission.

(c) **Hall tests** take place in a pre-booked location such as a hotel, where people are invited to attend to answer a few questions, usually being recruited from the street and being enticed by a give-away or refreshments. More complex tasks can be performed by the interviewee, for instance a display can be permanently set up and considered. Sometimes they may be carried out in a natural place for a particular product's consumption or usage: for example, a new brand of alcohol may be tested in pubs or restaurants.

The hall test is most appropriate for a situation with **test materials** that can be **evaluated** quickly such as a new pack design or advertisement. They are most commonly used for **quantitative research**, but they can include observation and qualitative techniques alongside a structured questionnaire. They may include usage of a product and an interview during which a respondent is asked to give his or her opinions about a product and evaluate it, as well as make a future usage and purchase declaration. An individual test usually lasts about **20 minutes**, although the simplest versions may only involve tasting a product and evaluating it on a scale.

(d) **Placement tests**. Respondents for these tests are recruited from omnibus surveys or street interviews, and are provided with the product to test in their own home, or whatever location is appropriate. Placement tests can be used for products that need to be tested over a period of time, such as household appliances or cosmetics. Results are collated by the respondent in a diary or similar format and the results are then sent to the tester, by post or online. While they may be expensive and time consuming to conduct, these surveys have the advantage that extended testing can be carried out in realistic scenarios.

(e) **Home interviews** are held in the interviewee's home (or doorstep), with the interviewer recruiting simply by knocking on doors. They can be pre-arranged by phone or by dropping a note through the door. Larger, in depth interviews often result but they are time-consuming, expensive and prone to interruption. Many people are reluctant even to answer their doors let alone let an interviewer in so recruiting for home interviews is often frustrating for the interviewer.

(f) **Business surveys** take place on the interviewee's business premises and are always pre-arranged. Again they are prone to interruption and/or last minute cancellation.

Exam tip

Hall tests and placement tests were examined in June 2005 and again in December 2006.

Action Programme 2

The next time you see someone conducting interviews in the street don't cross the road or avert your eyes: volunteer to take part and (without being too obvious about it) try to take note of the way questions are phrased, how much depends on the skill of the interviewer, and how easy the interviewer (who may or not be well trained) finds it to record your responses. Don't forget to make notes when you get the opportunity.

It must always be remembered that people taking part in interview surveys are **doing the researcher a favour**, so the least one can do is ensure that the interviewer is well-prepared and does not make the interviewee feel that his or her time is being wasted. Good preparation will also save time in the long run and reduce the costs of hiring freelance interviewers. Finally, it will result in getting the data that is actually needed. It is vital, therefore, that the questionnaire or interview schedule is clear, unambiguous, and accurate.

The interviewer's other tasks are:

(a) To **locate respondents** (stopping in street, calling house-to-house as instructed by the researcher)

(b) To **obtain respondents' agreement** to the interview (no mean feat).

(c) To **ask questions** (usually sticking strictly to the interview schedule/questionnaire's wording) and take down answers

(d) To **complete records**

Since the desired outcome of the survey is useful data, it is important to consider whether **interviewer bias** may affect the outcome. This comes about in selection of respondents (stopping people who look 'nice' rather than a reasonable cross-section) and handling the interview (not annoying the respondent so his or her answers are affected).

The **advantages of interviews** as a survey method over telephone and postal surveys are as follows.

(a) Respondent **suitability can be checked** at the outset by asking quota questions but more effectively by assessment of the respondent (young man, woman shopping with children), so that the target number of interviews is achieved.

(b) Respondents can be **encouraged to answer as fully as possible** and the interview is usually completed.

(c) Questions are **asked in the right order**, and all relevant questions are asked.

(d) The **use of show material** is properly administered.

(e) **Response rates are higher** than for other forms of survey.

2.1 Postal surveys 6/06

Approximately 25% of market research questionnaires are completed by postal survey. We are using the term 'postal' survey to cover all methods in which the questionnaire is given to the respondent and returned to the investigator without personal contact. Such questionnaires could be sent by post but might also be left near a store exit or delivered via door drops.

Postal questionnaires have the following **advantages** over personal interviews.

(a) The **cost per person** is likely **to be less**, so more people can be sampled, and central control is facilitated.

(b) It is usually possible to **ask more questions** because the people completing the forms (the respondents) can do so in their own time.

(c) **All respondents are presented with questions in the same way**. There is no opportunity for an interviewer to influence responses (interviewer bias) or to misrecord them.

(d) It may be **easier to ask personal or embarrassing questions** in a postal questionnaire than in a personal interview.

(e) Respondents **may need to look up information for the questionnaire**. This will be easier if the questionnaire is sent to their homes or places of work.

Action Programme 3

What are the advantages of personal interviews over postal questionnaires?

2.1.1 Enumerators

An **enumerator** will **deliver the questionnaire** and **encourage the respondent to complete it**. He will later visit the respondent again to collect the completed questionnaire and perhaps to help with the interpretation of difficult questions. This method results in a better response rate than for postal questionnaires.

2.2 Telephone surveys

Surveys conducted over the phone rather than face-to-face have the following advantages.

(a) The response is **rapid**.

(b) There is a **standard sampling frame** – the **telephone directory**, which can be systematically or randomly sampled.

(c) A **wide geographical area** can be covered fairly cheaply.

(d) It may be **easier to ask sensitive or embarrassing questions**.

But there are considerable **disadvantages** as well.

(a) A **biased sample** may result from the fact that a large proportion (about 10%) of people do not have telephones (representing certain portions of the population such as old people or students) and many of those who do are ex-directory.

(b) It is **not possible to use 'showcards'** or pictures.

(c) Due to the reputation of telesales, the **refusal rate is much higher** than with face-to-face interviews, and the interview often cut short.

(d) It is **not possible to see the interviewee's expressions** or to develop the rapport that is possible with personal interviews.

(e) The interview **must be short**.

Marketing at Work

'Do not call' was set up by the Federal Trade Commission in the United States in an attempt to stop unsolicited telemarketing calls to registered households. In September 2003, around 42 million telephone numbers had been registered with the service.

2.3 Incentives

It may be advisable to take active steps to **encourage better response rates** from questionnaires, surveys and telephone studies. Methods of achieving this include putting all respondents' names into a **prize draw** or offering a product or service **discount** to all respondents.

2.4 Web surveys

Web surveys are becoming more and more common. The Internet is ideal for surveys in some respects, but far less so in others.

(a) Questionnaires can be **generated dynamically** in response to the respondent's answers. For example if the respondent indicates no interest whatever in a particular topic then any questions relating to that topic can be skipped by the computer without the respondent even knowing the questions existed. Alternatively, if they indicate strong interest they may get additional questions that others would not see. This saves time for everybody.

(b) On the other hand **web users may not be typical** of the target market (not all of whom will have access to the Internet). **Design issues** are even more crucial than with paper-based questionnaires. All the same issues and pitfalls apply, but with several **additional factors** such as speed of processing, intuitive navigation through the questionnaire and security concerns.

Marketing at Work

Clients including Abbey National, McDonald's, Orange, Sainsbury's Bank and Sony Ericsson are using the results of a survey that used the Internet to investigate the lifestyles of 20,000 British people.

The survey covered five sections:

- Grocery retail and eating out
- Telecommunications
- Financial services
- Automotive
- Holiday and travel

Questions explored which factors drove customer satisfaction, loyalty and 'word of mouth' recommendation.

(www.research_live.com)

FAST FORWARD

Testing may be carried out on promotional materials and messages and on products (field tests) or on samples of entire markets.

2.5 Laboratory tests

Laboratory experiments are most often used for measuring response to **advertisements**, to **product design** and to **package design**. They can take place before the item being tested is generally released (pre-testing), or after (post-testing).

In theory an **artificial environment** is set up by the researcher in which most of the crucial factors which may affect the outcome of the research are controlled. However, in pre-tests in particular it can be **difficult to design an experiment** which isolates the impact of one factor in a product or package from all the other factors which make up the proposed item, and which are likely to be the subjects of other experiments.

2.6 Field tests

With some products it is difficult for consumers to form an immediate opinion based on a short trial in unfamiliar surroundings. These include products such as domestic appliances, cars and some items of office equipment. These are better **tested over time** in the **place where they will be used**. Some products are only intended to work over a period of time (such as anti-ageing cream).

In a field test **a product is tested in realistic surroundings**, that is in the environment in which it will be bought and/or consumed once launched. Whilst the researcher has less control over extraneous variables, field experiments do give a more realistic idea of future behaviour. They are also known as product or **placement tests**.

Field tests are usually carried out for products in what the marketer hopes is their final form. They are therefore **expensive** as the product has to be made and marketed in small quantities, and they are **risky** in that competitors will inevitably get a good look. Laboratory experiments are often preferred but there are some elements of the marketing mix, such as distribution, which do not lend themselves to laboratory tests.

There are **three main types** of field test.

(a) A sample of consumers **try the product out at home** and report findings, usually by completing a questionnaire. The consumers are often members of a carefully selected **consumer panel**. Such in-home placement tests are often used for toiletry and other personal products.

(b) **Retail outlets** are used as the site for testing merchandising, packaging and point-of-sale material (**store tests**). There should be a reasonable cross-section of stores, both by size and by region, and ideally a control group. Results are measured primarily by changes in sales by store, but sometimes also by interview surveys of consumers.

(c) **Test marketing** is an expensive but often vital experiment in which one or more marketing actions are **tried out in limited areas of the market** in order to predict sales volume, profitability, market share, consumer, retailer and distributor behaviour and regional variances. It is vital that the experiment be properly controlled since the prediction of a new product's success, or a successful change in the marketing mix of an existing product, very often depends on it. Mistakes can be expensive.

2.7 Continuous research

The object of continuous research is to **take measurements regularly** so as to monitor **changes in the market**, either consumer, business or internally. Often syndicated because of the set-up costs, continuous research is usually undertaken by a large market research organisation. It can focus on the same consumers over time (panel research) or on a changing body of consumers.

Some research is continuous in the sense that measurement takes place every day, while in other cases measurements are taken at regular intervals.

2.7.1 Omnibus surveys

FAST FORWARD

Omnibus surveys may be a cost effective way of obtaining certain types of information.

An **omnibus survey** is a master questionnaire run by market research companies who 'sell' space on the questionnaire to marketing organisations who need data. Because the market research companies undertake the sampling, administration, processing and analysis, and spread the cost over the organisations needing data, it is a cost-effective method of research for all concerned.

The master questionnaire usually contains some of the same questions (age, gender, occupation) every time, while the remainder of the questions are either continuous (the same questions in the same place on the questionnaire as were asked of a different group, say, one week earlier) or *ad hoc* (inserted on a first-come-first-served basis but in a sensible order).

2.7.2 Market tracking surveys

Where the market research company designs the whole questionnaire seeking data on a particular market from regular different samples of respondents, rather than a panel, there is a **market tracking survey**. The results are sold by the company to as many marketing organisations as possible. Sometimes information on product usage is combined with data on media exposure.

2.8 In-store testing

Product testing in store may be a **relatively quick and inexpensive method** of gathering information about customer attitudes towards a particular product. In-store testing can be a useful, convenient way to gain insights into expected consumer behaviour before a full product launch is implemented. Selected stores can be chosen to test a product and gather information about likely buyer behaviour when the product is launched. In-store testing is also a way of promoting the product before, during and after a launch.

3 Observation 12/04

FAST FORWARD

Observation takes various forms: **home audit**, **direct observation**, and the **use of physical and technological recording devices**.

Interviews and questionnaires depend on respondents answering questions on behaviour and attitudes truthfully. Sometimes it is necessary to **observe behaviour**, not only because respondents are unwilling to answer questions but because such questions do not record behaviour and are therefore unable to provide the researcher with answers.

The major categories of observations are as follows.

(a) **Home audit**. Also termed indirect observation, this involves the investigation of the respondent's home, office or premises so as to determine the extent of ownership of certain products/brands. (Note that the home audit and diary panels are termed **consumer panel** research.)

(b) **Direct observation**. This involves, not surprisingly, the direct observation of the behaviour of the respondent by the researcher. An event must meet three criteria to be a fit subject for direct observation.

  (i) The event being observed must only occupy a **short period** of time.

  (ii) It must be **frequently** performed.

(iii) The event must be **visible** (and so feelings, beliefs and attitudes are not suitable topics for this technique).

(c) **Recording devices**. Such devices record micro behaviour in laboratory settings and macro behaviour in natural settings.

(i) **Laboratory settings**

(1) **Psychogalvanometers** measure a subject's response to, say, an advertisement by measuring the perspiration rate (which tends to increase when the subject is excited).

(2) **Eye cameras** are used to assess those parts of, for example, an advertisement which attract most attention and those parts which are neglected.

(3) **Pupilometric cameras** are used in assessing the visual stimulation derived from an image.

(ii) In **natural settings** video and movie cameras are used to record behaviour. In such settings there is an increased chance of observing real behaviour but the researcher might have to wait a long time until the behaviour occurs.

(iii) Rather more prosaically, many retail outlets use **pressure mats** or automatic **sliding doors** to record basic information on number of shoppers.

During group discussion, **non-verbal communication** can be observed so as to assess the validity of a respondent's replies.

Observation can be **open** (the observer can be seen by the respondent) or **disguised** (the observer uses a physical disguise, a one-way mirror or a closed-circuit TV system, as is often the case in a natural setting), **structured** (the researcher must know what is to be observed) or **unstructured** (the situation does not allow for the data requirements to be predetermined).

Action Programme 4

Is the observation of the effectiveness of point-of-purchase promotional advertising material likely to be open or disguised?

Observation has the **advantage** over asking people questions of placing no reliance on respondents' memories, guesses or honesty – but it does have a number of **drawbacks**.

(a) It may not be feasible. You can enjoy watching a customer pick your product, and no other, off the shelf, but you will have no idea why they did so.

(b) It may be labour intensive (one observer can only observe a limited number of things). Timed video and CCTV are obviously of great assistance, and you can have several cameras, but you are unlikely to capture everything, and collating and interpreting the data may be highly time consuming.

(c) Attitudes and feelings cannot be observed. If a customer approaches a store and then turns round and walks away without entering you have no way of knowing why, just by watching.

The use of observation as a data collection method has been stimulated by advances in electronics. **EPOS** systems allow firms to virtually 'observe' stock on hand, inflows, outflows and the speed at which stock items are moving through the store. **CCTV** is useful to combat shoplifting, but arguably much more so because of the behaviours it can reveal.

3.1 Retail audit

Retail audits are used by organisations to assess consumer demand for their products.

At set intervals **researchers visit a sample of shops**, audit (count) the stock in question and record the details of any deliveries since the last audit. Using the fact that

sales = original stock + deliveries – final stock

they are able to calculate the sales of the product since the last audit.

Shops are segmented according to their type (multiples, independent, department) and by the volume of business. Those shops which sell the largest range of products in which the organisation is interested are usually the ones upon which the auditors concentrate.

Retail audits **investigate product types** and hence the client of the research company can be provided with information on their competitors' product as well as their own.

3.2 Mystery shoppers 12/03, 12/04

FAST FORWARD

There is a limit to the amount and type of information that can be captured by most forms of observation, although **mystery shopping** is one form that allows a wide range of marketing variables to be researched.

Mystery shopping my be carried out by researchers themselves or by specially recruited and trained members of the public. As the name suggests it involves a person posing as a genuine customer (not just in a shop, it could be **any sort of customer** for **any sort of business**) and reporting back on whatever aspect of the customer experience the researcher is interested in.

Exam tip

'Mystery shoppers' featured in the December 2003 exam in the context of monitoring the quality of a hotel's service.

Issues in using mystery shopping as a research technique include the following.

(a) A **suitable number** of different shoppers must be used because the results may be affected by the **characteristics of the shopper** as well as of the organisation being researched. The shoppers should fit the profiles of consumers in the organisation's genuine target markets.

(b) Some observations made will inevitably be **subjective** and this must be taken into account.

(c) **Credibility** is an issue with certain types of purchase: for instance people do not buy several cars a week. Certain types of purchase, particularly in financial services, involve the selling organisation checking the credentials of the customer.

(d) Mystery shoppers may need to be trained in **data collection skills**: they will not be very 'mysterious' if they fill in a data sheet during a face to face encounter with a selling organisation!

Marketing at Work

Mystery shopping research from Maritz Virtual Customers provides a trained, objective view of the experiences your customers have at the point of customer interaction, whether it's face-to-face, telephone, e-mail or Web-based. If your promise isn't being kept when those interactions occur your brand and your business will suffer.

The power of Virtual Customers, a wholly-owned unit of Maritz Research, is the ability to hold up a mirror through mystery shopping research, to reflect what actually happens in the delivery of a service or purchase of a product. We design the evaluation process to include your key drivers of customer satisfaction and customer loyalty. This process gives managers the powerful information needed to take action and improve business performance.

Maritz Virtual Customers plays a key role in Maritz' customer choice-experience-loyalty model by giving you insight into what customers really experience at the "moment-of-truth." You'll know whether your customers are being delighted or disappointed and receive the take-action intelligence you need to improve performance.

(www.virtualcustomers.com)

3.3 Recording devices

While questionnaires and diaries essentially record answers to direct questions, other devices are used to record **observations**, for instance of the order in which a consumer proceeds around a supermarket.

3.3.1 Manual recording systems

A consumer **diary** allows the consumer to record behaviour on or between different dates or even times of the day. The diary is completed every time a certain behaviour occurs, rather than behaviour being recalled at times specified by the researcher. It is thus an **accurate means of recording repetitive information** for, say, a consumer panel.

Diary-filling **can be very detailed and onerous** and it is rare that a household, even a member of a consumer panel, is asked to complete one for longer than two weeks. The problem is that the data recorded needs to be both accurate and up-to-date, whilst the room for error, with new brands on the market for instance, is vast.

3.3.2 Electronic recording systems

An explosion in market research data has been made possible by the development of **electronic recording devices**.

(a) **EPOS** (electronic point of sale systems) with scanners of bar-codes provide fast and accurate records of sales, times and prices.

(b) **Electronic questionnaires** and diaries, discussed above, allow information to be input directly into a computer system, so results can be reviewed at any time in the survey and range and topical checks applied.

(c) **Audio and video recording devices** may be used to record interviews, especially depth ones, and camcorders can be used to record consumer behaviour.

The key point about electronic recording devices is that **information recorded is complete**, so sampling and estimating are not required.

Marketing at Work

The impact of technology on marketing research is demonstrated by the widespread use of CAPI and CATI.

First, the paper questionnaire-carrying clipboard is being rapidly replaced for many applications by the laptop computer. Computer assisted personal interviewing (CAPI) has become the norm for face-to-face interviews, according to BMRB International, one of the UK's biggest market research agencies.

Computer-assisted telephone interviewing (CATI) is already firmly established as an alternative to the more laborious written questionnaires that telephone interviewers used to complete.

For both CAPI and CATI, interviewers tap survey answers straight into a computer, cutting down on data processing time and improving accuracy. Surveys can be more complex and closely targeted because the computer automatically selects the interviewer's 'routing' – which question should follow on from a particular answer.

3.4 In-home scanning

Consumer panel research has traditionally relied on diaries or home audits to collect data. However, both Neilsen and AGB have now launched new panels based on in-home scanning, where each household is equipped with a **hand-held laser scanner** or light pen for reading the bar-codes on the products they buy. This has revolutionised the consumer panel process because it obviates the need for diary completion and, plausibly, generates much higher levels of accuracy and comprehensiveness.

All panellists need to do is run the scanner or light-pen over the **bar-code** as they unpack their shopping. The bar-code instantly records the country of origin, the manufacturer, the product, and the product variant if applicable. Other **information can be keyed in** at the same time using the number keys attached to the scanner, including price, source of purchase, date of purchase, promotions, and who made the purchase.

Chapter Roundup

- **Questionnaire design** should be done methodically: **develop question topics**; **select question and response formats** and take care with **wording**; **determine the sequence**; **design the layout** and **pilot test**.
- **Questions** need to be **worded with precision**, avoiding ambiguity and lack of clarity, not conflating multiple issues, not making unjustified assumptions, making it easy and clear for respondents to answer.
- **Question types** include **Yes/No**, **multiple choice**, **ratings** and **scales**: the primary purpose is to facilitate statistical analysis. Two of the best known scales are the Likert scale and the Semantic Differential scale.
- As a general rule a questionnaire should **progress from the general to the particular** (funnelling). It may be helpful to avoid a pattern of negative responses by distributing questions about respective topics throughout the questionnaire rather than bunching them together.
- Questionnaire **length** will depend on the circumstances, but **short is better than long**. Clear instructions and layout are vital.
- Interviews are **classified according to where they occur** (in the street, in a shop, in the home). Despite possible interviewer bias interviews can improve the quality and rate of responses. Postal surveys are less costly and time consuming. Telephone surveys have some advantages, especially the ability to cover a wider geographical area, but have the disadvantage of lack of rapport and confusion with telesales.
- **Testing** may be carried out on promotional materials and messages and on products (field tests) or on samples of entire markets.
- **Omnibus surveys** may be a cost effective way of obtaining certain types of information.
- **Observation** takes various forms: **home audit**, **direct observation**, and the **use of physical and technological recording devices**.
- There is a limit to the amount and type of information that can be captured by most forms of observation, although **mystery shopping** is one form that allows a wide range of marketing variables to be researched.

Quick Quiz

1 At what point in the questionnaire design process should you 'determine sequence'?

2 What four questions should you ask yourself when designing a question on a questionnaire?

3 Write an example of a closed question.

4 What is wrong with this question?

   A BPP Study Texts are brilliant
   B BPP Study Texts are very useful
   C BPP Study Texts cover the syllabus very closely
   D BPP Study Texts are user friendly

5 Rewrite option A in the previous question using a Likert scale

6 List four advantages of administering a questionnaire by means of a face to face interview.

7 Which of the following statements is NOT correct?

   A Field tests should be carried out early in the product development cycle

   B It is possible to buy space on an omnibus survey for your own organisation's question

   C Web surveys allow questions to be generated dynamically depending on the answers to other questions

   D Postal questionnaires are likely to be longer than interview questionnaires

8 It is not possible to measure feelings by observation. True or false? Explain your answer.

9 List four issues that need to be considered when devising mystery shopper research.

10 What does CAPI stand for?

Answers to Quick Quiz

1 After you have determined the question topics, decided on question and answer formats and write the questions, but before final decisions are made about layout, pilot testing is carried out.

2 Why am I asking this question? What is it intended to find out? What exactly do I want to know? Will this question give me the information I need?

3 A closed question can be answered Yes or No or with a very short factual answer. For example, 'What is your date of birth?'.

4 This is intended to be an example of a very bad question. There is no indication of what to do (tick one or more options? Ring round one or more letters?). Option B in particular is far too vague: what does 'useful' mean? It is also a highly leading question, since there is no opportunity to do anything other than praise BPP Study Texts.

5 BPP Study Texts are brilliant

   5 Strongly agree
   4 Agree
   3 Don't know
   2 Disagree
   1 Strongly disagree

6 (a) Respondent suitability can be checked at the outset
(b) Respondents can be encouraged to answer as fully as possible
(c) Questions are asked in the right order, and all relevant questions are asked
(d) The use of show material is properly administered
(e) Response rates are higher than for other forms of survey

7 Option A is incorrect. Field tests are expensive and are usually carried out when a product is near to its final form.

8 False. Body language and eye movement in response to a stimulus can be revealing. However you cannot be completely sure without checking by some other means.

9 (a) The shoppers should fit the profiles of consumers in the organisation's genuine target markets.
(b) Some observations made will be **subjective**.
(c) **Credibility** may be an issue
(d) Mystery shoppers may need to be trained in **data collection skills**

10 Computer Assisted Personal Interviewing

Action Programme Review

1 This is a practical, ongoing exercise.

2 Don't forget to do this: it is not a waste of your time, it is a form of revision. And be sympathetic to the survey: you wouldn't want next year's CIM students wandering the streets giving frivolous answers to your carefully crafted questionnaire!

3 Large numbers of postal questionnaires may not be returned, may be returned only partly completed or may be returned very late. This may lead to biased results if those replying are not representative of all people in the survey. Response rates are likely to be higher with personal interviews, and the interviewer can encourage people to answer all questions. Low response rates are a major problem with postal questionnaires, but low response rates can be avoided by:

(a) Providing a stamped and addressed envelope or a box for the return of the questionnaire
(b) Giving a date by which you require the completed questionnaire
(c) Providing an incentive such as a lottery ticket for those who return questionnaires on time
(d) Using a good covering letter

Misunderstanding is less likely with personal interviews because the interviewer can explain questions which the interviewee does not understand.

Personal interviews are more suitable when deep or detailed questions are to be asked, since the interviewer can take the time required with each interviewee to explain the implications of the question. Also, the interviewer can probe for further information and encourage the respondent to think more deeply.

4 Disguised. A visible observer would discourage some customers.

Now try Questions 10 and 11 at the end of the Study Text

9

Sampling

Chapter topic list

Syllabus content – knowledge and skill requirement

- 4.6: The theory and processes involved in sampling

Introduction

Ideally, if you want to find out about something you **ask everyone involved** or look at every single example. But that is clearly **not practical** if you are researching a market with many thousands or millions of customers: it would cost too much and it would take too long.

Alternatively, you could examine a **'representative sample'** ... but just how do you get a sample that is representative?

This chapter tells you about a variety of approaches to sampling. In the middle it has some rather complicated-looking maths, including graphs, and some formulae and numerical examples.

However, **don't panic** if you find maths and statistics scary, as many people do. You may **in practice** be presented with statistical analyses prepared by experts and it would clearly be helpful to have some idea of what they meant and whether they could be trusted. Read this chapter with that in mind.

Exam tip

The CIM Overview and Rationale for this paper states clearly that students 'will not be tested on their ability to undertake statistical analysis'. So, the tip is: don't take a calculator!

You are, however, 'expected to show an understanding of various statistical techniques and their outputs'. You will gain that understanding from this chapter and the next.

1 Sampling **6/04, 12/05**

FAST FORWARD

Sampling is a key topic in marketing research. Various sampling methods are examined in this chapter.

Key concepts

A **population** in statistics simply means the set of individuals, items, or data from which a statistical sample is taken. For example you might send a questionnaire to a sample of 100 people who are aged 30 to 40: the population is ALL people aged 30 to 40.

Sampling is one of the most important tools of marketing research because in most practical situations a population will be far too large to carry out a complete survey.

A familiar example of sampling is a poll taken to try to predict the results of an election. It is not practical to ask everyone of voting age how they are going to vote week after week: it would take too long and cost too much. So a sample of voters is taken, and the results from the sample are used to estimate the voting intentions of everyone eligible to vote.

Occasionally a population (set of items) is small enough that **all of it can be examined**: for example, the examination results of one class of students. When the population is examined, the survey is called a **census**. This type of survey is quite rare, however, and usually the researcher has to choose some sort of sample.

You may think that using a sample is very much a **compromise**, but you should consider the following points.

(a) It can be shown mathematically that once a certain sample size has been reached, **very little extra accuracy** is gained by examining more items.

(b) It is possible to **ask more questions** with a sample.

(c) The **higher cost** of a census may **exceed the value** of results.

(d) **Things are always changing**. Even if you took a census it could be out of date by the time you completed it.

1.1 The choice of a sample

One of the most important requirements of sample data is that it should be **complete** in the sense that it covers all relevant aspects of the population to be examined. If this requirement is not met, then the sample will be **biased**.

For example, suppose you wanted to survey the weekly productivity of workers in a factory, and you went along every Monday and Tuesday for a few months to measure their output. Would these data be complete? The answer is no. You might have gathered very thorough data on what happens on Mondays and Tuesdays, but you would have missed out the rest of the week. It could be that the workers, keen and fresh after the weekend, work better at the start of the week than at the end. If this is the case, then your data will give you a **misleadingly high productivity figure**. Careful attention must therefore be given to the sampling method employed to produce a sample.

FAST FORWARD

A sample can be **selected** using **random sampling**, **quasi-random sampling** (systematic, stratified and multistage sampling) or **non-random sampling** (quota and cluster sampling). Ensure that you know the characteristics, advantages and disadvantages of each sampling method.

1.2 Random sampling

To ensure that the sample selected is **free from bias**, random sampling must be used. Inferences about the population being sampled can then be made validly.

A simple random sample is a sample selected in such a way that **every item in the population has an equal chance of being included**.

For example, if you wanted to take a random sample of library books, it would **not be good enough to pick them off the shelves, even if you picked them at random**. This is because the **books which were out on loan** would stand no chance of being chosen. You would either have to make sure that all the books were on the shelves before taking your sample, or find some other way of sampling (for example, using the library index cards).

A random sample is **not necessarily a perfect sample**. For example, you might pick what you believe to be a completely random selection of library books, and find that every one of them is a detective thriller. It is a remote possibility, but it could happen. The only way to eliminate the possibility altogether is to take 100% survey (a census) of the books, which, unless it is a tiny library, is impractical.

1.2.1 Sampling frames

If random sampling is used then it is necessary to construct a sampling frame. A sampling frame is simply a **numbered list of all the items in the population**. Once such a list has been made, it is easy to select a random sample, simply by generating a list of random numbers using random number tables or a computer.

A sampling frame should have the following characteristics.

- **Completeness**. Are all members of the population included on the list?
- **Accuracy**. Is the information correct?
- **Adequacy**. Does it cover the entire population?
- **Up to dateness**. Is the list up to date?
- **Convenience**. Is the sampling frame readily accessible?
- **Non-duplication**. Does each member of the population appear on the list only once?

Action Programme 1

Why is a telephone directory an unsuitable sampling frame?

Action Programme 2

You want to take a random sample of people who live in a particular area. Why would the electoral register not be a satisfactory sampling frame?

In many situations it might be **too expensive** to obtain a random sample, in which case quasi-random sampling is necessary, or else it may not be possible to draw up a sampling frame.

1.3 Quasi-random sampling

Quasi-random sampling, which provides a **good approximation to random sampling**, necessitates the existence of a sampling frame. There are **three main methods** of quasi-random sampling.

1.3.1 Systematic sampling

Systematic sampling may provide a good approximation to random sampling. It works by selecting **every nth item** after a random start. For example, if it was decided to select a sample of 20 from a population of 800, then every 40th (800 ÷ 20) item after a random start in the first 40 should be selected. The starting point could be found using the lottery method or random number tables. If (say) 23 was chosen, then the sample would include the 23rd, 63rd, 103rd, 143rd ... 783rd items.

The gap of 40 is known as the **sampling interval**.

The investigator must ensure that there is no regular pattern to the population which, if it coincided with the sampling interval, might lead to a biased sample. In practice, this problem is often overcome by choosing multiple starting points and using varying sampling intervals whose size is selected at random.

1.3.2 Stratified sampling

In many situations **stratified sampling** is the best method of choosing a sample. The **population must be divided into strata or categories**.

If we took a random sample of all marketers in the country, it is conceivable that the entire sample might consist of members of the CIM working in commercial companies. Stratified sampling removes this possibility as random samples could be taken from each type of employment, the number in each sample being proportional to the total number of marketers in each type (for example those who are lecturers, those in commerce, those in the public sector and those in market research and agencies).

Note, however, that stratification requires prior knowledge of each item in the population. Sampling frames do not always contain this information. Stratification from the electoral register as to age structure would not be possible because the electoral register does not contain information about age.

1.3.3 Multistage sampling

The population is first **divided into quite large groups**, usually on a geographic basis, and a small sample of these groups is selected at random. Each of the groups selected is **subdivided into smaller groups** and again, a smaller number of these is selected at random. This process is **repeated as many times as necessary** and finally, a random sample of individuals in each of the smallest groups is taken. A fair approximation to a random sample can be obtained.

1.4 Non-random sampling

Non-random sampling is used **when a sampling frame cannot be established**.

1.4.1 Quota sampling

In quota sampling randomness is forfeited in the interests of **cheapness and administrative simplicity**. Investigators are told to interview all the people they meet up to a certain quota. A large degree of bias could be introduced accidentally. For example, an interviewer in a shopping centre may fill his quota by only meeting people who can go shopping during the week. In practice, this problem can be **partly overcome by subdividing the quota** into different types of people, for example on the basis of age, gender and income, to ensure that the sample mirrors the structure or stratification of the population. The interviewer is then told to interview, for example, 30 males between the ages of 30 and 40 from social class B. The actual choice of the individuals to be interviewed, within the limits of the **quota controls**, is left to the field worker.

Action Programme 3

The number of marketers and their sex in each type of work in a particular country are as follows.

	Female	*Male*	*Total*
Lecturers	100	100	200
Commercial companies	400	300	700
Public sector	100	200	300
Marketing research and agencies	500	300	800
			2,000

What would an investigator's quota be, assuming that a sample of 200 is required?

1.5 Cluster sampling **6/04**

Cluster sampling involves **selecting one definable subsection of the population** as the sample, that subsection taken to be representative of the population in question. The pupils of one school might be taken as a cluster sample of all children at school in London.

Action Programme 4

A publishing company carries out a national survey of adults' reading habits. To reduce travelling costs, the country is first divided into constituencies. A sample of 50 constituencies is then selected at random. Within each of these constituencies, 5 polling districts are selected, again using random techniques. Interviewers will visit a random selection of 30 people on the electoral register in each of the districts selected. What sampling method is the company using?

2 The size of a sample **12/04**

As well as deciding on the appropriateness of a particular sampling method for a given situation, the size of the sample actually selected must also be given consideration.

Although, in certain circumstances, statistical processes can be used to calculate sample sizes, as we'll see in a moment there is **no universal law** for determining the size of the sample. Researchers may simply rely on their **experience** from other studies similar to the project in hand. Two general considerations should, however, be borne in mind.

(a) The larger the size of the sample, the more accurate the results.

(b) There reaches a point after which there is little to be gained from increasing the size of the sample.

Despite these principles other, more administration-type factors, play a role in determining sample size.

(a) **Money** and **time** available

(b) **Degree of precision required**. A survey may have the aim of discovering residents' reaction to a road widening scheme and hence a fairly small sample, producing imprecise results, would be acceptable. An enquiry into the safety of a new drug would, on the other hand, require an extremely large sample so that the information gained was as precise as possible.

(c) **Number of subsamples required.** If a complicated sampling method such as stratified sampling is to be used, the overall sample size will need to be large so as to ensure adequate representation of each subgroup (in this case, each stratum).

3 Statistics and sampling 6/04

FAST FORWARD

According to the **central limit theorem**, if a large number of samples are taken from the population, their means calculated and the means plotted as a frequency distribution, this distribution (the sampling distribution of the mean) will be very close to being **normally distributed**.

3.1 Research data and distributions

Once it has been collected research data can be organised and summarised in various ways for presentation purposes. One useful way is to prepare a table that shows how many times each value appears. A **'frequency distribution'** is an analysis of the number of times (the frequency) each particular value occurs in (is 'distributed amongst) a set of items.

A **probability distribution** is the same except that it replaces actual numbers with proportions of the total. To take a very simple example, in a statistics test, the marks out of ten awarded to 50 students might be as follows (note this is a census of all students who took the test, not a sample).

Marks out of 10	*Number of students (frequency distribution)*	*Proportion or probability (probability distribution)*
0	0	0.00 or 0%
1	0	0.00 or 0%
2	1	0.02 or 2%
3	2	0.04 or 4%
4	4	0.08 or 8%
5	10	0.20 or 20%
6	15	0.30 or 30%
7	10	0.20 or 20%
8	6	0.12 or 12%
9	2	0.04 or 4%
10	0	0.00 or 0%
	50	1.00 or 100%

A graph of the probability distribution would look like this. You'll see the significance of this in a moment.

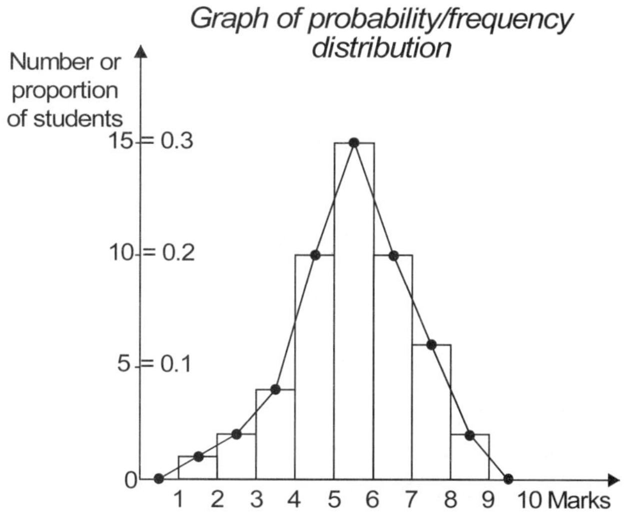

The **area under the curve** represents the total number of students whose marks have been recorded, 50 people. The area under the curve is 100% (the total of all the probabilities) of the sample.

There are a number of different probability distributions but we shall confine our attention to just one: **the normal distribution**.

3.2 The normal distribution

The normal distribution is important because **many probability distributions are close enough to a normal distribution** to be treated as one without any significant loss of accuracy. That opens up lots of possibilities for research data.

The normal distribution can be drawn as a graph, and it would be a bell-shaped curve.

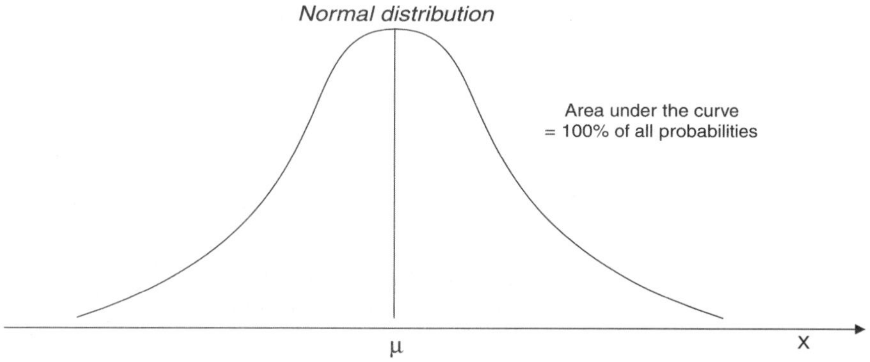

The normal curve is **symmetrical**. The symbol μ is the average or 'mean' of the distribution and the left hand side of the area under the curve to the left of μ is the mirror image of the right hand side.

3.3 The standard deviation and the normal distribution

For any normal distribution, the dispersion of values around the mean can be measured exactly in terms of a value called the **standard deviation**. You need not worry about how the standard deviation is calculated.

The entire curve represents all the possible outcomes and the normal curve is symmetrical; therefore **50%** of values are **greater** than the mean value, and **50% less than** the mean value.

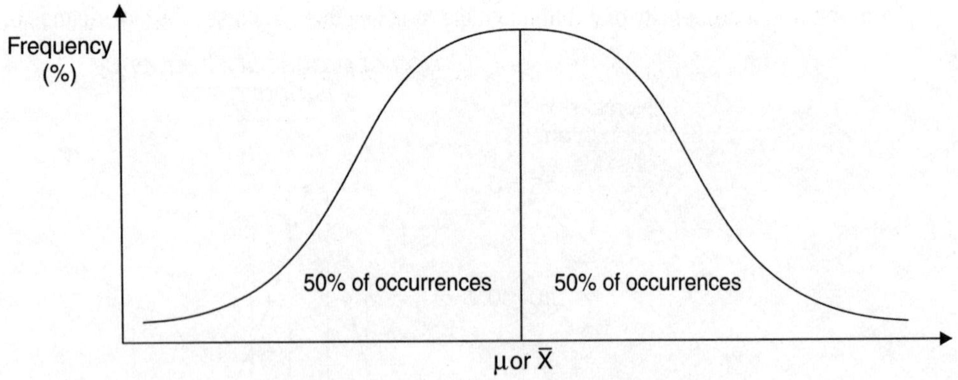

The normal distribution also has the following very important properties.

(a) About **68%** of frequencies have a value within **one standard deviation** either side of the mean. Thus if a normal distribution has a mean of 80 and a standard deviation of 3, 68% of the total outcomes would occur within the range plus or minus (±) one standard deviation from the mean, that is, within the range 77 – 83. Since the curve is symmetrical, 34% of the values must fall in the range 77 – 80 and 34% in the range 80 – 83.

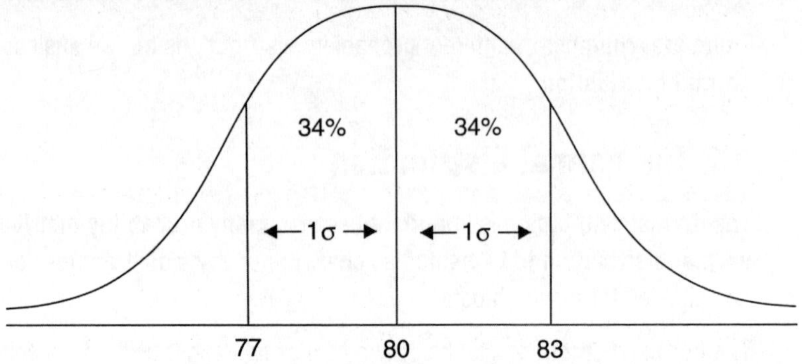

(b) About **95%** of the frequencies in a normal distribution occur in the range **± 1.96** standard deviations from the mean.

In our example 95% of the frequencies in the distribution would occur in the range

$$80 \pm 1.96 \times 3$$
$$= 80 \pm 5.88$$
$$= 74.12 \text{ to } 85.88$$

Half of 95% is 47½% , so 47½% of outcomes would be in the range 74.12 to 80 and the other 47½% would be in the range 80 to 85.88.

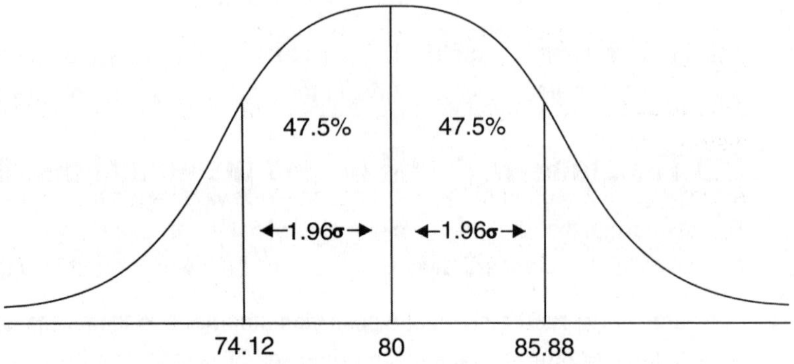

(c) About **99%** of the frequencies occur in the range **± 2.58** standard deviations from the mean.

In our example, 99% of frequencies would lie in the range

$80 \pm 2.58\ (3)$
$= 80 \pm 7.74$
$= 72.26$ to 87.74.

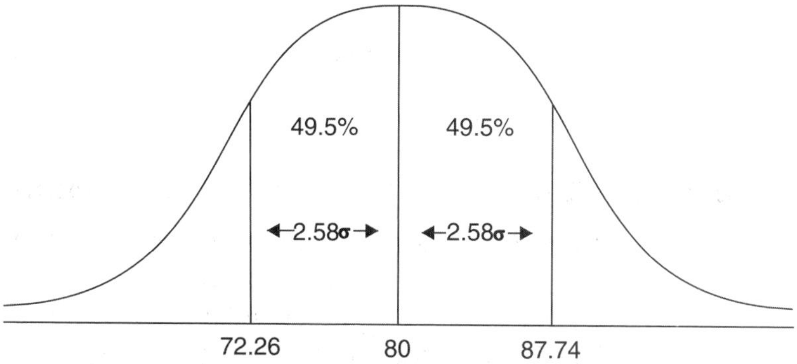

Although there is an infinite number of normal distributions, depending on values of the mean μ and the standard deviation σ, the way the frequencies are distributed around the mean is **exactly the same for all normal distributions**.

A **normal distribution table**, shown at the end of this text, gives the proportion of the total between the mean and a point above or below the mean for any multiple of the standard deviation.

Distances above or below the mean are expressed in numbers of standard deviations z.

$$z = \frac{x - \mu}{\sigma}$$

where z = the number of standard deviations above or below the mean
x = the value of the variable under consideration
μ = the mean
σ = the standard deviation

3.4 Sampling distribution of the mean

Suppose that we wish to estimate the mean of a population, say the average weight of potatoes consumed by households in a week. A sample of, say, 100 households might be taken, and the mean weight per household of the sample might be, say, 5.8 kg.

Another sample of 100 households might then be taken and the mean weight might be, say, 6.3 kg.

A large number of samples might be taken and the mean of each sample calculated. These means are like the test marks we looked at earlier. They will not all be the same but we can count up the number of times each value occurs and plot the results as a distribution. This type of distribution is called a 'sampling distribution of the mean'.

A sampling distribution of the mean has the following important properties.

(a) It is very close to being a normal distribution, and the larger the sample the more closely will the sampling distribution approximate to a normal distribution. The statistical rule that a sampling distribution of sample means is normally distributed is known as the **central limit theorem.**

(b) The **mean** of the sampling distribution is the **same as** the **population** mean, μ.

(c) The sampling distribution has a standard deviation which is called the **standard error** of the mean. This is calculated as the standard deviation of the population divided by the square root of the size of each sample: $\sigma / \sqrt{n}$. As we'll see, this statistic is important when calculating what size of sample needs to be taken to obtain useful results.

(The standard deviation *of the population* (σ) is not normally known. To overcome this problem the standard deviation *of a sample* is taken as the best estimate of the standard deviation of the whole population, so that se = $s/\sqrt{n}$, where s is the standard deviation of a sample.)

3.5 Confidence levels, limits and intervals

FAST FORWARD

Armed with knowledge of the central limit theorem and properties of the sampling distribution of the mean, we can say, with a certain level of confidence and using sample data, the range within which the true population mean falls.

From our knowledge of the properties of a normal distribution, together with the rule that sample means are normally distributed around the true population mean, with a standard deviation equal to the standard error, we can **draw some conclusions** about sample data collected as part of research study.

(a) With 68% probability, the population mean lies within the range: sample mean $\pm$ one standard error.

(b) With 95% probability, the population mean lies within the range: sample mean $\pm$ 1.96 standard errors.

(c) With 99% probability, the population mean lies within the range: sample mean $\pm$ 2.58 standard errors.

These degrees of certainty (such as 95%) are known as **confidence levels**, and the ends of the ranges (such as sample mean + 2.58 standard errors) around the sample mean are called **confidence limits**. The ranges (such as sample mean $\pm$ one standard error) are called **confidence intervals**.

Thus we have a **very useful research tool** for estimating the essential characteristics of an entire population simply by finding out about a small number of its members.

3.6 Sampling distribution of a proportion

The arithmetic mean or average is a very important statistic, and sampling is often concerned with estimating the mean of a population.

Many surveys, however, especially those concerned with attitudes or opinions about an issue or the percentage of times an event occurs (for example, the proportion of returned items out of the total number of items sold) attempt to estimate a proportion rather than an arithmetic mean.

Suppose for example, that we wished to know what proportion of an electorate intends to vote for the Jacobin party at the forthcoming general election. Several samples might be obtained, and the proportion of pro– Jacobin voters in a sample might vary, say from 37% to 45%. The central limit theorem would apply, and the proportion of pro-Jacobin voters in each sample could be arranged into a sampling distribution (the sampling distribution of a proportion) with the following features.

(a) It is normally distributed.
(b) It has a mean equal to the proportion of pro-Jacobin voters in the population.
(c) It has a standard deviation equal to the standard error of a proportion.

The formula for the standard error of a proportion is $\sqrt{[pq/n]}$

where p is the proportion in the population (eg 5%)
q is 1 – p (100% – 5% = 95%)
n is the size of the sample.

We use the sample proportion p as an estimate of the population proportion.

For example, suppose a researcher wishes to know what proportion of people in a certain area regularly travel by bus. Of a sample of 400 people, 285 said they did so. Estimate the population proportion with 99% confidence.

The sample proportion is 285/400 = 0.7125.

The standard error is $\sqrt{\dfrac{0.7125 \times (1 - 0.7125)}{400}} = 0.0226$

The 99% confidence interval for the population proportion is

$$\begin{aligned} & 0.7125 \pm (2.58 \times 0.0226) \\ = \quad & 0.7125 \pm 0.0583 \\ = \quad & 0.6542 \text{ to } 0.7708 \end{aligned}$$

With 99% confidence we can say that between 65% and 77% of people in that area regularly travel by bus.

4 Sample sizes using statistics

FAST FORWARD

As well as being able to do this, we are also able to calculate the **size of the sample** required to obtain a sufficient degree of **accuracy** at a given level of **confidence** in the estimation of the population mean.

Suppose that an organisation wants to find out the average income to within £10 of all those in a particular market segment. A previous investigation estimated it to be £18,000, with a standard deviation of £50. How could the organisation decide on the **size** of the sample required to be able to estimate the true average salary to within £10?

We know that, at the 95% level of confidence, the population mean equals a sample mean plus or minus 1.96 standard errors.

If we require the estimate to be within ± £10 then 1.96 standard errors = 10 and a bit of algebra will give us the size of the sample we need to take.

$\therefore\ 1.96 \times \sigma / \sqrt{n} = 10$

$\therefore\ \dfrac{1.96 \times £50}{\sqrt{n}} = 10$

$\therefore\ \left(\dfrac{1.96 \times £50}{10}\right)^2 = n = 96.04$, say 97 (we have to round up)

A sample size of 97 is therefore required to be able to estimate the true average income to within ± £10 and be 95% confident of our answer.

In general terms the size of sample required to estimate a population mean with a sufficient degree of accuracy (r) at a given level of confidence = $(1.96\sigma/r)^2$. (An estimate must be provided for the standard deviation (σ) even before the sample is collected.) At the 99% confidence level, 1.96 is replaced by 2.58.

4.1 Selecting a sample size in order to estimate a proportion

A similar approach can be taken to the problem of deciding a sample size to obtain the proportion of a population with sufficient accuracy.

If we require an estimate of the proportion which is accurate to within ± r% then we know that at the 95% level of confidence:

r = 1.96 standard errors = $1.96\sqrt{[pq/n]}$

$$r^2 = \frac{1.96^2 \times pq}{n}$$

$$n = \frac{1.96^2 \times pq}{r^2}$$

At the 99% confidence level, 1.96 is replaced by 2.58.

Suppose an organisation wishes to estimate how many people would take up a promotional offer. Because of the potential cost implications they require a result that is within 0.5% of the true proportion, and want to be 99% confident of the result. An initial sample indicated that p = 0.02. What size of sample should be examined?

$p = 0.02$, therefore $q = 1 - p = 0.98$
$r = 0.5\% = 0.005$

At a 99% level of confidence

$$n = \frac{2.58^2 \times 0.02 \times 0.98}{0.005^2}$$

$$= 5{,}218.6 \text{ units, say } 5{,}219 \text{ units}$$

The sample would need to consist of 5,219 units.

If we have no initial idea of the population proportion, we work out a required sample size using p = 0.5, as this gives the largest possible value for n. We will thus at least achieve the required accuracy. (You would need to ask 16,641 people in the example above.)

5 Problems with sample data

FAST FORWARD

There are many **potential problems** with sample data including **bias**, **unrepresentative data**, and **insufficient data**, perhaps because of non-response.

There are several faults or weaknesses which might occur in the design or collection of sample data. These are as follows.

(a) **Bias**. In choosing a sample, unless the method used to select the sample is the random sampling method, or a quasi-random sampling method, there will be a likelihood that some 'units' (individuals or households etc) will have a poor, or even zero chance of being selected for the sample. Where this occurs, samples are said to be biased. A biased sample may occur in the following situations.

    (i) The sampling frame is out of date, and excludes a number of individuals or 'units' new to the population.

    (ii) Some individuals selected for the sample decline to respond. If a questionnaire is sent to 1,000 households, but only 600 reply, the failure of the other 400 to reply will make the sample of 600 replies inevitably biased.

    (iii) A questionnaire contains leading questions, or a personal interviewer tries to get respondents to answer questions in a particular way.

(b) **Insufficient data**. The sample may be too small to be reliable as a source of information about an entire population.

(c) **Unrepresentative data**. Data collected might be unrepresentative of normal conditions. For example, if an employee is asked to teach a trainee how to do a particular job, data concerning the employee's output and productivity during the time he is acting as trainer will not be representative of his normal output and productivity.

(d) **Omission of an important factor**. Data might be incomplete because an important item has been omitted in the design of the 'questions'.

(e) **Carelessness**. Data might be provided without any due care and attention. An investigator might also be careless in the way he gathers data.

(f) **Confusion of cause and effect (or association)**. It may be tempting to assume that if two variables appear to be related, one variable is the cause of the other. Variables may be associated but it is not necessarily true that one causes the other.

(g) Where questions call for something **more than simple 'one-word' replies**, there may be difficulty in interpreting the results correctly. This is especially true of 'depth interviews' which try to determine the reasons for human behaviour.

One method of checking the accuracy of replies is to insert control questions in the questionnaire, so that the reply to one question should be compatible with the reply to another. If they are not, the value of the interviewee's responses are dubious, and may be ignored. On the other hand, the information that the interviewee is genuinely confused about something, and so offers contradictory answers, may be valuable information itself, or it may reflect the way the questions are structured.

5.1 Non-sampling error

A non-sampling error is an error that results solely from the manner in which the observations are made, and leads to inaccurate conclusions being drawn from the group being studied. It can occur whether a total population or a sample is being used. The simplest example of a non-sampling error is inaccurate measurements due to poor procedures or data input errors. Unintended errors may result from any of the following.

- The manner in which the response is elicited – no two interviewers are alike, and questions may be worded poorly
- The suitability of the persons surveyed – some may give deliberately inaccurate answers
- The purpose of the study – if the respondent knows what it is, it may affect the responses given
- The personal biases of the interviewer or survey writer – questionnaires must be designed to draw out useful responses
- Non-response – either through refusal or non-availability

5.2 Non-response

Non-response (of a sample member) cannot be avoided. It can, however, (apart from in mail surveys) be kept at a reasonable level. Experience has shown that the non-response part of a survey often differs considerably from the rest. The types of non-response are as follows.

(a) **Units outside the population**. Where the field investigation shows that units no longer exist (eg demolished houses), these units should be considered as outside the population and should be subtracted from the sample size before calculating the non-response rate.

(b) **Unsuitable for interview**. This is where people who should be interviewed are too infirm or too unfamiliar with the language to be interviewed.

(c) **Movers**. People who have changed address since the list was drawn up cannot be interviewed.

(d) **Refusals**. Some people refuse to co-operate.

(e) **Away from home**. People might be away from home for longer than the field work period and call-back might not be possible.

(f) **Out at time of call**.

These sort of problems occur chiefly in **random** sample surveys. Some of the above do not apply when interviewing is done in factories, colleges or offices. In quota sampling (c), (e) and (f) do not appear. Although the interviewer may miss some people for these reasons, he or she simply continues until he or she fills the quota.

Social change can influence the level of non-response. Rising crime means that householders may be afraid to answer the door to strangers and there are other employment opportunities for 'doorstep interviewers'. Response rates are therefore slipping as more people either refuse to be or cannot be interviewed.

Marketing at Work

The director general of the Market Research Society, the industry's professional body, says falling response levels are not just a UK phenomenon. He is concerned that the quality of research will begin to be affected, for the lower response rates are, the greater the departure from ideal cross-sections of opinion, and the less accurate findings are likely to be.

Another problem is that of **'data fatigue'**, as the public becomes tired of filling in questionnaires and more cynical about the real motives of 'market researchers' because of 'sugging' (selling under the guise of research) and 'frugging' (fundraising under the guise of research).

5.3 How to deal with non-response

Taking **substitutes** (such as the next house along) is no answer because the substitutes may differ from the non-respondents. Instead the interviewer can try to increase the response rate.

(a) Little can be done about **people not suitable** for interview.

(b) **People who have moved** are a special category. It is usually not practical to track them down. It is acceptable to select an individual from the new household against some rigorously defined procedure.

(c) To minimise **'refusals'**, keep questionnaires as brief as possible, use financial incentives, and highly skilled interviewers. Refusal rates tend to be low (3-5 per cent).

(d) People **'away from home'** may be contacted later, if this is possible.

(e) People **'out at time of call'** is a common problem. The researcher should plan the calling time sensibly (for example, as most breadwinners are out at work in the day-time, call in the evening). Try to establish a good time to call back – or arrange an appointment.

Exam tip

The problem of non-response was the subject of a question in the December 2003 exam. In June 2007, types of non-sampling error were examined. These can include inadequate coverage, inaccurate measurement, poor processing and non-response.

Chapter Roundup

- **Sampling** is a key topic in marketing research. Various sampling methods were examined in this chapter.
- A sample can be **selected** using **random sampling**, **quasi-random sampling** (systematic, stratified and multistage sampling) or **non-random sampling** (quota and cluster sampling). Ensure that you know the characteristics, advantages and disadvantages of each sampling method.
- According to the **central limit theorem**, if a large number of samples are taken from the population, their means calculated and the means plotted as a frequency distribution, this distribution (the sampling distribution of the mean) will be very close to being **normally distributed**.
- Armed with knowledge of the central limit theorem and properties of the sampling distribution of the mean, we can say, with a certain level of confidence and using sample data, the range within which the true population mean falls.
- As well as being able to do this, we can also able to calculate the **size of the sample** required to obtain a sufficient degree of **accuracy** at a given level of **confidence** in the estimation of the population mean.
- There are many **potential problems** with sample data including **bias**, **unrepresentative data**, and **insufficient data**, perhaps because of non-response.

Quick Quiz

1. What factors make sampling worthwhile rather than a compromise?
2. What is a simple random sample?
3. What is a sampling frame?
4. What is stratified sampling?
5. What is cluster sampling?
6. List three administrative factors which may affect the size of a sample.
7. Define confidence intervals, confidence levels and confidence limits.
8. List five faults or weaknesses that may occur in the collection of sample data.
9. Define 'data fatigue'.

Answers to Quick Quiz

1. Very little extra accuracy is achieved by larger sample if done effectively; it gives the opportunity to ask more questions; higher cost of more respondents may reduce value of results; could be out-of-date by the time of completion.
2. A sample selected in such a way that every item in the population has an equal chance of being included.
3. A numbered list of all the items in the population.
4. The population is divided into strata or categories.
5. One definable sub-section of the population is taken to be representative of the population in question.
6. Money/time; degree of precision required; number of sub-samples required.
7. These are defined in Section 3.5.
8. Bias; insufficient data; unrepresentative data; omission of an important factor; carelessness; confusion of cause and effect; ambiguity.
9. The public becomes tired of filling in questionnaires.

Action Programme Review

1. Not everyone has a telephone and not all of those who do have a telephone are listed.
2. (a) Those under 18 are not included on the register since they are not entitled to vote.

   (b) Mobile individuals such as students are frequently not registered where they actually live.

   (c) The register is not up to date and so those who have recently moved to the area are omitted and those who have recently left the area are still included.
3. The investigator needs to interview 200/2,000 × 100% = 10% of the population.

   Using quota sampling, the investigator would interview the first 10 (100 × 10%) male marketing lecturers that he met, and the first 40 (400 × 10%) female marketers in commercial companies.

	Female	*Male*	*Total*
Lecturers	10	10	20
Commercial companies	40	30	70
Other commercial	10	20	30
Marketing research and agencies	50	30	80
			200

4. Cluster sampling.

Now try Questions 12 and 13 at the end of the Study Text

Part E
Presenting and evaluating information

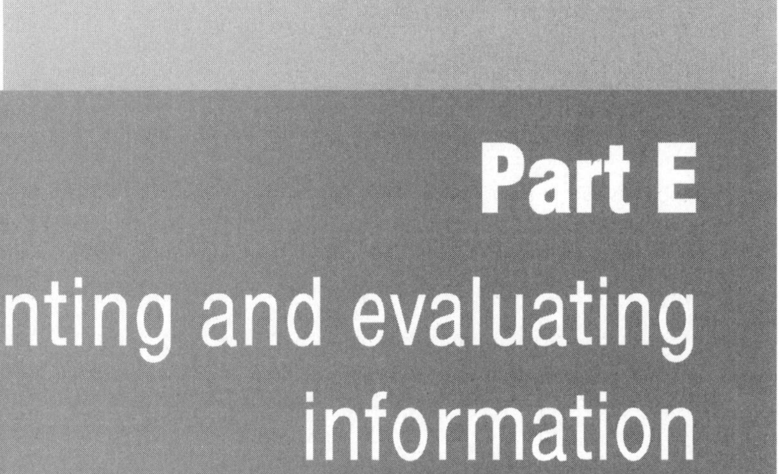

10

Analysing data

Chapter topic list

Syllabus content – knowledge and skill requirements

- 5.1: Use techniques for analysing qualitative and quantitative data
- 5.4: Use research and data to produce actionable recommendations for a marketing plan or to support a business decision

Introduction

We begin this chapter with some reassuring remarks about how you don't need to be a mathematical genius to draw valid conclusions from research data, and how sometimes it pays to ignore the evidence entirely!

As we'll see in a moment, methods of making sense of **qualitative** data really amount to no more than the ability to organise words (in other words comments made by customers) into a form that allows you to recognise patterns. To some extent you can do this with **quantitative** data too, but the very fact that it is in numerical form means that there are **other more scientific** possibilities for analysis.

As Wilson (2002) points out: 'many student's eyes glaze over when confronted by formulas and statistics. Thankfully many of the analysis and questionnaire design software packages ... remove the onerous tasks of applying formulas and calculating statistical outcomes. However, researchers do need to develop an **awareness and understanding** of the statistical techniques available and the meaning of their outputs.'

Much of this chapter is therefore devoted to descriptions and illustrations of some of the more useful statistical techniques. Some are simple concepts, like averages and scattergraphs; others sound a bit scarier.

(a) Hypothesis testing and the chi-squared test are both ways of testing out whether your **assumptions and expectations** about a market are **borne out by the evidence** collected from a sample.

 (i) **Hypothesis** testing looks at the **average** value
 (ii) The **chi-squared** test looks at the **pattern** of values.

(b) Correlation and regression are way of measuring how far the value of one thing is related to the value of another, such as the value of sales of ice cream and the temperature.

Put in these simple terms it should be obvious how statistics might help us make or change **marketing decisions**. Keep that in mind and don't get bogged down by the figures.

1 Analysing research data

FAST FORWARD

Data may sometimes be successfully **analysed** on the basis of intuition or previous experience, but a **scientific approach** is likely to be more credible to most research clients.

Some approaches to how the value and validity of data may be assessed are relatively unscientific.

(a) **Common sense**. Clearly data which is dated, which emanates from dubious sources or which is based on unrepresentative samples should be treated with extreme caution, if not totally disregarded.

(b) **Statistical approaches**. There are a variety of sampling methods for survey data as already described, which are appropriate to different situations. All of them involve some degree of risk (some probability of error). The degree of risk of statistical error can, however, be computed as we have seen.

(c) **Expert judgement depends on the expertise**. The same data can be interpreted differently by different people – you have only to look at differences between economists or between politicians of different parties on the latest figures to see ample evidence of this. The following array – 98.7, 98.6, 98.6, 98.4, 98.1, 98.1 – might be regarded by a statistician as a declining trend but to a marketing manager the figures may represent a very steady state, especially if they were percentages of actual sales against budgeted sales for the last six years. The marketing manager might be wise to consult more than one expert before making a decision.

(d) **The intuitive approach**. Some people have a better feel for figures than others and seem able to judge the value and validity of data intuitively. For example, it is said that Rank Xerox ignored survey findings that there was no market for a dry copier and in doing so went on to become a world leader in this field.

(e) **The questioning approach**. Always question the origin and the basis of the data. Ask for further information. An actual spend of 180% of budget is not important if the amount concerned is only £10. A much smaller variance on a much larger amount could, however, be quite serious. Recognise that human errors occur when manipulating data, that bias can occur in questionnaire design: ask to see the questionnaire, check the figures.

Action Programme 1

Suggest possible reasons why Rank Xerox could have received a negative response on the market for a dry copier.

1.1 Analysing qualitative data — Pilot Paper, 6/07

FAST FORWARD

Qualitative data collected from focus groups and interviews can be subjected to various kinds of **content analysis** such as **tabulation** or **spider diagrams** and there are some software packages specially designed to facilitate such analysis.

The qualitative data you have collected from focus groups and depth interviews and the like will most probably be in the form of **transcripts** of tapes and interviewers' notes. A large volume of such data may seem unmanageable at first but there are a variety of techniques that you can use to make sense of it all. This is called **'content analysis'**.

(a) **Tabulation**. A table is created with columns for the different kinds of respondents and rows for the research objectives. Here is a very basic example.

	Men	Women
Attitude towards watching sports		
Attitude towards playing sports		

The comments and quotes from the transcripts are then entered into the appropriate box. This makes it much easier to make comparisons and can give rise to some quantitative data ('six out of ten women said ...').

Provided researchers are not allowed to add their own categories the task can be shared between several people with consistent results. On the other hand the method could be considered to be too inflexible: collected data that does not 'fit' anywhere might be discarded even though it is valuable.

(b) **Cut and paste**. This is identical to the tabular method except that data is not entered afresh but simply 'lifted' from the original transcript, so preserving accuracy. A word processing package or a spreadsheet would be used.

(c) **Spider diagrams** or **mind maps**. The research issue is placed at the centre of a sheet of paper and the key themes that emerge and relevant quotes and comments from the transcripts responses are placed around it.

Factors influencing how customers assess price

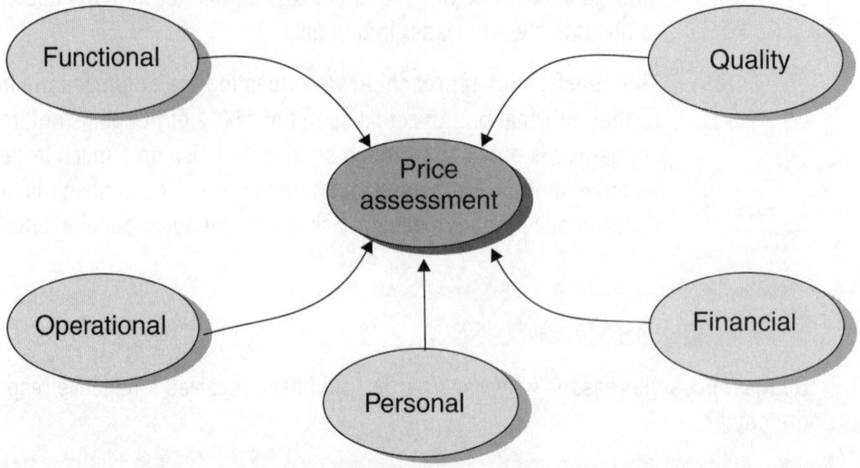

This makes it easier to include comments that don't 'fit' when using the tabulation method. The complexity of the interrelationships between items can be shown more clearly, via the placement of the comments and the use of interconnecting lines. Because the method is less rigid, there is no guarantee that two researchers would analyse the data in the same way, however.

(d) **Annotation.** As you might guess this entails the researcher categorising the items in a transcript by adding marginal comments, or perhaps using different coloured highlighter pens (or the equivalent in a word processor or spreadsheet). This leaves the actual data intact, so it is still possible to see how the full conversation flowed.

(e) **Computerised analysis** is possible with varying degrees of sophistication. Some programs might simply count the number of times a particular word or phrase appears; others can recognise patterns and related concepts.

Marketing at Work

QSR N6 is the fast, powerful, latest version of the most widely used qualitative research analysis software NUD*IST.

The programs in the NUD*IST line since their launch in 1987 have always been tool-based – providing researchers with interlocking tools for doing many sorts of qualitative research. This approach leaves it to the user to select the tools they want and to use them in the way they want. N6 is designed to take this approach further, making the access to data more direct and use of the tools more intuitive.

There are tools for handling large surveys or small "in-depth" analytical projects. Access to import and export facilities for statistics, database, and table-handling programs (such as SPSS, Excel, Access) ensure easy and comprehensive interaction between quantitative and qualitative aspects of the project – if needed. N6 introduces the ability to scope the exported material to include different subsets of the data in the results.

The Merge program allows multiple researchers to bring their work together. And if graphic visualization is important to your work, export to the extremely powerful analytically oriented Decision Explorer and the visually oriented Inspiration program.

A fundamental and unique feature of QSR's software is a node system of "containers" for ideas, topics, concepts and the like, that may or may not be used to code text or label documents. If you want to manage ideas, the nodes can be organised in a linked system of topics, thesaurus-like, that makes it easier to create, document and catalog ideas and topics, to rearrange and update your node catalogs or "trees", and to view and manipulate your data from the point of view of nodes, instead of the point of view of documents.

N6 has all the "unparalleled" search tools of the NUD*IST line, including simple or pattern-based (wildcard) text search and a complete set of ways of studying and comparing the coding of nodes (Node Search). In N6, text and node search are accessible core tools, simple to run. Both windows can stay on-screen permanently, inviting inquiry that moves between them.

(*www.qsrinternational.com.au*)

Exam tip

The Pilot paper asks for an explanation of two approaches that can be used to analyse transcripts. The June 2007 paper asked how you would analyse qualitative data for presentation to a client.

1.2 Preparing quantitative data for statistical analysis

Before **quantitative** data can be analysed statistically by computer it needs to be **entered** into the computer in some way if it was not collected in digital form in the first place, either by direct typing or by scanning technologies. The concerns here are the same as those for getting **clean data** into the organisation's database.

For ease and speed of analysis the data may also need to be **coded** in some way: for example if one of the options that respondents could have chosen was 'Green' then Green might be allocated a numerical code of, say, 6. This is much faster for the computer to process and also avoids possible inconsistencies.

2 Interpreting statistical information 6/04

FAST FORWARD

Quantitative data can be subjected to **statistical analysis** of varying degrees of complexity: to indicate useful characteristics such as **frequency, averages, dispersion, correlation** and **trends.**

Statistics are raw 'data'. They must be **processed** in some way to create **'information'** which is **meaningful and helpful** for a particular purpose. This section looks very briefly at some of the ways of using statistical data: the most important methods are described in more depth in the sections that follow this one.

2.1 Averages

Key concept

An **average** is a value which is 'typical' or representative of a set of data, a measure of its 'central tendency'.

The main types of average are as follows.

(a) The **arithmetic mean**, often shown by the symbol $\bar{x}$ ('x bar'). This is found by adding up all the items in the set, then dividing by the number of items in the set.

Eg: customer complaints per month over a six month period.

January	*February*	*March*	*April*	*May*	*June*
0	26	0	5	3	2

The average number of complaints is $\frac{0+26+0+5+3+2}{6} = \frac{36}{6} = 6$ per month.

The problem with this is that **extremes** (like the 26) **distort** the average: the actual monthly complaints are not as bad as 6 – which also disguises the fact that you had a real problem in February!

(b) The **median**: the **middle value**, when you arrange the data in ascending order. (If there is an even number of items, the median is mid-way between the middle two.) For example, here are our monthly complaints reordered:

0 0 2 3 5 26

↑

Median = 2.5

(c) The **mode**: the **most frequently occurring** value in a set of data. So the mode for our monthly customer complaints is 0!

You can probably now begin to appreciate why Disraeli said 'There are three kinds of lies: Lies, damned lies and statistics'. It is very easy to use averages to disguise the true facts.

2.2 Frequency distribution

As we saw in the previous chapter one type of classification often used in the organisation of large sets of data (and their presentation, as we will see later) is a **frequency distribution**.

Key concept

A **frequency distribution** is a method of classification in which the data is divided into segments or classes, and the number of items of data that fall into (or are observed in) each class is called the class frequency.

Classes might be ranges of age, costs/numbers/frequency of products purchased, time spent or errors made. You can compare the relative frequency of one class against another, or against the same class over time, to show trends.

2.2.1 Example

Given below is a set of raw data on the number of minutes in each hour reported spent on the telephone by 40 sales office staff.

19	15	1	24	5	19	27	34	14	23
9	5	4	18	41	17	15	19	23	14
34	11	16	17	28	29	31	11	21	12
8	5	16	6	17	29	7	9	23	18

As a frequency distribution, the data would be organised as follows. For example, count up how many times a number between 0 and 10 occurs.

	Time spent per hour (minutes)	*Number of workers*	
Classes	0 – 9	10	*Class frequencies*
	10 – 19	17	
	20 – 29	9	
	30 – 39	3	
	40 – 60	1	
	Total	40	*Total frequency*

A **cumulative frequency distribution** uses 'ceilings' instead of ranges to define classes: 'under 10, under 20' etc. But the class 'under 20' **includes** 'under 10' as well as '10 to 19': the frequency distribution accumulates. To use our example:

Time spent per hour (minutes)	*Number of workers = cumulative frequency*	
Under 10	10	
Under 20	10 + 17 = 27	
Under 30	10 + 17 + 9 = 36	
Under 40	10 + 17 + 9 + 3 = 39	
Under 60	10 + 17 + 9 + 3 + 1 = 40	(Total sample)

2.3 Trends

Key concepts

A **time series** is a set of data recorded at intervals over a period of time (eg monthly sales or customer complaint figures for the year).

A **trend** is an underlying movement (upwards or downwards) in a time series over the long term.

Patterns which can be observed in business time series include the following.

(a) **Trends**. Figures (for example, sales revenue, or number of women in managerial positions) may show a **positive trend** (there is an increase, in **each** successive set of data, or in general over time), or **negative trend** (that is, there is a regular decrease or downward movement).

(b) **Seasonal patterns or variations** that is, observable peaks and troughs at the same times of each successive year. There may be a repeated **seasonal pattern** (peak at Christmas, falling to low during Summer holidays, rising steeply to a peak at Christmas again, say). There may also be a **general trend:** the peaks and troughs get higher (or lower) from one year to the next. Look at the graph below.

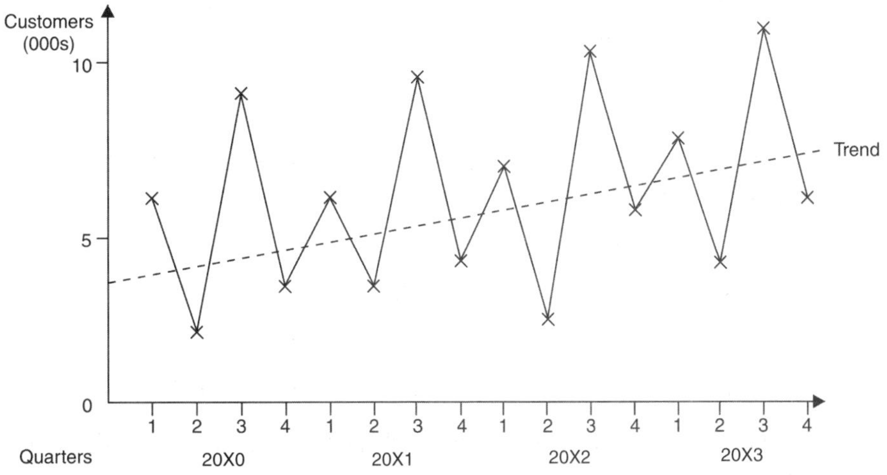

(c) **Cyclical variations**, reflecting the 'larger' pattern of the swing in an economy (usually over many years) from 'boom' to 'bust' and back again.

(d) **Random variations:** irregular ups and downs reflecting all the unpredictable factors that lie behind data gathered over time. The underlying or overall trend or seasonal cyclical pattern need not be altered.

Marketing at Work

'..... a certain charity ..... sent a test mailing to existing donors, asking for an additional contribution for a key project. It presented three boxes for respondents to tick, marked £15, £25 or £50 for this extra donation. The overall results were as follows: mailed 20,000; response rate 2.27 per cent; responders 453; money received £15,025; average gift £33.17.

On this basis, a roll-out to 200,000 was undertaken, with the goal of raising £150,000. But despite a similar response rate, the sum received fell short by more than £25,000. So what happened? Why did the average gift drop so dramatically (from £33.17 to £27.82)? Could this have been predicted?

In fact, the test result proved inaccurately high because of a single exceptional donation of £2,500 – which distorted the figures badly. This one donation changed the average gift from £22.71 to £33.17.

Marketing Week

Action Programme 2

What do you notice about the following findings?

(a) **Car ownership per home of those owning at least one car**

		Number owned by age of head of household		
Cars per home	*All homes*	*Head of household Aged < 45*	*Head of household Aged 45-64*	*Head of household Aged >65*
One	70%	65%	58%	80%
Two	25%	30%	30%	18%
Three	5%	5%	12%	2%

(b) **Growth of the US online market ($bn)**

	1996	*1997*	*2001*
Business-to-business sales	6	8	183
Travel	0.5	0.6	7.4
Financial services	0.8	1.2	5

2.4 Summarising statistical data

Some essential points to look out for in summarising statistical data include the following.

(a) **What is the 'argument' or 'story' of the data: what point does it make?**

It may help if you think about this as if you were writing a press release – as you may be asked to do. What is newsworthy about the findings revealed by the figures or graph? (Are Italians slow to take up e-commerce compared to the rest of Europe? Are women more likely than men to respond positively to direct mail?) Ask yourself what information the organisation will be able to **use**.

(b) **What comparisons are suggested?**

Mentally translate figures into slices of a pie chart, or bars of a bar chart (see the next chapter) to see some possibilities. Is one brand's market share bigger than others? Is a disproportionate amount spent on one promotional medium compared to others?

(c) **What trends or correlations can be observed?**

These are particularly useful concepts in summarising the importance of data and indicating what (if anything) needs to be done. A trend suggests change (for good or bad). A correlation suggests that if you manipulate one variable, you will get change in another. Mentally translate figures into a line graph or scatter diagram to see the possibilities. Is e-commerce penetration rising and projected to rise further? Does a reduction in PR spend correlate with rising product returns?

(d) **How reliable and meaningful is the data?**

Are apparent anomalies, surprises or trends accounted for by the age of the data (when was it gathered?), the size and constitution of the research sample (was it large and random enough to represent a genuine cross-section?), the question asked (was it ambiguous or leading?).

(e) **Are you interpreting the data correctly?**

3 Hypothesis testing 6/04

FAST FORWARD

You may also be expected to be aware of and understand the value of various methods of **hypothesis testing**. A hypothesis test is made by comparing the result from a sample with what we would expect if the null hypothesis were true. If the gap between the reality and the expectation is too wide, we reject the null hypothesis.

Hypothesis testing is the process of establishing the significance of the results of sample data for beliefs (hypotheses) about the population.

For example, suppose a sample of 150 people has been taken asking them how much they would be willing to pay for a new product. The mean price for the sample was £45 with a standard deviation of £10. However the marketing manager is convinced that the majority of people will not pay more than £40.

Is the sample consistent with the 'hypothesis' that the average acceptable price is £40?

3.1 Equal or not equal?

To apply a hypothesis test, we begin by stating an initial view, called the **null hypothesis**, that the average acceptable price is equal to £40. The alternative hypothesis will be that it is not equal to £40.

Next, we select a significance level, which indicates how severely we are testing the null hypothesis. Here, we will use 5%. A level of 5% is a common choice. The lower the significance level, the lower the probability of wrongly rejecting the null hypothesis, but the higher the probability of wrongly accepting it.

Our choice of 5% means that we shall assume that the sample mean (£45) is consistent with our estimated population mean (£40) provided that the sample mean is within what would be a 100% – 5% = 95% confidence interval around a sample mean equal to the mean given by the null hypothesis.

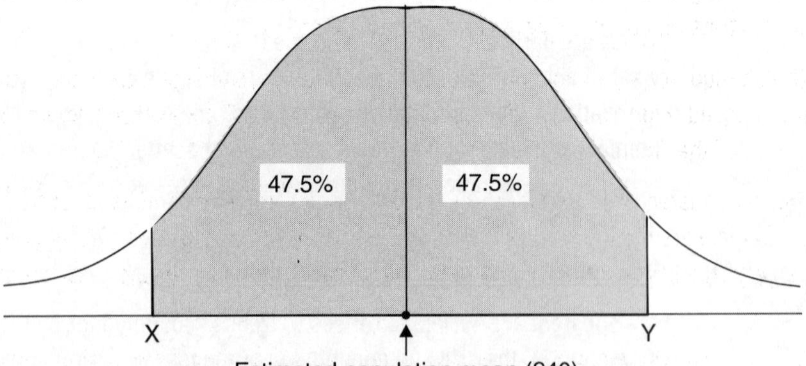

You may prefer to think of this in terms of the diagram above. If the sample mean of £45 is within the range from X to Y, we will conclude that our null hypothesis is acceptable.

X and Y are each 1.96 standard errors from the mean. From our sample, we can calculate the standard error as $10/\sqrt{150} = 0.816$. We can now test the hypothesis.

(a) The sample mean is £5 higher than our hypothesised population mean

(b) This is $5/0.816 = 6.1$ standard errors above the mean.

(c) At the 5% level of significance we would expect the sample mean to be within 1.96 standard errors of the hypothesised mean. It is not, and so at this level of significance, we reject the null hypothesis.

3.1.1 Conclusion

The average acceptable price is not £40, and the marketing manager is wrong. He or she should read this book!

Note that if we had got a sample mean within 1.96 standard errors of the hypothesised mean, this would not have proved that the null hypothesis was true. It would only have shown that we did not have enough evidence to reject the null hypothesis.

3.2 Procedure for hypothesis testing

The general procedure for hypothesis testing is as follows.

(a) Establish a hypothesis, for example that the mean value of all a company's invoices is £200. This is the null hypothesis (H_0). Also state an alternative hypothesis (H_1), for example that the mean value is not £200.

(b) Calculate the standard error ($\sigma/\sqrt{n}$) and the Z value ($(\overline{x} - \mu)/se$).

(c) Test the hypothesis. Are the sample results near enough what we would expect to get if the null hypothesis were true? What we expect is determined by the **significance level** selected. This is the chance we take of wrongly rejecting the null hypothesis.

(d) Having tested the hypothesis, draw a conclusion.

4 The chi-squared test 6/04

FAST FORWARD

A **chi-squared test** can test the hypothesis that two variables are unconnected. Expected frequencies are computed, and are then compared with observed frequencies. A chi-squared test can also be used to test whether observed data fit a given distribution. Again, expected frequencies are computed and compared with observed frequencies.

In sampling and in significance testing of sample results, we often use the normal distribution and concentrate on **comparing means or proportions**.

The chi-squared distribution is another distribution used in significance testing. (Chi-squared is pronounced 'Kigh squared' after the Greek letter 'chi'). You will often find chi-squared referred to by means of the Greek letter itself: χ^2.

The chi-squared distribution can be used to test a sample of items in order to decide whether the items in the sample are distributed according to a preconceived or expected distribution **pattern**. It compares the **frequencies** in the various categories rather than the mean or proportion that might be calculated from them.

Because they test whether something conforms to a certain pattern or not, χ^2 tests are often referred to as **goodness-of-fit tests**. The χ^2 test is a flexible method for distinguishing statistically significant data from data that is affected only by chance, with a view to directing control efforts to the places where they can be of most value.

Significance testing with the chi-squared test involves two steps.

(a) Calculating a chi-squared statistic.

(b) Seeing whether this statistic exceeds a certain critical point value, to establish the significance of the figures in the sample.

4.1 Observed and expected frequencies

χ^2 is used as a test of significance by comparing the actual or observed results of a sample against the results which would be expected, given a pre-conceived idea of how the population is distributed.

It is usual to test a null hypothesis. The null hypothesis states that the differences between the actual and expected frequencies arose purely by chance, and so there is no significant difference between observed results from the sample and the results that we would have expected.

What we have to do, then, is to compare the observed frequency of each category in the sample with its expected value.

We must have a list of observed results or frequencies and a corresponding list of expected results or frequencies.

A chi-squared statistic is calculated by taking the difference between each of the observed and expected frequencies, squaring the difference, and dividing this square by the expected frequency.

$$\chi^2 = \sum \frac{(O-E)^2}{E}$$

where O is the observed frequency (sometimes labelled 'A' for actual frequency) and E is the expected frequency of each item in the sample.

4.2 Example: a chi-squared test

Let's begin with a simple example.

The Genteel Stores Group operate a chain of department stores around the country. The marketing director has been stating for some years that the group's stores appeal more to older people than to younger people, and that the age distribution of the store's customers is as follows.

Age group of customers	*Proportion*
Under 20 years	5%
20 and under 30 years	10%
30 and under 40 years	15%
40 and under 50 years	20%
50 and under 60 years	30%
60 and under 70 years	15%
70 and over	5%

A survey of customers coming into the group's stores has just been carried out. The survey took a sample of 400 customers, and their ages were as follows.

Age	*Number*
Under 20	26
20 – 30	63
30 – 40	64
40 – 50	82
50 – 60	94
60 – 70	56
70 and over	15
	400

Solution

We can use the chi-squared test to decide whether the marketing director's estimate of the age distribution of customers could be correct or not.

To do this, we start by calculating a chi-squared statistic. Listing observed and expected frequencies for the sample side by side, we get the following.

Age group	*Observed O*		*Expected E*	*(O-E)*	*(O-E)²*	*(O-E)²/E*
Under 20	26	(5%)	20	6	36	1.80
20 – 30	63	(10%)	40	23	529	13.23
30 – 40	64	(15%)	60	4	16	0.27
40 – 50	82	(20%)	80	2	4	0.05
50 – 60	94	(30%)	120	–26	676	5.63
60 – 70	56	(15%)	60	–4	16	0.27
70 and over	15	(5%)	20	–5	25	1.25
	400		400		χ^2 =	22.50

The chi-squared statistic has been obtained, and is 22.50. We can now use this in a significance test, to establish whether or not we should accept the marketing director's estimate of customer age distribution.

4.3 Evaluating χ^2

You may have realised that since χ^2 is a measure of the difference between observed and expected frequencies, then the higher its value, the more likely it will be that the difference between the observed and expected results is significant. If $\chi^2 = 0$, there would be no difference at all between observed and expected results.

The different figures in the $(O-E)^2/E$ column that make up the overall χ^2 statistic reflect the size of the difference between O and E in each category. In the example above the 20-30 and 50-60 age groups have the largest differences between observed and expected frequencies.

Thus we begin the test of significance by establishing a null hypothesis: that there is no significant difference between observed and expected frequencies. χ^2 should be 0 if there were no difference at all. However, since we have only used one set of sample results then some deviation between observed and expected frequencies is likely to occur. Provided that this deviation is 'reasonably likely' to occur, then the null hypothesis may be assumed to be correct.

The decision rule will be that the null hypothesis will be accepted if it is probable at a certain level of significance that the difference between observed and expected results arose just by chance.

4.4 Using the chi-squared distribution table

The level of significance is referred to in chi-squared tables as a probability level, for example 10%, 5%, or 1% and so on. What this means for our purposes is that if the null hypothesis is really correct, then the probability that our chi-squared statistic will exceed a critical point value (given in chi-squared distribution tables) is 10%, 5% or 1% and so on according to the probability level that we select for our decision rule.

Suppose, for example, that we decide that the null hypothesis will be accepted unless there is only a 5% or smaller probability that a difference between observed and expected results would arise if the null hypothesis were true. We would look for a critical point value in the 5% probability level column in our chi-squared distribution tables.

A chi-squared distribution table is shown at the end of this text. Look at it carefully.

(a) The table has a column for each probability level that we might decide to test.

(b) There is a row for differing degrees of freedom.

(c) For each probability level and number of degrees of freedom, the table gives us a critical point value.

So before we can identify the critical point value that we are looking for, we need to know how many degrees of freedom there are.

The rules for the number of degrees of freedom vary depending upon how the χ^2 test is used. For our purposes it is sufficient to know that when we are comparing the actual and expected distributions of sample results in a list of classes or categories, the number of degrees of freedom is (n–1), where n is the number of classes or categories in the list.

4.5 The results of the test

We can now go back to our example of the age distribution of customers of the department store group, and complete the chi-squared test.

(a) Our χ^2 statistic is 22.5.

(b) There are seven age groups, and so n = 7.

(c) This gives us (7 – 1) = 6 degrees of freedom.

(d) If we test at the 5% level of significance, the critical point value, from the table (probability 5%, degrees of freedom 6) is 12.59.

Our χ^2 statistic (22.5) exceeds the critical point value (12.59), and since there is only a 5% probability or less that this could happen if the null hypothesis were correct, our conclusion is that the null hypothesis should be rejected.

In other words, the observed age distribution of customers is significantly different from the marketing director's estimate.

4.6 Attributes and types

Another application of the χ^2 test is when we wish to test the association or correspondence between two or more attributes. In other words, we might want to test whether one type of people (or items) might have the same range of attributes as other types, or whether there is a significant difference between them.

When comparisons of these kinds are made, the data is usually arranged in a table, known as a **contingency table**. (Contingency in this sense means 'close connection'.) An example might help to illustrate the nature of this type of goodness-of-fit test. As with the previous examples we shall then go on to calculate χ^2 and make the significance test.

4.7 Example: contingency tables

An investigation is being carried out into delays in the payment of invoices by the customers of a particular company, MPL Tables Ltd. Details of the current debtors situation are as follows.

	Attribute as a debtor			
Type of customer	*Slow payer (> 3 months)*	*Average payer (1 and <3 months)*	*Prompt payer (< 1 month)*	*Total*
Large private companies	8	17	6	31
Small private companies	20	25	22	67
Quoted companies	11	16	9	36
Local authorities	6	8	2	16
	45	66	39	150

You are required to prepare a statistical analysis to determine whether there is any relationship between the type of customer and its attribute as a payer. Use the 5% level of significance.

Solution

The attribute that we are looking at here is status as a payer, and we want to compare this attribute for four types of customer. The problem is to decide whether different types of customer have different payment habits, or whether all customers are much the same in the time they take to pay their debts to MPL Tables.

There are four 'samples' (four different types of customer), and there are three 'attributes' to compare – slow payers, average payers and prompt payers. These are set out in a table of observed frequencies. What we have to do next is establish a similar table for expected frequencies.

The total number of customers (of all types) is 150.

45 or 30% are slow payers
66 or 44% are average payers
39 or 26% are prompt payers

The null hypothesis is that there is no difference between the distribution of status as debtors among each type of customer ie all types of customer consist of 30% slow payers, 44% average payers and 26% prompt payers. These are the expected proportions. For example consider the 31 large private companies. 30% of 31 (ie 9.3) are expected to be slow payers, 44% (ie 13.6) average payers and the remaining 26% (ie 8.1) are expected to be prompt payers.

A contingency table can now be drawn up, as follows.

Type of customer	*Slow* Observed	*Slow* Expected (30%)	*Average* Observed	*Average* Expected (44%)	*Prompt* Observed	*Prompt* Expected (26%)
Large private companies	8	9.3	17	13.6	6	8.1
Small private companies	20	20.1	25	29.5	22	17.4
Quoted companies	11	10.8	16	15.8	9	9.4
Local authorities	6	4.8	8	7.0	2	4.2
	45	45.0	66	66.0	39	39.0

(*Attribute as a debtor*)

There are 12 pairs of observed and expected frequencies in this 4 × 3 table.

$$\chi^2 = \sum \frac{(O-E)^2}{E}$$

	O	*E*	*(O-E)*	*(O-E)*^{2}	$\frac{(O-E)^2}{E}$
Slow payers					
Large private companies	8	9.3	−1.3	1.69	0.18
Small private companies	20	20.1	−0.1	0.01	0.00
Quoted companies	11	10.8	+0.2	0.04	0.00
Local authorities	6	4.8	+1.2	1.44	0.30
Average payers					
Large private companies	17	13.6	+3.4	11.56	0.85
Small private companies	25	29.5	−4.5	20.25	0.69
Quoted companies	16	15.8	+0.2	0.04	0.00
Local authorities	8	7.0	+1.0	1.00	0.14
Prompt payers					
Large private companies	6	8.1	−2.1	4.41	0.55
Small private companies	22	17.4	+4.6	21.16	1.22
Quoted companies	9	9.4	−0.4	0.16	0.02
Local authorities	2	4.2	−2.2	4.84	1.16
				χ^2 =	5.11

Our value for χ^2 is 5.11. (If you are working through this example you may have slight rounding differences.) We must now determine whether 5.11 is below the critical point in the χ^2 distribution at the 5% level of significance.

In χ^2 goodness-of-fit tests with a contingency table, the number of degrees of freedom is

$v = (m-1)(n-1)$

where the contingency table is of a size m × n (ie m rows, n columns).

In our example, the contingency table has four rows and three columns. The degrees of freedom are therefore (4–1)(3–1) = 3 × 2 = 6.

From the χ^2 critical points table, the critical point at the 5% level of significance when there are 6 degrees of freedom = 12.59.

The value of χ^2 in our test is 5.11, well below the critical point.

We therefore accept the null hypothesis: there is no significant difference between the payment pattern for different types of customer.

In this test, a 'sample' was taken at a particular point in time, when the company had 150 debtors. The debtors position is constantly changing. If we knew the status of every potential customer at every point in time, we would expect χ^2 to be 0 if the null hypothesis is true. Since however, the situation does change and at any point in time variations might occur, we cannot expect a zero value of χ^2. Hence the need to establish a level of significance for the test of the null hypothesis.

Action Programme 3

What is the difference between a 'type' and an 'attribute'?

Exam tip

As a final point it is worth warning you not to get so immersed in the figures that you lose sight of the obvious. For example, if you look back at the table above you can see at a glance that nearly half of the company's customers are small private companies – the type most likely to yield to pressure to pay up more promptly (larger customers would just go elsewhere). Be alert to the obvious if you are asked to **comment** on figures in an exam question or in real life.

5 Correlation and regression 6/04

FAST FORWARD

When the value of one variable is related to the value of another, they are said to be **correlated**. Two variables might be perfectly correlated, partly correlated or uncorrelated. Correlation can be positive or negative.

Key concept

Correlation is the measurement of the nature and strength of association between two variables.

Do price cuts coincide with changes in sales volume? If so, do sales go **up** when prices go down, or do they go **down** (in which case, perhaps the lower price is affecting the perception of our product's quality)? Is there an association (close enough to base decisions on) between hours worked and employee absenteeism?

One way of showing the correlation between two related variables is on a **scattergraph** or scatter diagram, plotting a number of pairs of data on the graph. For example, a scattergraph showing monthly selling costs against the volume of sales for a 12-month period might be as follows.

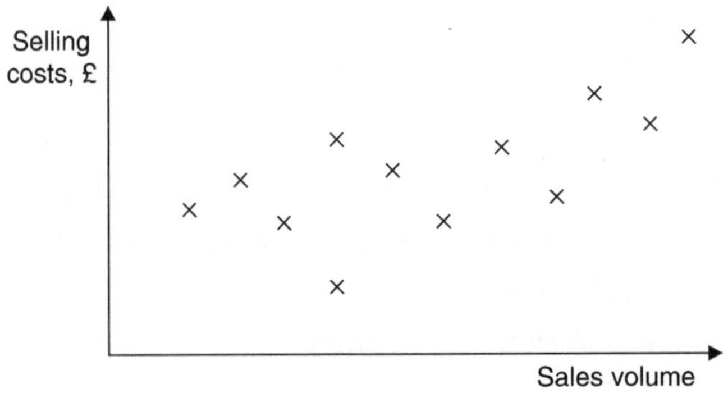

This scattergraph suggests that there is some correlation between selling costs and sales volume, so that as sales volume rises, selling costs tend to rise as well.

5.1 Degrees of correlation

Two variables can be one of the following.

(a) Perfectly correlated
(b) Partly correlated
(c) Uncorrelated

These differing degrees of correlation can be illustrated by scatter diagrams.

(a) **Perfect correlation**

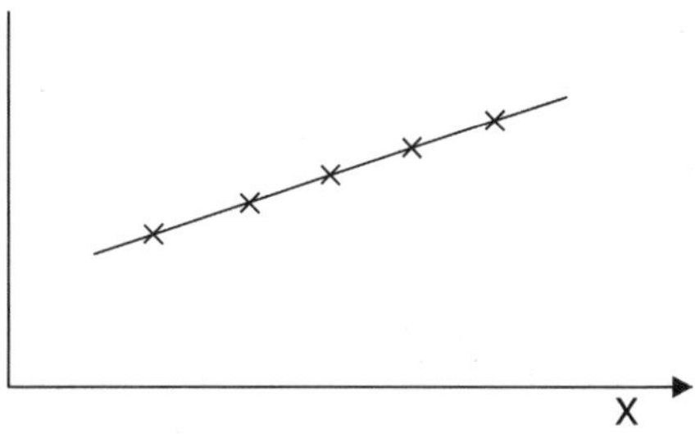

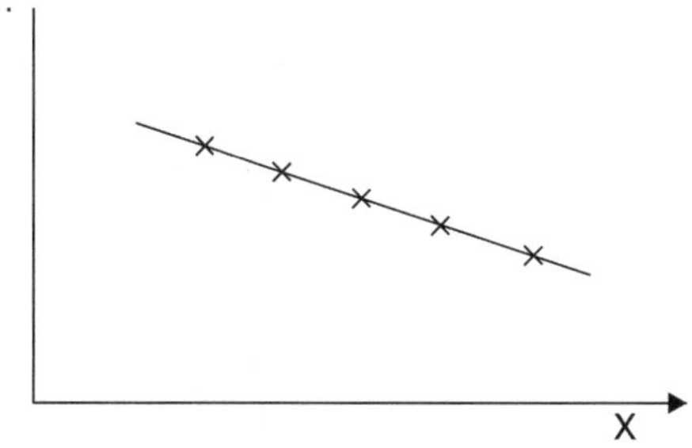

All the pairs of values lie on a straight line. An exact **linear relationship** exists between the two variables.

(b) **Partial correlation**

(i

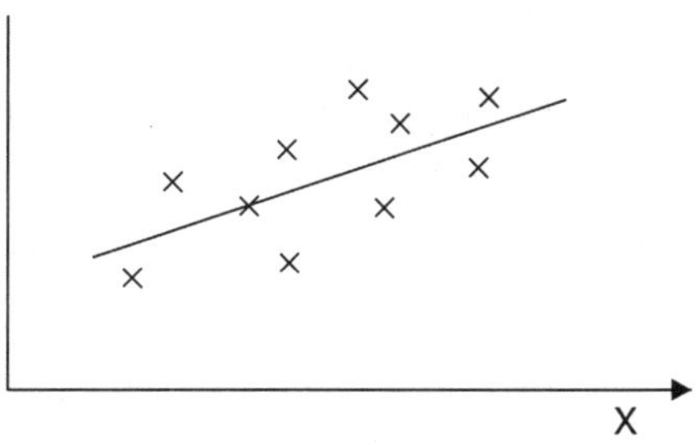

(I

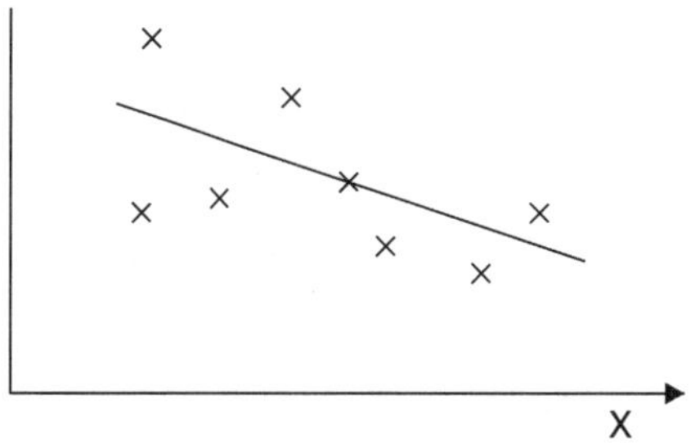

In (i), although there is no exact relationship, low values of X tend to be associated with low values of Y, and high values of X with high values of Y.

In (ii) again, there is no exact relationship, but low values of X tend to be associated with high values of Y and vice versa.

(c) **No correlation**

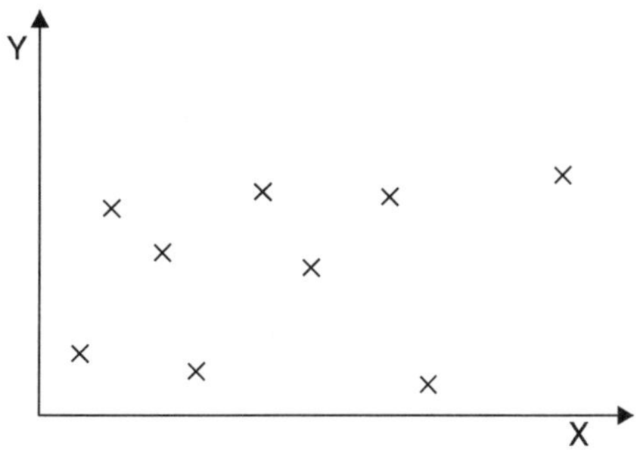

The values of these two variables are not correlated with each other.

5.2 Positive and negative correlation

Correlation, whether perfect or partial, can be positive or negative.

(a) **Positive correlation** means that low values of one variable are associated with low values of the other, and high values of one variable are associated with high values of the other.

(b) **Negative correlation** means that low values of one variable are associated with high values of the other, and high values of one variable with low values of the other.

5.3 The correlation coefficient

FAST FORWARD

The **degree of correlation** between two variables is measured by the **product moment correlation coefficient**, **r**. The nearer r is to +1 or –1, the stronger the relationship.

The degree of correlation between two variables can be measured, and we can decide, using actual results in the form of pairs of data, whether two variables are perfectly or partially correlated, and if they are partially correlated, whether there is a high or low degree of partial correlation.

This degree of correlation is measured by the Pearsonian correlation coefficient (the coefficient of correlation), r (also called the 'product moment correlation coefficient').

There are several formulae for the correlation coefficient, although each formula will give the same value. One of them is as follows.

$$\text{Correlation coefficient, } r = \frac{n\Sigma XY - \Sigma X\Sigma Y}{\sqrt{[n\Sigma X^2 - (\Sigma X)^2][n\Sigma Y^2 - (\Sigma Y)^2]}}$$

where X and Y represent pairs of data for two variables X and Y, and n is the number of pairs of data used in the analysis.

r must always fall between –1 and +1. If you get a value outside this range you have made a mistake.

r =	+1	means that the variables are perfectly positively correlated
r =	–1	means that the variables are perfectly negatively correlated
r =	0	means that the variables are uncorrelated

5.4 Example: the correlation coefficient

The cost of output at a factory is thought to depend on the number of units produced. Data have been collected for the number of units produced each month in the last six months, and the associated costs, as follows.

Month	*Output* *'000s of units* X	*Cost* *£'000* Y
1	2	9
2	3	11
3	1	7
4	4	13
5	3	11
6	5	15

Assess whether there is there any correlation between output and cost.

Solution

$$r = \frac{n\Sigma XY - \Sigma X\Sigma Y}{\sqrt{[n\Sigma X^2 - (\Sigma X)^2][n\Sigma Y^2 - (\Sigma Y)^2]}}$$

We need to find the values for the following.

(a) ΣXY Multiply each value of X by its corresponding Y value, so that there are six values for XY. Add up the six values to get the total.

(b) ΣX Add up the six values of X to get a total. $(\Sigma X)^2$ will be the square of this total.

(c) ΣY Add up the six values of Y to get a total. $(\Sigma Y)^2$ will be the square of this total.

(d) ΣX^2 Find the square of each value of X, so that there are six values for X^2. Add up these values to get a total.

(e) ΣY^2 Find the square of each value of Y, so that there are six values for Y^2. Add up these values to get a total.

Workings

X	*Y*	*XY*	X^2	Y^2
2	9	18	4	81
3	11	33	9	121
1	7	7	1	49
4	13	52	16	169
3	11	33	9	121
5	15	75	25	225
ΣX = 18	ΣY = 66	ΣXY = 218	ΣX^2 = 64	ΣY^2 = 766

$(\Sigma X)^2 = 18^2 = 324$ $(\Sigma Y)^2 = 66^2 = 4{,}356$

$n = 6$

$$r = \frac{(6\times 218)-(18\times 66)}{\sqrt{(6\times 64-324)\times(6\times 766-4{,}356)}}$$

$$= \frac{1{,}308-1{,}188}{\sqrt{(384-324)\times(4{,}596-4{,}356)}}$$

$$= \frac{120}{\sqrt{60\times 240}} = \frac{120}{\sqrt{14{,}400}} = \frac{120}{120} = 1$$

There is perfect positive correlation between the volume of output at the factory and costs which means that there is a perfect linear relationship between output and costs.

5.5 The coefficient of determination, r^2

FAST FORWARD

The **coefficient of determination**, r^2, measures the proportion of the total variation in the value of one variable that can be explained by the variation in the value of the other variable.

Unless the correlation coefficient r is exactly or very nearly +1, –1 or 0, its meaning or significance is a little unclear. For example, if the correlation coefficient for two variables is +0.8, this would tell us that the variables are positively correlated, but the correlation is not perfect. It would not really tell us much else. A more meaningful analysis is available from the square of the correlation coefficient, r^2, which is called the coefficient of determination. r^2

r^2 (alternatively R^2) measures the proportion of the total variation in the value of one variable that can be explained by variations in the value of the other variable. In the exercise above, r = –0.992, therefore r^2 = 0.984. This means that over 98% of variations in sales can be explained by the passage of time, leaving 0.016 (less than 2%) of variations to be explained by other factors.

Similarly, if the correlation coefficient between a company's output volume and maintenance costs was 0.9, r^2 would be 0.81, meaning that 81% of variations in maintenance costs could be explained by variations in output volume, leaving only 19% of variations to be explained by other factors (such as the age of the equipment).

Note, however, that if r^2 = 0.81, we would say that 81% of the variations in y can be explained by variations in x. We do not necessarily conclude that 81% of variations in y are caused by the variations in x. We must beware of reading too much significance into our statistical analysis.

5.6 Correlation and causation

FAST FORWARD

Correlation and regression analysis do not indicate cause and effect. Even if r = 1, the correlation could still be spurious, both variables being influenced by a third.

If two variables are well correlated, either positively or negatively, this may be due to pure chance or there may be a reason for it. The larger the number of pairs of data collected, the less likely it is that the correlation is due to chance, though that possibility should never be ignored entirely.

If there is a reason, it may not be causal. For example, monthly net income is well correlated with monthly credit to a person's bank account, for the logical (rather than causal) reason that for most people the one equals the other.

Even if there is a causal explanation for a correlation, it does not follow that variations in the value of one variable cause variations in the value of the other. For example, sales of ice cream and of sunglasses are well correlated, not because of a direct causal link but because the weather influences both variables.

Having said this, it is of course possible that where two variables are correlated, there is a direct causal link to be found.

5.7 Spearman's rank correlation coefficient

In the examples considered above, the data were given in terms of the values of the relevant variables, such as the number of hours. Sometimes however, they are given in terms of order or rank rather than actual values. When this occurs, a correlation coefficient known as Spearman's rank correlation coefficient, R should be calculated using the following formula.

$$\text{Coefficient of rank correlation } R = 1 - \left[\frac{6\Sigma d^2}{n(n^2-1)}\right]$$

where n = number of pairs of data

d = the difference between the rankings in each set of data.

The coefficient of rank correlation can be interpreted in exactly the same way as the ordinary correlation coefficient. Its value can range from –1 to +1.

5.8 Example: the rank correlation coefficient

The examination placings of seven students were as follows.

Student	*Statistics placing*	*Economics placing*
A	2	1
B	1	3
C	4	7
D	6	5
E	5	6
F	3	2
G	7	4

Required

Judge whether the placings of the students in statistics correlate with their placings in economics.

Solution

Correlation must be measured by Spearman's coefficient because we are given the placings of students, and not their actual marks.

$$R = 1 - \frac{6\Sigma d^2}{n(n^2 - 1)}$$

where d is the difference between the rank in statistics and the rank in economics for each student.

Student	*Rank Statistics*	*Rank Economics*	*d*	d^2
A	2	1	1	1
B	1	3	2	4
C	4	7	3	9
D	6	5	1	1
E	5	6	1	1
F	3	2	1	1
G	7	4	3	9
			$\Sigma d^2 =$	26

$$R = 1 - \frac{6 \times 26}{7 \times (49 - 1)} = 1 - \frac{156}{336} = 0.536$$

The correlation is positive, 0.536, but the correlation is not strong.

5.9 Lines of best fit

Correlation enables us to determine the strength of any relationship between two variables but it does not offer us any method of **forecasting values** for one variable, Y, given values of another variable, X.

If we assume that there is a linear relationship between the two variables, however, and we determine the equation of a straight line (Y = a + bX) which is a good fit for the available data plotted on a scattergraph, we can use the equation for forecasting: we can substitute values for X into the equation and derive values for Y.

There are a number of techniques for estimating the equation of a line of best fit. We will be looking at the **scattergraph** method and **simple linear regression** analysis. Both provide a technique for estimating values for a and b in the equation

Y = a + bX

where X and Y are the related variables and
a and b are estimated using pairs of data for X and Y.

Marketing at Work

With such a large repository of data at its disposal, it is small wonder that BBC is using data analysis techniques and propensity modelling to gain a greater understanding of its evader audiences (people who don't buy a TV licence), and to convert them to payers.

Three years ago OgilvyOne was asked to develop an evasion propensity scoring model to identify evaders and potential evaders. It's a propensity model with a twist, in that it focuses on prospects least likely to become customers.

The aims of the model were straightforward: to target evaders by postcode; to identify evader sub-groups and characteristics; and to direct a communications strategy based on these.

The existing TVL customer database was enhanced with financial data from Equifax and lifestyle and socio-economic variables from Claritas to get a better understanding of the customer groups. More than 400 variables were finally distilled to 27 key variables in a multiple linear regression model, with the evasion rate as the dependent variable. This became known as the Evader Score Model (ESM).

Direct Response, 30 January 2003

5.10 The scattergraph method

FAST FORWARD

The **scattergraph method** involves the use of judgement to draw what seems to be a line of best fit through plotted data. **Linear regression analysis** (the least squares method) is another technique for estimating a line of best fit.

The scattergraph method is to plot pairs of data for two related variables on a graph, to produce a scattergraph, and then to use judgement to draw what seems to be a line of best fit through the data.

For example, suppose we have the following pairs of data about sales revenue and advertising expenditure.

Period	*Advertising expenditure*	*Sales revenue*
	£	£
1	17,000	180,000
2	33,000	270,000
3	34,000	320,000
4	42,000	350,000
5	19,000	240,000
6	41,000	300,000
7	26,000	320,000
8	27,000	230,000

These pairs of data can be plotted on a scattergraph (the horizontal axis representing the independent variable and the vertical axis the dependent) and a line of best fit might be judged as the one shown below. It is drawn to pass through the middle of the data points, thereby having as many data points below the line as above it.

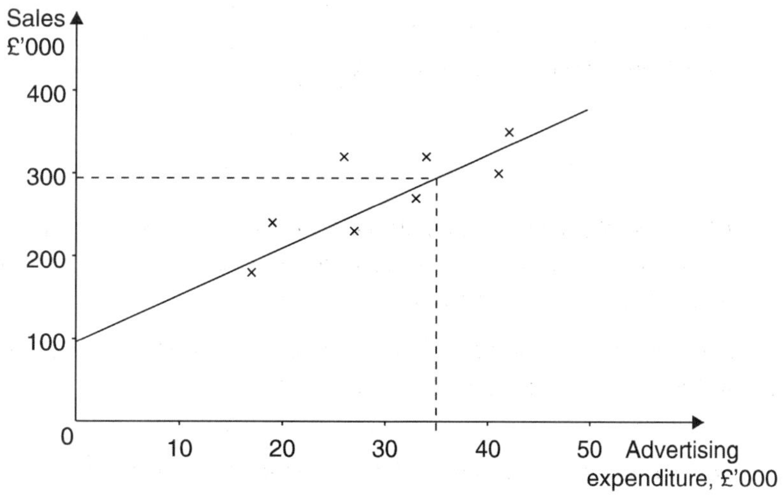

Suppose the company to which these data relate wants a forecast sales figure, given a marketing decision to spend £35,000 on advertising. An estimate of sales can be read directly from the scattergraph as shown (£290,000).

5.11 Least squares method of linear regression analysis

This method involves using the following formulae for a and b in Y = a + bX.

$$b = \frac{n\Sigma XY - \Sigma X \Sigma Y}{n\Sigma X^2 - (\Sigma X)^2}$$

$$a = \overline{Y} - b\overline{X}$$

where n is the number of pairs of data

$\overline{X}$ is the average X value of all the pairs of data

$\overline{Y}$ is the average Y value of all the pairs of data

There are some points to note about these formulae.

(a) The line of best fit that is derived represents the regression of Y upon X.

A different line of best fit could be obtained by interchange in X and Y in the formulae. This would then represent the regression of X upon Y (X = a + bY) and it would have a slightly different slope.

(b) Since $a = \overline{Y} - b\overline{X}$, it follows that the line of best fit must always pass through the point $(\overline{X}, \overline{Y})$.

(c) If you look at the formula for b and compare it with the first formula we gave for the correlation coefficient (Paragraph 5.3) you should see some similarities between the two formulae.

5.12 Example: the least squares method

(a) Given that there is a fairly high degree of correlation between the output and the costs detailed in Paragraph 5.4 (so that a linear relationship can be assumed), calculate an equation to determine the expected level of costs, for any given volume of output, using the least squares method.

(b) Prepare a budget for total costs if output is 22,000 units.

(c) Confirm that the degree of correlation between output and costs is high by calculating the correlation coefficient.

Solution

(a) *Workings*

X	Y	XY	X^2	Y^2
20	82	1,640	400	6,724
16	70	1,120	256	4,900
24	90	2,160	576	8,100
22	85	1,870	484	7,225
18	73	1,314	324	5,329
ΣX = 100	ΣY = 400	ΣXY = 8,104	ΣX^2 = 2,040	ΣY^2 = 32,278

n = 5 (There are five pairs of data for x and y values)

$$b = \frac{n\Sigma XY - \Sigma X\Sigma Y}{n\Sigma X^2 - (\Sigma X)^2} = \frac{(5\times 8{,}104)-(100\times 400)}{(5\times 2{,}040)-100^2}$$

$$= \frac{40{,}520-40{,}000}{10{,}200-10{,}000} = \frac{520}{200} = 2.6$$

$$a = \overline{Y} - b\overline{X} = \frac{400}{5} - 2.6\times\left(\frac{100}{5}\right) = 28$$

$$Y = 28 + 2.6X$$

where Y = total cost, in thousands of pounds
X = output, in thousands of units.

Note that the fixed costs are £28,000 (when X = 0 costs are £28,000) and the variable cost per unit is £2.60.

(b) If the output is 22,000 units, we would expect costs to be

$28 + 2.6 \times 22 = 85.2 =$ £85,200.

(c) $$r = \frac{520}{\sqrt{200\times(5\times 32{,}278-400^2)}} = \frac{520}{\sqrt{200\times 1{,}390}} = \frac{520}{527.3} = +0.99$$

5.13 The reliability of regression analysis forecasts

As with all forecasting techniques, the results from regression analysis will not be wholly reliable. There are a number of factors which affect the reliability of forecasts made using regression analysis.

(a) It assumes a linear relationship between the two variables (since linear regression analysis produces an equation in the linear format) whereas a non-linear relationship might exist.

(b) The technique assumes that the value of one variable, Y, can be predicted or estimated from the value of one other variable, X. In reality the value of Y might depend on several other variables, not just X.

(c) When it is used for forecasting, it assumes that what has happened in the past will provide a reliable guide to the future. For example, if a line is calculated for total costs of production, based on historical data, the estimate could be used to budget for future costs. However, if there has been cost inflation, a productivity agreement with the workforce, a move to new premises, the dismissal of large numbers of office staff and the introduction of new equipment, future costs of production might bear no relation to costs in the past.

5.14 Multivariate data analysis

FAST FORWARD

More advanced techniques such as **factor analysis** and **multiple regression** are needed when trying to analyse the relationship between more than two variables.

Most researchers would use a **statistical software package** to help with all of the more complicated statistical techniques.

If you need to analyse the relationship between **more than two variables** (multivariate analysis) more advanced techniques are needed. You'll probably be relieved to know that the details are beyond the scope of this book, but this list will give you an idea of what can be done. Some of this is possible in a spreadsheet package such as Excel, but if you need techniques like this you would probably buy a statistical software package.

- **Cluster analysis**: classifies people into mutually exclusive groups
- **Conjoint analysis**: measures the relative importance of variables
- **Factor analysis**: simplifies data by reducing a large number of variables into groups
- **Multiple discriminant analysis**: classifies people into the relevant segment on the basis of measured variables
- **Multiple regression analysis**: the relationship between three or more variables
- **Perceptual mapping**: brand positioning

Chapter Roundup

- **Data** may sometimes be successfully **analysed** on the basis of intuition or previous experience, but a **scientific approach** is likely to be more credible to most research clients.
- **Qualitative data** collected from focus groups and interviews can be subjected to various kinds of **content analysis** such as **tabulation** or **spider diagrams** and there are some software packages specially designed to facilitate such analysis.
- **Quantitative data** can be subjected to **statistical analysis** of varying degrees of complexity: to indicate useful characteristics such as **frequency**, **averages**, **dispersion**, **correlation** and **trends**.
- You may also be expected to be aware of and understand the value of various methods of **hypothesis testing**. A hypothesis test is made by comparing the result from a sample with what we would expect if the null hypothesis were true. If the gap between the reality and the expectation is too wide, we reject the null hypothesis.
- A **chi-squared test** can test the hypothesis that two variables are unconnected. Expected frequencies are computed, and are then compared with observed frequencies. A chi-squared test can also be used to test whether observed data fit a given distribution. Again, expected frequencies are computed and compared with observed frequencies.
- When the value of one variable is related to the value of another, they are said to be **correlated**. Two variables might be perfectly correlated, partly correlated or uncorrelated. Correlation can be positive or negative.
- The **degree of correlation** between two variables is measured by the **product moment correlation coefficient, r**. The nearer r is to +1 or –1, the stronger the relationship.
- The **coefficient of determination**, r^2, measures the proportion of the total variation in the value of one variable that can be explained by the variation in the value of the other variable.
- **Correlation and regression analysis do not indicate cause and effect**. Even if $r = 1$, the correlation could still be spurious, both variables being influenced by a third.
- Spearman's **rank correlation coefficient** is used when data is given in terms of order or rank rather than actual values.
- The **scattergraph method** involves the use of judgement to draw what seems to be a line of best fit through plotted data. **Linear regression analysis** (the least squares method) is another technique for estimating a line of best fit.
- More advanced techniques such as **factor analysis** and **multiple regression** are needed when trying to analyse the relationship between more than two variables.
- Most researchers would use a **statistical software package** to help with all of the more complicated statistical techniques.

Quick Quiz

1 What is the main drawback of using a spider graph to analyse qualitative data when there is a very large amount of data to analyse?

2 What does 'the mean' mean?

3 If you list the number of users of e-mail under the age of 10, under the age of 20, under the age of 30 and under the age of 40, you are compiling a:

Correlation	Time series
Frequency distribution	Cumulative frequency distribution

4 What is a trend?

5 Which of the options listed below is *not* illustrated by the following diagram?

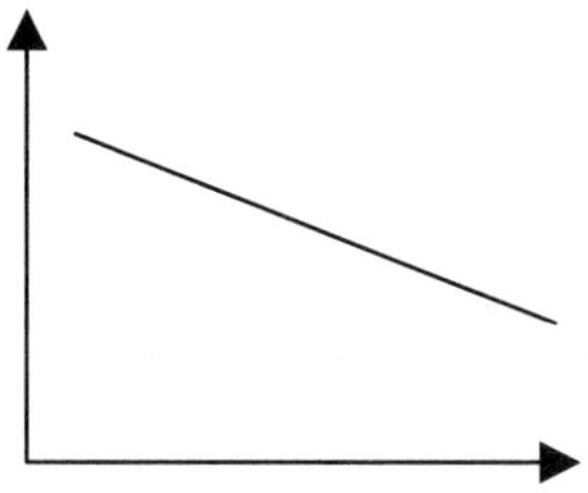

A Line graph
B Positive correlation
C Negative correlation
D Trend

6 Complete this sentence: Hypothesis testing is the process of establishing the significance of the results of sample data for ....

7 Complete the sentence: The chi-squared distribution can be used to test a sample of items in order to decide whether the items in the sample are ....

8 Complete the sentence: The chi-squared test can also be used when we want to see whether one type of people or items ....

9 Positive correlation means that low values of one variable are associated with ...... values of the other. Negative correlation means that low values of one variable are associated with ...... values of the other. Fill in the gaps.

10 Regression can be used for .... the value of one variable when you know the value of another. Fill in the gap.

Answers to Quick Quiz

1 If there is a large amount of data then it is likely that several people will be needed to do the analysis, and the spider graph method does not guarantee consistency in the way different people do the analysis.

2 The mean is the best know type of average, calculated by adding up all the values and dividing by the number of values. It can be distorted by isolated extreme values.

3 Cumulative frequency distribution

4 An underlying movement (upwards or downwards) in a time series over the long term.

5 B

6 Hypothesis testing is the process of establishing the significance of the results of sample data for **beliefs about the population.**

7 The chi-squared distribution can be used to test a sample of items in order to decide whether the items in the sample are **distributed according to a preconceived or expected distribution pattern**.

8 The chi-squared test can also be used when we want to see whether one type of people or items **have the same range of attributes as other types**.

9 Positive: low ... low. Negative: low ... high

10 **Forecasting**

Action Programme Review

1 The negative response to Rank Xerox's survey on the potential market for dry copiers could have been due to some of the following factors.

(a) The wrong people were asked.

(b) People did not understand the dry copying concept (technologically).

(c) The benefits of dry copying were not made clear.

(d) The survey was conducted at an unfavourable time (when respondents had spent all their budget) and were therefore not willing to countenance any potential extra expenditure.

(e) The question design was faulty.

(f) Human errors were made in computing results.

(g) Statistical errors were made in computing results.

(h) Competitors sabotaged the research.

(i) The questionnaire might have been too long, thus causing irritation.

(j) Interviewers could have been biased.

2 Some of the points you may have picked up on include the following.

(a) This looks a bit like a frequency distribution – but isn't. It doesn't tell us what percentage of one-car owners, for example, are in which age bracket: the percentages don't add up to 100% across the rows, but down the columns. The data tells us what percentage of each age groups owns one, two and three cars. We may note that in any age group, people are most likely to own one car. However, people are more likely to own three cars in the 45-64 age bracket than at any other time, and are least likely to own more than one car in the bracket > (over) 65. You might also suggest that this can be explained by family life cycle factors: at the beginning of family/career launch, income is more likely to be available for one or two cars; at career peak, the family may be more likely to afford a third car; on retirement and post-dependent-family, there is much more likelihood that one car will suffice.

(b) You may note the exponential growth of on-line consumption in all sectors: approx 33%, 20% and 50% respectively in the single year 1996-1997, and 2,187%, 1,135% and 316% over the 5 years to 2001! If you were in the travel business, for example, you may simply have noted that growth for 2001 is $7.4bn – more than 12 times the figure of $0.6 bn posted in 1997.

However, you might be suspicious (because of the gap in years) that data is old: no source or date is give, after all. Perhaps the 2001 figures are only projections made in 1998: you may want to confirm the figures for 2001 and intervening years.

3 It depends on how you are looking at the problem. A large company (type) may be a slow, average or prompt payer (attribute). A slow payer (type) may be a large, small quoted or local authority organisation (attribute).

Now try Question 14 at the end of the Study Text

BPP LEARNING MEDIA

11

Reports and presentations

Chapter topic list

Syllabus content – knowledge and skill requirements

- 5.2: Preparation of a research report aimed at supporting marketing decisions
- 5.3: Planning and design of an oral presentation of market research results
- 5.4: Use of research and data to produce actionable recommendations for a marketing plan or to support a business decision

Introduction

The final stage of the marketing research process is the presentation of findings to the client, either in the form of a written report or as an oral presentation, or more usually both.

There are differences in these methods of course – in particular a report is more formal and you cannot control the conditions in which it is read – but there are many similarities in the techniques that can be used.

Exam tip

General points here about presentation may be familiar from your earlier studies, but it does no harm to be reminded: that is one of the principles of good communication!

Do not be intimidated or constrained by anything you read here. There are no hard rules about presentation and if you can think of a better way of organising a report or structuring a presentation than the standard way, then by all means use it.

1 The audience thinking sequence **Pilot Paper, 12/06**

FAST FORWARD

Whenever you are **communicating** in a **report** or in a **presentation** you should take into account the **audience's thinking sequence**: Respect the client's importance; Consider the client's needs; Demonstrate how your information helps the client; Explain the detail that underpins your information; Remind the client of the key points; Suggest what the client should do now.

Wilson (2002) suggests that the researcher should take account of the typical 'thinking sequence' that people go through when you are communicating with them.

(a) **Respect the client's importance**: in other words don't waste their time with irrelevant, badly structured or presented, over-long information.

(b) **Consider the client's needs**: the client needs to make a marketing decision.

(c) **Demonstrate how your information helps the client**: relate the research findings to the original objectives

(d) **Explain the detail that underpins your information**: why should your findings be believed? Because you have evidence that 'Nine out of ten dogs prefer ...' or whatever. This is the place for tables and charts and apt quotes from respondents.

(e) **Remind the client of the key points**

(f) **Suggest what the client should do now**: there will usually be a variety of options. It is the client's decision, but it is usual to give recommendations.

The researcher knows more about the subject matter of the report or presentation than the report user. It is important that this information should be communicated impartially, so that the report user can make his own judgements.

(a) Any assumptions, evaluations and recommendations should be clearly signalled as such.

(b) Points should not be over-weighted (or omitted as irrelevant) without honestly evaluating how objective the selection is.

(c) Facts and findings should be balanced against each other.

(d) A firm conclusion should, if possible, be reached. It should be clear how and why it was reached.

The researcher must also **recognise the needs and abilities of the audience**.

(a) Beware of 'jargon', overly technical terms and specialist knowledge the user may not share.

(b) Keep your vocabulary, sentence and paragraph structures as simple as possible, for clarity (without patronising an intelligent user).

(c) Bear in mind the type and level of detail that will interest the user and be relevant to his/her purpose.

(d) The audience may range from senior manager to junior operational staff to complete layman (a non-executive director, say). Your vocabulary, syntax and presentation, the amount of detail you can go into, the technical matter you can include and the formality of your report structure should all be influenced by such concerns.

Exam tip

The needs and requirements of the audience will impact upon report preparation. This was the topic of a question at the December 2006 sitting.

2 Research reports 6/05, 6/07

FAST FORWARD

A **research report** typically has the following elements: **Title page**; **list of contents**; **executive summary**; **introduction/problem definition**; **research method** (and limitations); **research findings**; **conclusions**; **appendices**.

Exam tip

Writing reports, and the use of tables to present data was the subject of a question on the June 2005 paper. In June 2007, candidates were asked to set out some key guidelines for structuring and writing market research reports.

Various techniques can be used to make the content of a research report easy to identify and digest.

- The material in the report should be in a logical order
- The relative importance of points should be signalled by headings
- Each point may be numbered in some way to help with cross-reference
- The document should be easy on the eye, helped by different font sizes, bold, italics, capitals, spacing.

A typical report structure is shown on the next page.

(a) **Headings**. There is a 'hierarchy' of headings: there is an overall title and the report as a whole is divided into sections. Within each section main points have a heading in bold capitals, sub-points have a heading in bold lower-case and sub-sub-points have a heading in italics. (Three levels of headings within a main section is usually considered the maximum number that readers can cope with.) It is not necessary to underline headings.

(b) **References**. Sections are lettered, A, B etc. Main points are numbered 1, 2 and so on, and within each division paragraphs are numbered 1.1, 1.2, 2.1, 2.2. Sub-paragraphs inherit their references from the paragraph above. For instance the first sub-paragraph under paragraph 1.2 is numbered 1.2.1.

(c) **Fonts**. Word processors offer you a wealth of fonts these days, but it is best to avoid the temptation. It is often a good idea to put headings in a different font to the main text, but stop there: two fonts is quite enough!

The example on the next page is by no means the only way of organising a report, of course: you might choose to reference sub-paragraphs 1.2(a), 1.2(b). You might use roman numerals, although we advise against this. If your report turns out to be longer than you expected and you get up to paragraph XLVIII you are likely to confuse many of your readers.

TITLE	Arial 48 pt Bold Capitals
SECTION A	Arial 28 pt Bold Capitals
1 HEADING STYLE 1	Arial 18 pt Capitals Bold
1.1 Paragraph	Times New Roman 12 pt
Heading style 2	Arial 16 pt Bold
1.2 Paragraph	Times New Roman 12 pt
1.2.1 Sub-paragraph	Times New Roman 12 pt Indented
1.2.2 Sub-paragraph	Times New Roman 12 pt Indented
Heading style 3	Arial 14 pt Italic
1.3 Paragraph	Times New Roman 12 pt
Heading style 2	Arial 16 pt Bold
1.4 Paragraph	Times New Roman 12 pt
2 HEADING STYLE 1	Arial 18 pt Capitals Bold
2.1 Paragraph etc.	Times New Roman 12 pt
SECTION B	Arial 28 pt Bold Capitals
etc.	

A detailed report on an extensive research study may run to many pages, and may therefore require these elements.

(a) **Title page** (also giving contact information)

(b) A **list of contents**: the major headings and sub-headings. Most word processing software can produce these automatically.

(c) A **summary** of findings (to give the reader an initial idea of what the report is about). This is usually called the **executive summary**, the implication being that senior managers don't have time to read it all.

(d) **Introduction/problem definition**: this is likely to be very similar to the rationale and objectives set out in the research brief and proposal.

(e) **Research method (and limitations)**: again this is likely to be similar to the equivalent section in the proposal, although it must be updated if anything had to be changed during the implementation of the research or if the research did not go to plan (lower than expected response rates).

(f) **Research findings**: this is the main body of the report

(g) **Conclusions**: this section should point out the implications of the findings for the client with reference to the initial problem.

(h) Supporting **appendices**: these might include the questionnaire used or the original discussion document, more detailed tables of figures, lists of secondary sources used. Appendices contain subsidiary detailed material that may well be of interest to some readers, but which might lessen the impact of the findings if presented in full detail in the body of the report.

(i) Possibly, an **index**.

Action Programme 1

You work in a marketing consultancy called The Brand Tracker Partnership. As marketing assistant you are involved in a variety of activities, ranging from marketing research on behalf of clients to assisting in the marketing of the Brand Tracker Partnership itself.

The firm has been commissioned to undertake research into the women's fragrance market by Sian Singh, the brand manager of Georgie, a perfume made by the leading cosmetics manufacturer Lanroche.

The raw data was collected by a colleague and is very disorganised. It needs to be analysed and put into an appropriate format for the client to read.

Marketing research data

Annual advertising spend	£'000
Georgie	955
Possession	1,870
Esta Lauda	877
Eternal	1,206
Ana	1,049
Charly Klein	698

Marketing research was conducted during December 200X. A sample of 300 women aged between 16-55, which was representative of the fragrance buying market, was questioned by means of a survey. Following a telephone survey, four focus groups were held in different hotels around the country to obtain further qualitative information.

Desk research, using secondary data sources published by MEAL and SalesMonitor, was analysed to produce advertising expenditure and industry sales figures. In addition, advertising in women's magazines and below the line promotional activity in retail outlets were monitored over a period between October to December 200X.

Reasons for purchase

	% saying
I tried it in the shop	55
It is the one I usually buy or wear	53
I wanted to try something new/different	32
I saw it advertised in a magazine	25
I smelt it on someone else	19
I smelt a scratch-and-sniff ad	16
I saw it advertised on television	14
Advice from the sales assistant	12

	% saying
There was a money off offer	8
It was cheaper than the others	6

Thirty two fragrances were named as being bought or requested and received as gifts indicating that it is a fragmented market. However, eleven major brands had 73 per cent of total market share.

Of those mentioned, 64 per cent sell for more than £15 per 30 ml. Lady, Carlie and Max Maxa were ranked as the least expensive perfumes. ABC1s are no more likely to buy or receive premium priced fragrances than anyone else, with figures indicating that fragrances generally have a flat class profile. Charly Klein and Carlie draw more than two thirds of buyers from the 16-25 age group, with Cachet concentrated amongst those in their 30s. Ana, Georgie and Eternal appear to have popularity with all age groups. Channelle and Esta Lauda were popular amongst the older market – mainly those in the 40-55 age group.

Fragrances bought

Brand	*% market share*
Channelle	3.7
Max Maxa	2.0
Cachet	2.0
Possession	10.5
Georgie	8.8
Lady	7.2
Ana	13.0
Eternal	11.0
Charly Klein	5.5
Esta Lauda	5.0
Carlie	4.3

Price was not considered to be important except amongst buyers of Carlie. Of these, 34 per cent gave cheapness as the reason for purchase. Brand recognition levels were generally high for many fragrances. Newer entrants into the market such as, Cachet, Georgie and Possession, achieved high recall levels possibly influenced by the impact of point of sale and in-store promotional activity. Advertising expenditure was generally high amongst most brands.

Sampling is very important both on the counter and through scent strips in magazines.

Spontaneous ad recall	%
Ana	22
Possession	18
Eternal	12
Georgie	12
Channelle	9
Charly Klein	8
Max Maxa	7
Cachet	5
Esta Lauda	3
Lady	2
Carlie	2

Required

Write a short report for Sian Singh, using the market research data shown here.

3 Presenting findings 6/05

FAST FORWARD

Tables, graphs, charts and **illustrations** of various kinds can **greatly enhance** the **value** of a report because they make it easier to take in information at a glance. This was specifically examined on the June 2005 paper.

3.1 Tables

Tables present data in rows and columns. This form of presentation makes it easier to understand large amounts of data. A railway timetable is a familiar example.

Charing Cross	15:38	16:08	16:18	16:28	16:37	16:45	16:58
Waterloo	15:41	16:11	16:21	16:31	16:40	16:48	17:01
London Bridge	15:49	16:19	16:29	16:39	16:48	16:56	17:09
New Cross	16:01	16:31	16:41	-	17:00	17:08	17:21
Lewisham	16:06	16:36	16:46	16:50	17:05	17:13	17:26

Suppose you arrive at London Bridge at 16:42 and you want to go to Lewisham. Using a table like the one above there are at least three things that this timetable tells you.

(a) You can **look up a specific value** by seeing where rows and columns meet. Since you know it is 16:42 you can quickly see from the timetable that your next train is due in six minutes (at 16:48) and will arrive in Lewisham at 17:05.

(b) You can work your way around the table from your original starting point and **test out other scenarios**. For instance, you can see that if you had arrived at London Bridge a few minutes earlier you could have got a fast train. If you are not sure that six minutes is long enough to buy a cup of coffee and a bar of chocolate you can get a slightly later train to Lewisham which will give you 14 minutes.

(c) You can read across rows (or down columns) and **compare values**. For future reference you can note (by reading right across the London Bridge row) that from 16:19 onwards there is a train to Lewisham roughly every ten minutes.

Tables are a simple way of presenting numerical information. Figures are displayed, and can be compared with each other: relevant totals, subtotals, percentages can also be presented as a summary for analysis.

A table is two-dimensional (rows and columns): so it can only show two variables: a sales analysis for a year, for example, might have rows for months, and columns for products.

SALES FIGURES FOR 2005

	Product A	*Product B*	*Product C*	*Product D*	*Total*
Jan	370	651	782	899	2,702
Feb	718	312	748	594	2,372
Mar	548	204	585	200	1,537
Apr	382	616	276	359	1,633
May	132	241	184	223	780
Jun	381	216	321	123	1,041
Jul	679	612	733	592	2,616
Aug	116	631	343	271	1,361
Sep	421	661	868	428	2,378
Oct	211	158	653	479	1,501
Nov	306	243	676	404	1,659
Dec	898	759	796	394	2,847
Total	5,162	5,334	6,965	4,966	22,427

You are likely to present data in tabular form very often. Here are the key points to remember.

(a) The table should have a clear **title**.

(b) All columns and rows should be clearly **labelled**.

(c) Where appropriate, there should be **sub-totals** and a **right-hand total column** for comparison.

(d) A total figure is often advisable at the **bottom of each column** of figures also, for comparison. It is usual to double-underline totals at the foot of columns.

(e) **Numbers** should be **right-aligned** and they are easier to read if you use the **comma separator** for thousands.

(f) **Decimal points should line up**, either by using a decimal tab or by adding extra noughts (the latter is preferable, in our opinion).

(g) A grid or border is optional: see what looks best and is easiest to read. (In the above example we've used a grid to illustrate the alignment of numbers more clearly.)

(h) Tables should not be packed with too much data. If you try to get too much in the information presented will be difficult to read.

3.1.1 Columns or rows?

Often it will be obvious what information should go in the columns and what should go in rows. Sometimes, it won't matter too much which way round you have the rows and columns. Here are some points to remember.

(a) It is usually easier to read across a short line than a long one. That means that it is usually **better to have a long thin table** than a short wide one: lots of rows rather than lots of columns. If you had a price list of five hundred products each of which came in 3 different sizes. You would probably tabulate the information like this, without even considering the other possibility (it wouldn't fit on the paper or screen, anyway, if you had products in columns).

Product	*Large*	*Medium*	*Small*
A001	12.95	11.65	9.35
A002	14.50	12.50	10.50
A003	Etc.	Etc.	Etc.
A004			
A005			
Etc.			

(b) However, most people find it easier to compare figures by reading across than by reading down. For example in the previous version of the sales figures it is easier to compare product totals, but in the version below it is easier to compare monthly totals.

	Jan	*Feb*	*Mar*	*Apr*	*May*	*Jun*	*Jul*	*Aug*	*Sep*	*Oct*	*Nov*	*Dec*	*Total*
Product A	370	718	548	382	132	381	679	116	421	211	306	898	5,162
Product B	651	312	204	616	241	216	612	631	661	158	243	759	5,334
Product C	782	748	585	276	184	321	733	343	868	653	676	796	6,965
Product D	899	594	200	359	223	123	592	271	428	479	404	394	4,966
Total	2,702	2,372	1,537	1,633	780	1,041	2,616	1,361	2,378	1,501	1,659	2,847	22,427

(c) If you are not sure what your audience will most want to compare it might be helpful to give them both versions, if practicable.

3.2 Line graphs

In business, line graphs are usually used to illustrate **trends over time** of figures such as sales or customer complaints.

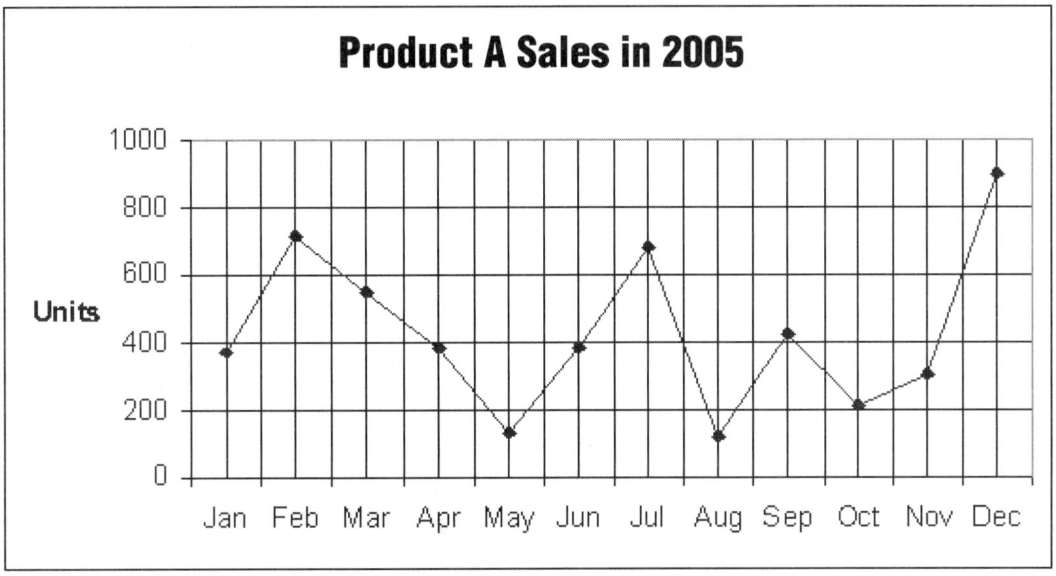

The figures are plotted on a grid and then joined by a line that reflects the 'ups and downs' of the figure, over a period of time. Note that it is conventional to show **time** on the **horizontal** axis.

Now the trend in sales is shown instantly, in a way that is probably not immediately apparent from a column or row of figures. This **encourages us to ask questions**: for instance why did sales drop in the early months of the year and suddenly shoot up in June and July?

By using different symbols for the plotted points, or preferably by using different colours, several lines can be drawn on a line graph before it gets too overcrowded, and that means that **several trends** (for example the sales performance of different products) can be compared.

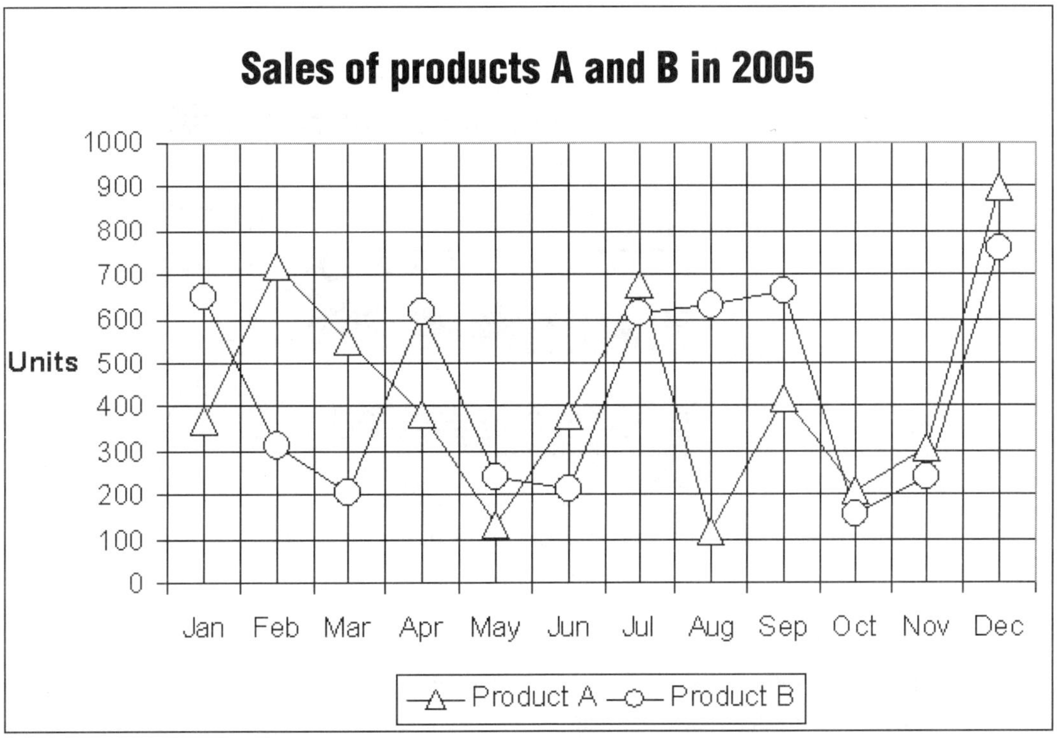

The scale of the vertical axis should be just large enough for you to tell with reasonable accuracy the sales figure at any given point during the period. In the example above we have used a scale of 100 and you can tell, for instance that sales of product A in April were a little less than 400 (check in the table given above).

3.3 Charts

3.3.1 Bar charts

The bar chart is one of the most common methods of visual presentation. Data is shown in the form of bars which are the same in width but variable in height. Each bar represents a different item, for example the annual production cost of different products or the number of hours required to produce a product by different workteams.

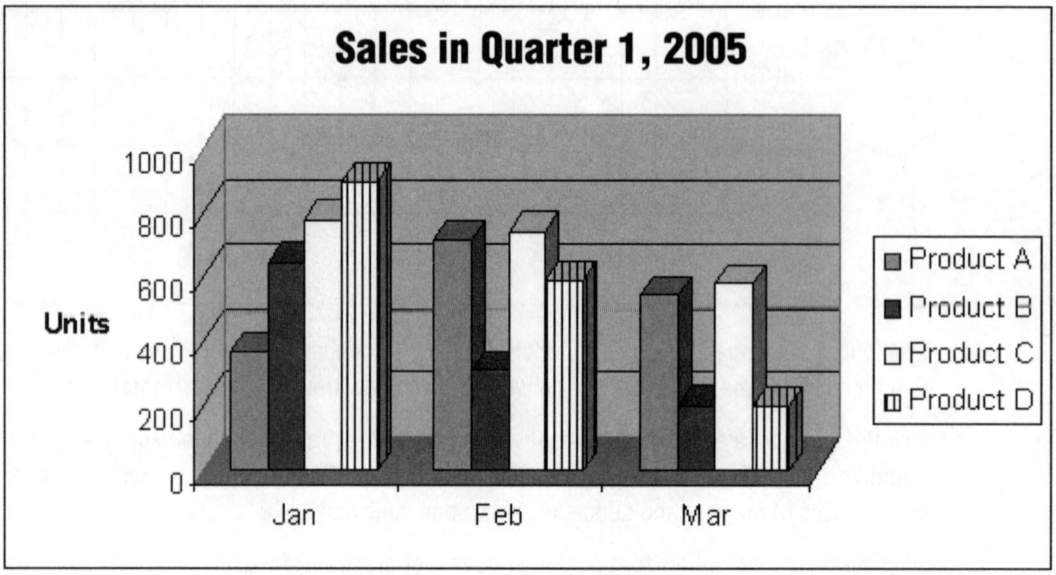

As you can see, here we are more interested in comparing a few individual items in a few individual months (although you can still get a visual impression of trends over time).

Horizontal presentation is also possible.

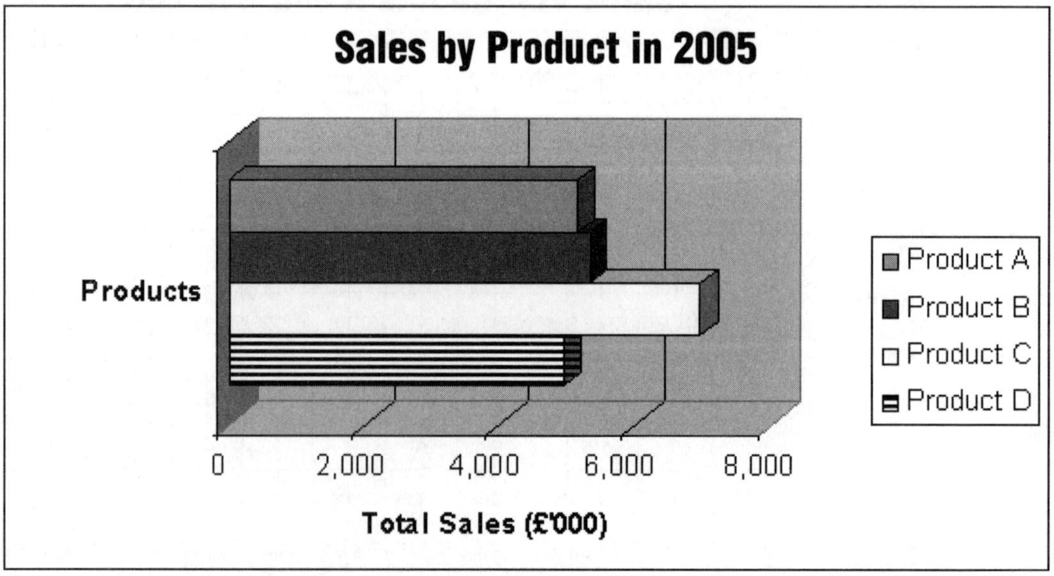

There are no hard and fast rules about whether you should use vertical or horizontal presentation. However, these guidelines may help.

(a) If you are showing **trends over time** (for instance January to March) **vertical bars** look best

(b) If you are showing **differences at a single point in time** (the end of 2005, for instance) you might prefer **horizontal** bars.

3.3.2 Pie charts

A pie chart shows the **relative** sizes of the things that make up a total.

Pie charts are most effective where the number of slices is small enough to keep the chart simple, and where the difference in the size of the slices is large enough for the eye to judge without too much extra information.

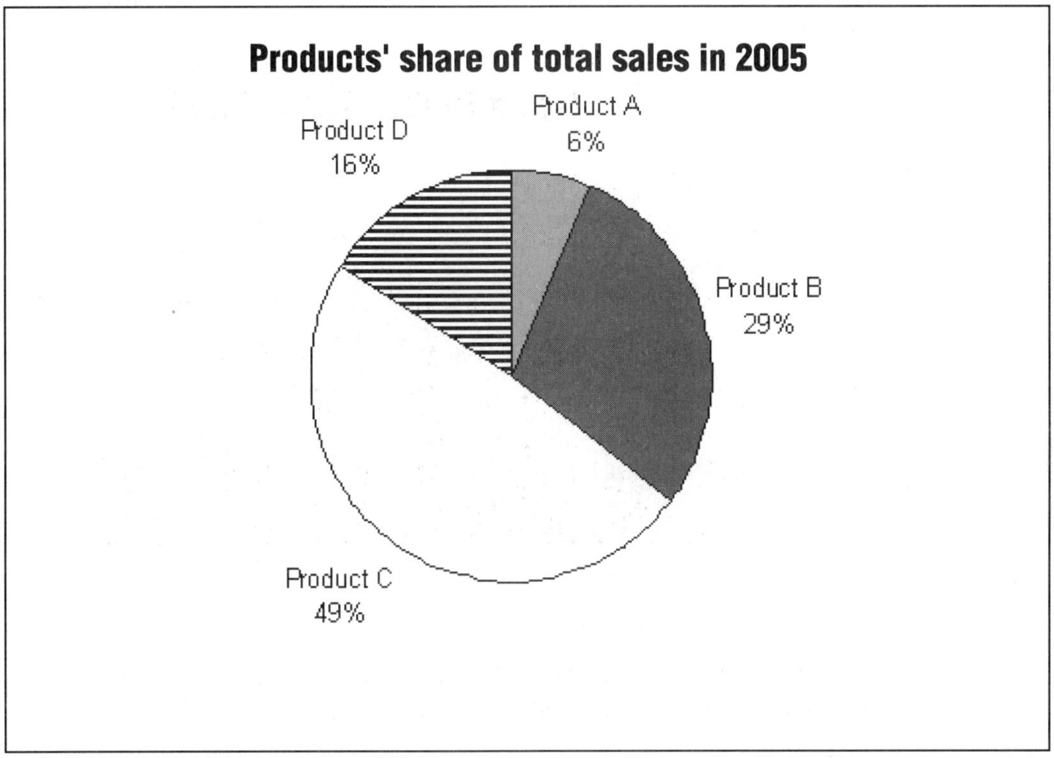

3.4 Flow charts, organisation charts and other labelled diagrams

Flow charts and organisation charts are useful ways of presenting and summarising information that involves a series of **steps** and **choices** and/or **relationships** between the different items.

On the following pages there are some examples of this type of presentation.

If you choose any of these forms of presentation here are some points to bear in mind.

(a) Be consistent in your use of layout and symbols (and colours, if used). For instance, in our flow chart example below a decision symbol is consistently a diamond with italic text; a YES decision consistently flows downwards; a NO decision consistently flows to the right.

(b) Keep the number of connecting lines to a minimum and avoid lines that 'jump over' each other at all costs.

(c) Keep the labels or other text brief and simple.

(d) Hand-drawn diagrams should be as neat and legible as possible. If they are likely to be seen by a lot of people (not just your team) it is better to use a business graphics programme like Microsoft Visio.

(e) Everyone can draw … but only so well. If you are not expert you can waste an enormous amount of time playing with computer graphics. If it needs to be really beautifully presented and you are not an expert sketch it quickly by hand and then give it to a professional!

3.4.1 A flowchart

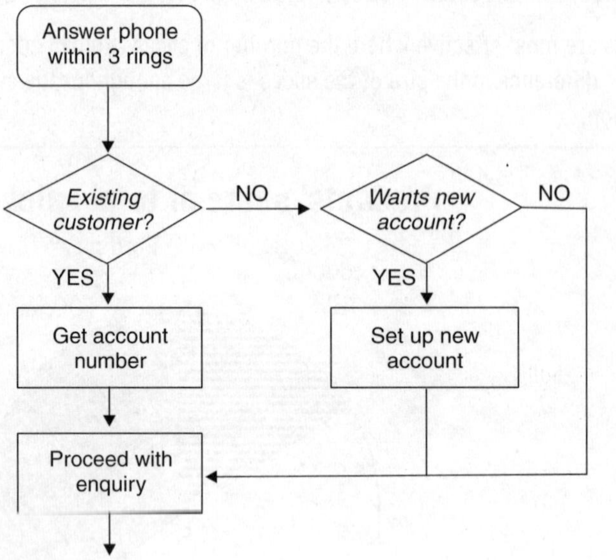

3.4.2 An organisation chart

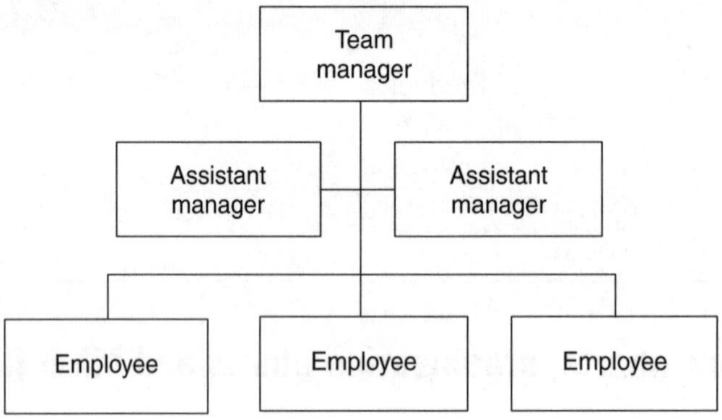

3.5 Pictograms

A pictogram is a simple graphic image in which the **data is represented by a picture or symbol**, with a clear key to the items and quantities intended. Different pictures can be used on the same pictogram to represent different elements of the data. For example a pictogram showing the number of people employed by an organisation might use pictures of … people!

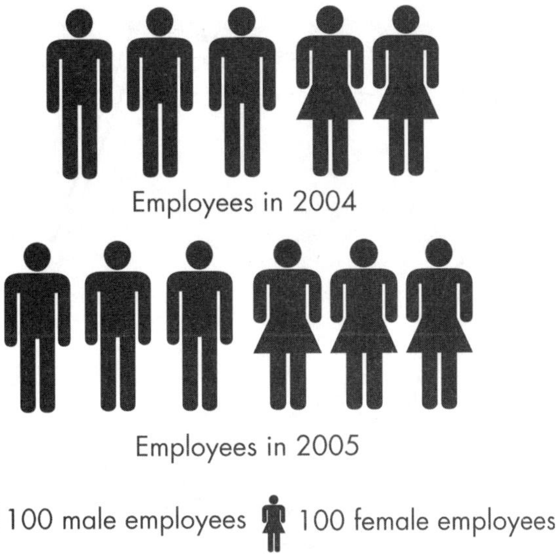

You can see quite easily that the workforce has grown and that the organization employs far more female workers than before.

Pictograms present data in a simple and appealing way. They are **often used on television**. Watch out for them next time you are watching a news item involving numbers (number of trains late, number of new jobs created, and so on).

- The symbols must be clear and simple.
- There should be a key showing the number that each symbol represents.
- Bigger quantities are shown by more symbols, not bigger symbols.

Bear in mind, however, that pictograms are **not appropriate** if you need to give **precise** figures. You can use portions of a symbol to represent smaller quantities, but there are limits to what you can do.

150 female employees

Over 100 employees, mostly male. But how many others and what sex are they?

3.6 Drawings and graphics

A labelled drawing may sometimes be the best way of presenting a lot of information in a small space. Imagine how difficult it would be to explain all the information you get from the following diagram if you could only use words!

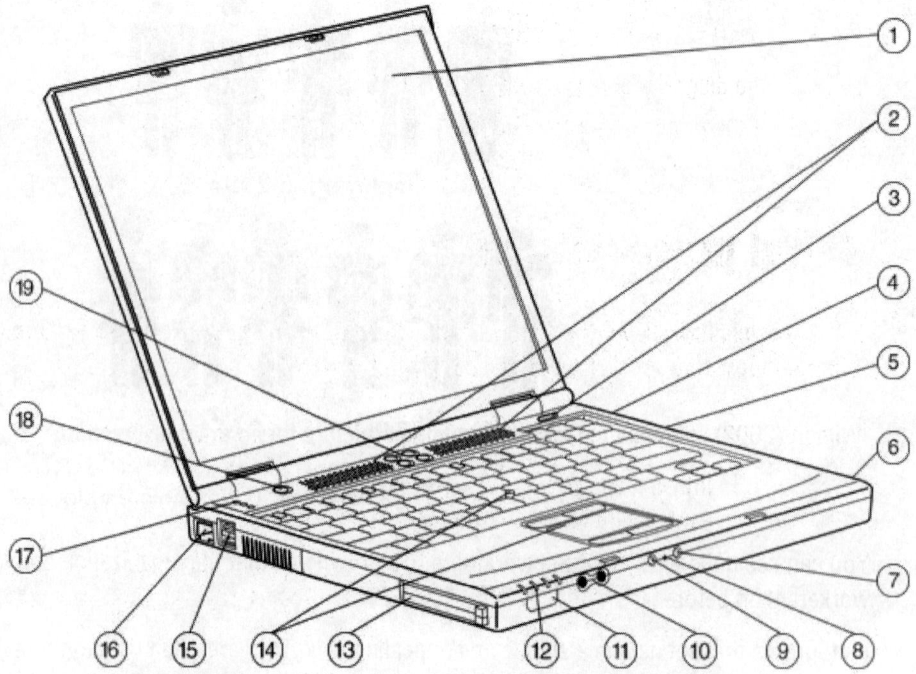

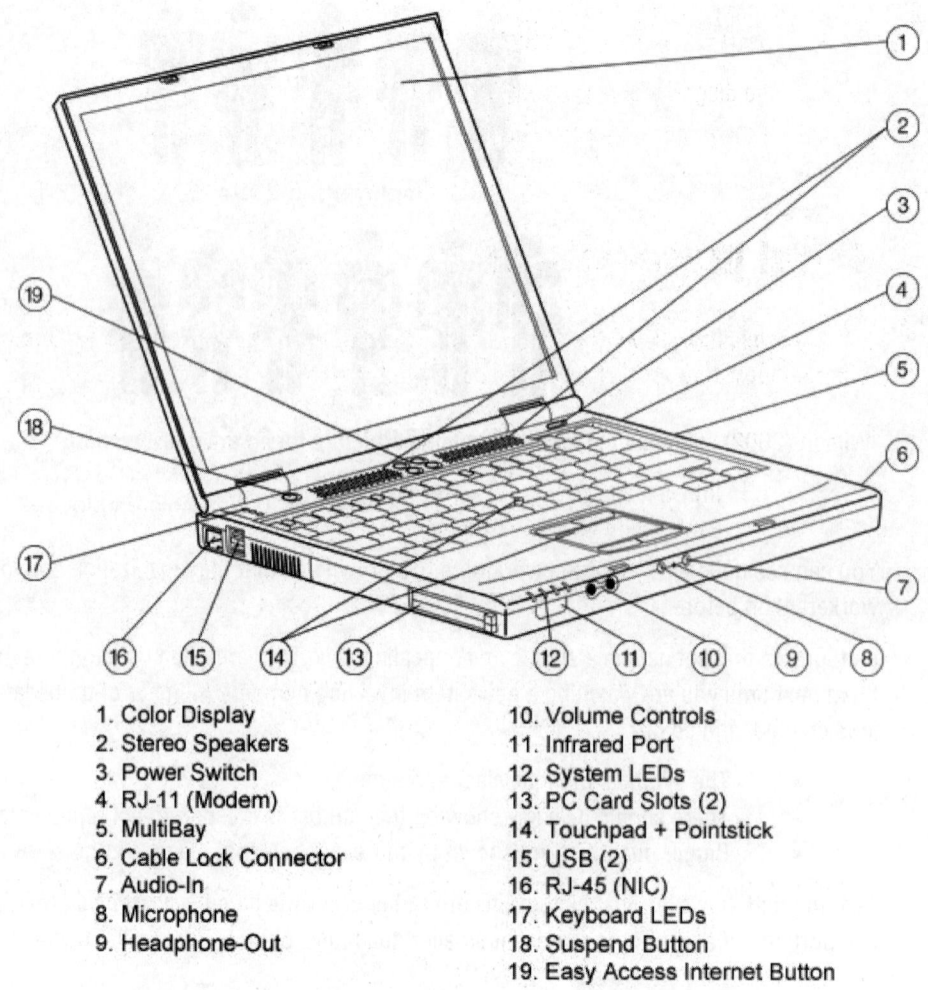

1. Color Display
2. Stereo Speakers
3. Power Switch
4. RJ-11 (Modem)
5. MultiBay
6. Cable Lock Connector
7. Audio-In
8. Microphone
9. Headphone-Out
10. Volume Controls
11. Infrared Port
12. System LEDs
13. PC Card Slots (2)
14. Touchpad + Pointstick
15. USB (2)
16. RJ-45 (NIC)
17. Keyboard LEDs
18. Suspend Button
19. Easy Access Internet Button

3.7 Product positioning maps

Although they may be called **'maps'** these are really a form of **scatter diagram**. **Two key attributes** of a product are taken and competing products are graded to fit between the extremes of possessing an attribute or not possessing it.

For example a package delivery service may be **fast** or **slow**, and it may deal with **large** or **small** packages.

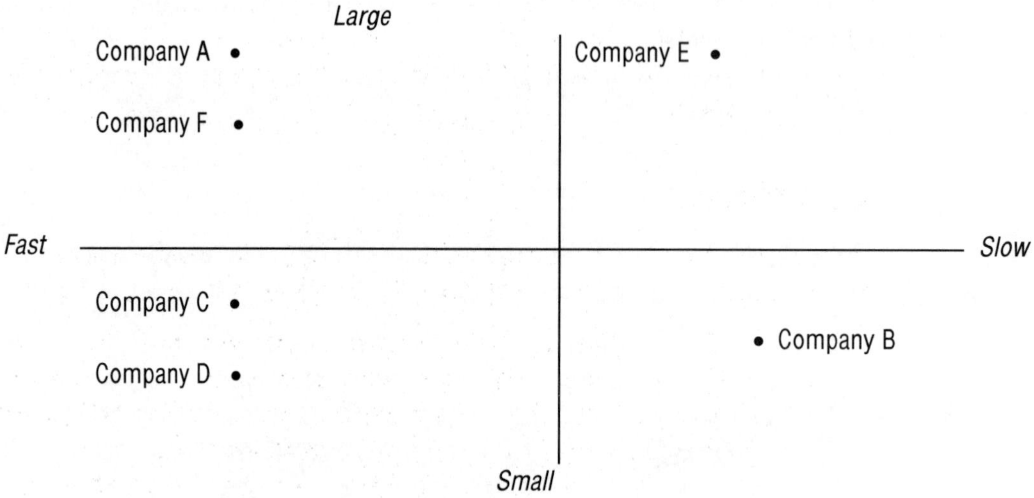

Action Programme 2

Interpret the diagram above.

4 Oral presentations 6/05, 12/06

FAST FORWARD

An **oral presentation** would have the following structure: **Introduction**; **Explanation of research methodology**; **Key findings**; **Conclusions/recommendations**; **Questions**.

Wilson (2002) suggests the following outline structure for an oral presentation.

- Introduction
- Explanation of research methodology
- Key findings
- Conclusions/recommendations
- Questions

This is not unlike the structure of a report, and many of the same points apply. However, **live interaction** with the audience has its own issues.

Action Programme 3

What presentations, conferences, or speech-making occasions have you attended recently? For each, note:

- The style of speech (formal/informal etc)
- The length of the speech
- Any visual aids used

How effective was the speaker in targeting each of these elements to

(a) The purpose of the speech and
(b) The needs of the audience?

FAST FORWARD

Matters to consider when preparing and delivering presentations include **audience motivation**, **physical factors** in the presentation room, **content**, **clarity**, adding **emphasis and interest**, and **controlling nerves** and **body language**.

4.1 Audience

The audience's **motivations** and **expectations** in attending a presentation will, as we have seen, influence their perceptions of you and your message. Why might they be at your presentation?

(a) **They need specific information from the presentation**. An audience which is deliberately seeking information, and intending to use it to further their own objectives, is highly motivated. If their objectives match the speaker's (say, in a training seminar, where both trainer and trainees want improved job performance as the outcome), this motivation aids the speaker. It is therefore important to gauge, as far as possible, what this highly-motivated group **want** to hear from you, and **why**.

(b) **They are interested in the topic of the presentation**. The audience may have a general expectation that they will learn something new, interesting, or useful on a topic that they are pre-disposed to gather information about: it is up to the speaker to hold their attention by satisfying the desire for relevant information. They may also have some prior knowledge, on which the speaker can build: there will be a fine line to tread between boring the audience by telling them what they already know, and losing them by assuming more knowledge than they possess.

(c) **They are required to be there**.

   (i) Attendance may be **compulsory**, whether or not those attending are motivated or interested in the subject matter. In this case, you can at least find out the size and composition of your audience, but unless motivation and interest can be stimulated by the presentation, compulsory attendance may simply create resistance to the message.

   (ii) Attendance may be **recommended by a superior**, in which case even if the participants are not interested in the subject matter, they may be motivated to pay attention because they perceive it to be in their own interest to do so.

   This is known as a **captive audience**. Note that it is a double-edged sword: the audience may be compelled to listen to you, but they are actually **less** likely to listen attentively, co-operatively and with positive results, unless you can motivate them to do so once you have them in front of you.

(d) **They expect to be entertained**. The topic of the presentation may be entertaining or the audience may expect the speaker to put information across in an entertaining manner – perhaps using humour or illustration. The organisation culture may encourage the idea that attending meetings and conferences is equivalent to rest and recreation: a bit of a 'day out' for the participants, more useful for the networking in the coffee breaks than the technical content of the presentations. As a speaker, you will have to ensure that you do not fulfil such expectations at the expense of your primary objectives – but be aware that the entertainment-seekers are also a potential audience for your message: it may be possible to arouse more motivated interest.

Taking into account any **specific** audience needs and expectations, your message needs to have the following qualities.

(a) **Interest**. It should be lively/entertaining/varied or relevant to the audience's needs and interests, or preferably both.

(b) **Congeniality**. This usually means positive, supportive or helpful in some way (eg in making a difficult decision easier, or satisfying a need).

(c) **Credibility**. It should be **consistent** in itself, and with known **facts**; apparently **objective**; and from a source perceived to be **trustworthy**.

(d) **Accessibility**. This means both:

   (i) **Audible/visible**. (Do you need to be closer to the audience? Do you need a microphone? Enlarged visual aids? Clearer articulation and projection?)

   (ii) **Understandable**. (What is the audience's level of knowledge/education/ experience in general? Of the topic at hand? What technical terms will need to be avoided or explained? What concepts or ideas will need to be explained?)

4.2 Physical preparation

At the planning stage, you might also consider physical factors which will affect the audience's concentration: their ability and willingness to keep listening attentively and positively to your message. Some of these may not be in your control, if you are not planning the meeting or conference or arranging the venue, but as far as possible, give attention to the following.

(a) **Listening conditions**. Try and cut out background noise – conversations outside the room, traffic, loud air conditioning or rattling slide projector, say. (There may be a trade-off between peace and quiet, and good ventilation, also required for alertness: be sensible about the need to open a door or window or switch on a fan.)

(b) **Freedom from interruption and distraction**. Do not let the focus shift from the speaker and his message to outside views of people passing by. Arrange not to be disturbed by others entering the room. Announce, if appropriate, that questions and comments will be invited at the end of the session.

(c) **Ventilation, heating and lighting**. A room that is too stuffy, or draughty, too hot or cold, too bright or too dim to see properly, can create physical discomfort, which shifts attention from the speaker and his message to the listener.

(d) **Seating and desking**. Excessive comfort can impair alertness – but uncomfortable seating is a distraction. Combined with inadequate arrangements for writing (since many people may wish or need to take notes), it can cause severe strain over a lengthy talk.

(e) **Audibility and visibility**. Inadequate speaking volume or amplification is a distraction and a strain, even if it does not render the message completely inaccessible. Excessive volume and electronic noise is equally irritating. Visibility requires planning not just of effective visual aids (clear projection in suitable light, adequately enlarged) but also of seating plans, allowing unobstructed 'sight lines' for each participant.

(f) **Seating layout**. Depending on the purpose and style of your presentation, you may choose formal classroom-like rows of seating, with the speaker in front behind a podium, or informal group seating in a circle or cluster in which the speaker is included. The formal layout enhances the speaker's credibility, and may encourage attention to information, while the informal layout may be more congenial, encouraging involvement and input from the whole group.

(g) **Time**. Listeners get tired over time – however interesting the presentation: their concentration span is limited, and they will not be able to listen effectively for a long period without a break.

- (i) If you have the choice (and a limited volume of information to impart), a ten-minute presentation will be more effective than a one-hour presentation.
- (ii) If the volume of information or time allotted dictate a lengthy talk, you will need to build in reinforcements, breaks and 'breathers' for your listeners, by using repetition, summary, jokes/anecdotes and question-and-answer breaks.
- (iii) Bear in mind, too, that the time of day will affect your listeners' concentration, even if your presentation is a brief one: you will have to work harder if your talk is first thing in the morning, late in the day (or week), or approaching lunch-time.

(h) **The speaker's appearance**. It should already be obvious that the appearance of the speaker may sabotage his efforts if it is uncongenial or unappealing, lacks credibility or the authority expected by the audience or is distracting in some way.

Action Programme 4

In what other research circumstances besides the final presentation might the researcher find it useful to think about physical factors that will affect his or her audience's concentration?

4.3 Content

Armed with your clearly-stated objectives and audience profile, you can plan the **content** of your presentation.

One approach which may help to clarify your thinking is as follows.

Prioritise	Select the **key points** of the subject, and a **storyline** or theme that gives your argument a unified sense of 'direction'. The **fewer** points you make (with the most emphasis) and the clearer the **direction** in which your thoughts are heading, the easier it will be for the audience to grasp and retain your message.
Structure	Make notes for your presentation which **illustrate** simply the **logical order** or **pattern** of the key points of your speech.
Outline	Following your structured notes, **flesh out** your message. • **Introduction** • **Supporting evidence, examples and illustrations** • **Notes** where **visual aids** will be used • **Conclusion**
Practise	Rehearsals should indicate difficult logical leaps, dull patches, unexplained terms and other problems: adjust your outline or style. They will also help you gauge and adjust the **length** of your presentation.
Cue	Your outline may be too detailed to act as a cue or **aide-memoire** for the talk itself. **Small cards**, which fit into the palm of the hand may be used to give you: • **Key words** for each topic, and the logical links between them • Reminders for when to use **visual aids** • The **full text** of any detailed information you need to quote

An effective presentation requires two key structural elements.

(a) An **introduction** which:

- Establishes your credibility
- Establishes rapport with the audience
- Gains the audience's attention and interest (sets up the problem to be solved, uses curiosity or surprise)
- Gives the audience an overview of the **shape** of your presentation, to guide them through it: a bit like the scanning process in reading.

(b) A **conclusion** which:

- **Clarifies and draws together** the points you have made into one main idea (using an example, anecdote, review, summary)
- **States or implies what you want/expect your audience to do** following your presentation

- Reinforces the audience's **recall** (using repetition, a joke, quotation or surprising statistic to make your main message **memorable**).

4.4 Clarity

Your structured notes and outline should contain cues which clarify the **logical order**, shape or progression of your information or argument. This will help the audience to **follow you** at each stage of your argument, so that they arrive with you at the conclusion. You can signal these logical links to the audience as follows.

(a) **Linking words or phrases**

Therefore ... [conclusion, result or effect, arising from previous point]
As a result ...

However ... [contradiction or alternative to previous point]
On the other hand ...

Similarly ... [confirmation or additional example of previous point]
Again ...

Moreover ... [building on the previous point]

(b) **Framework**: setting up the structure

'Of course, this isn't a perfect solution: There are advantages and disadvantages to it. It has the advantages of .... But there are also disadvantages, in that ... '

(c) You can use more elaborate devices which summarise or repeat the previous point and lead the audience to the next. These also have the advantage of giving you, and the listener, a 'breather' in which to gather your thoughts.

Other ways in which content can be used to clarify the message include the following.

(a) **Examples and illustrations** – showing how an idea works in practice.

(b) **Anecdotes** – inviting the audience to relate an idea to a real-life situation.

(c) **Questions** – rhetorical, or requiring the audience to answer, raising particular points that may need clarification.

(d) **Explanation** – showing how or why something has happened or is so, to help the audience understand the principles behind your point.

(e) **Description** – helping the audience to visualise the person, object or setting you are describing.

(f) **Definition** – explaining the precise meaning of terms that may not be shared or understood by the audience.

(g) The use of **facts, quotations or statistics** – to 'prove' your point.

Your **vocabulary and style** in general should contribute to the clarity of the message. Remember to use short, simple sentences and non-technical words (unless the audience is sure to know them): avoid jargon, clichés, unexplained acronyms, colloquialisms, double meanings and vague expressions (like 'rather', 'good'). Remember, too, that this is **oral** communication, not written: use words and grammatical forms that you would **normally use in speaking** to someone – bearing in mind the audience's ability to understand you, and the formality of the occasion.

Visual aids will also be an important aspect of content used to signal the structure and clarify the meaning of your message. We discuss them specifically below.

4.5 Adding emphasis

Emphasis is the 'weight', importance or impact given to particular words or ideas. This can largely be achieved through delivery – the tone and volume of your voice, strong eye contact, emphatic gestures – but can be reinforced in the content and wording of your speech. Emphasis can be achieved by a number of means.

(a) **Repetition:** 'If value for money is what the market wants, then value for money is what this brand must represent.'

'One in five customers has had a quality complaint. That's right: one in five.'

(b) **Rhetorical questions:** 'Do you know how many of your customers have a quality complaint? One in five. Do you think that's acceptable?'

(c) **Quotation:** '"Product quality is the number one issue in customer care in the new millennium." That's the conclusion of our survey report.'

(d) **Statistical evidence:** 'One in five of your customers this year have had a quality complaint: that's 10% more complaints than last year. If the trend continues, you will have one complaint for every two satisfied customers – next year!'

(e) **Exaggeration:** 'We have to look at our quality control system. Because if the current trend continues, we are going to end up without any customers at all.'

4.6 Adding interest

Simple, clear information often lacks impact, and will only be interesting to those already motivated by the desire for the information. The speaker will need to balance the need for clarity with the need to get the key points across. All the devices discussed so far can be used for impact.

Here are some further suggestions.

(a) **Analogy, metaphor, simile** etc – comparing something to something else which is in itself more colourful or interesting.

(b) **Anecdote or narrative** – as already mentioned, telling a story which illustrates or makes the point, using suspense, humour or a more human context.

(c) **Curiosity or surprise** – from incongruity, anticlimax or controversy. Verbatim quotes from customers can be very useful in this respect.

(d) **Humour**. This is often used for entertainment value, but also serves as a useful 'breather' for listeners, and may help to get them on the speaker's side. (Humour may not travel well, however: the audience may not be on the speaker's wavelength at all, especially in formal contexts. Use with caution.)

4.7 Controlling nerves

Stage-fright can be experienced before making a phone call, going into an interview or meeting, or even writing a letter, but it is considerably more acute, for most people, before standing up to talk in front of a group or crowd of people. Common fears are to do with **making a fool of oneself**, forgetting one's **lines**, being unable to answer **questions**, or being faced by blank incomprehension or **lack of response**. Fear can make vocal delivery hesitant or stilted and **body language** stiff and unconvincing.

A **controlled amount of fear**, or stress, is actually **good for you**: it stimulates the production of **adrenaline**, which can contribute to alertness and dynamic action. Only at excessive levels is stress harmful, degenerating into **strain**. If you can **manage your stress** or stage-fright, it will help you to be **alert** to feedback from your audience, to think 'on your feet' in response to questions, and to project vitality and enthusiasm.

(a) **Reduce uncertainty and risk**. This means:

(i) **Preparing thoroughly** for your talk, including rehearsal, and anticipating questions

(ii) **Checking** the venue and facilities meet your expectations

(iii) **Preparing** whatever is necessary for your own confidence and comfort (glass of water, handkerchief, note cards)

(iv) **Keeping your notes to hand**, and in order, during your presentation.

(b) **Have confidence in your message**. Concentrate on the desired outcome: that is why you are there. Believe in what you are saying. It will also make it easier to project enthusiasm and energy.

(c) **Control physical symptoms.** Breathe deeply and evenly. Control your gestures and body movements. Put down a piece of paper that is visibly shaking in your hand. Pause to collect your thoughts if necessary. Smile, and maintain eye contact with members of the audience. If you **act** as if you are calm, the calm will **follow**.

4.8 Non-verbal messages

Any number of body language factors may contribute to a speaker **looking confident and relaxed**, or nervous, shifty and uncertain. **Cues** which indicate confidence – without arrogance – may be as follows.

(a) An upright – but not stiff – **posture**: slouching gives an impression of shyness or carelessness.

(b) **Movement** that is purposeful and dynamic, used sparingly: not constant or aimless pacing, which looks nervous.

(c) **Gestures** that are relevant, purposeful and flowing: not indecisive, aggressive, incomplete or compulsive. Use gestures **deliberately** to reinforce your message, and if possible keep your hands up so that gestures do not distract the audience from watching your face. In a large venue, gestures will have to be exaggerated – but practise making them look **natural**. Watch out for habitual, irrelevant gestures you may tend to make.

(d) **Eye-contact** with the audience maintains credibility, maintains the involvement of the audience and allows you to gather audience feedback as to how well you are getting your message across. Eye-contact should be **established immediately**, and **re-established** after periods when you have had to look away, to consult notes or use visual aids.

The most effective technique is to let our gaze wander (purposefully) across the whole audience, **involving** them all, without intimidating anybody: establish eye-contact long enough for it to be registered, to accompany a point you are making, and then move on.

4.9 Visual aids

FAST FORWARD

Visual aids include slides (acetates and PowerPoint), videos, flipcharts, handouts and props and demonstrations.

Key concept

The term **visual aids** covers a wide variety of forms which share two characteristics.

(a) They use a visual image.

(b) They act as an aid to communication. This may seem obvious, but it is important to remember that visual aids are not supposed to be impressive or clever for their own sake, but to support the message and speaker in achieving their purpose.

A number of media and devices are available for using visual aids. They may be summarised as follows.

Equipment/medium	Advantages	Disadvantages
Slides: photographs, text or diagrams projected onto a screen or other surface	• Allow colour photos: good for mood, impact and realism • Pre-prepared: no speaker 'down time' during talk • Controllable sequence/ timing: pace content/audience needs	• Require a darkened room: may hinder note-taking • Malfunction and/or incompetent use: frustration and distraction
Film/video shown on a screen or TV monitor	• Moving images: realism, impact: can enhance credibility (eye witness effect)	• Less flexible in allowing interruption, pause or speeding up to pace audience needs
Overheads: films or acetates (hand drawn or printed) projected by light box onto a screen behind/above the presenter	• Versatility of content and presentation • Low cost (for example, if hand written) • Clear sheets: can be used to build up images as points added	• Require physical handling: can be distracting • Risk of technical breakdown: not readily adaptable to other means of projection
Presentation software: for example, Microsoft PowerPoint. PC-generated slide show (with animation, sound) projected from PC to screen via data projector	• Versatility of multi-media: impact, interest • Professional design and functioning (smooth transitions) • Use of animation to build, link and emphasise as points added	• Requires PC, data projector: expensive, may not be available • Risk of technical breakdown: not readily adaptable to other means of projection • Temptation to over-complexity and over-use: distraction
Flip charts: large paper pad mounted on frame – sheets are 'flipped' to the back when finished with	• Low cost, low-risk • Allows use during session (for example, to 'map' audience views, ideas) • Can be pre-prepared (for example, advertising 'story boards') • Easy to refer back	• Smaller, still, paper-based image: less impact • Hand-prepared: may lack perceived quality (compared to more sophisticated methods)
Handouts: supporting notes handed out for reference during or after the session	• Pre-prepared • Audience doesn't need to take as many notes: reminder provided	• Audience doesn't need to take as many notes: may encourage passive listening.
Props and demonstrations: objects or processes referred to are themselves shown to the audience	• Enhances credibility (eye witness effect) • Enhances impact (sensory solidity)	• May not be available • Risk of self-defeating 'hitches'

The following illustrations show two of the media discussed above, demonstrating some of their key features – and showing how a picture can be a helpful 'break' from reading or hearing lots of verbal content!

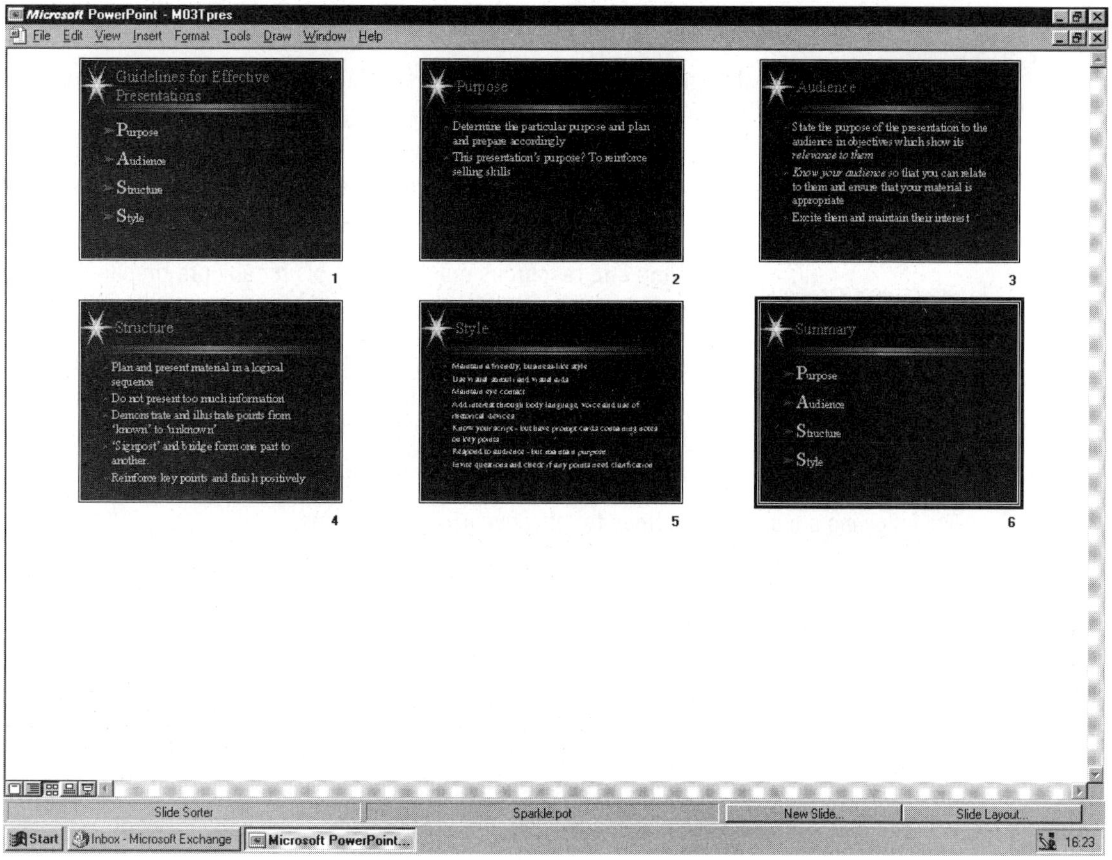

Whatever medium or device you are using, visual aids are **versatile** with regard to **content**: maps, diagrams, flowcharts, verbal notes, drawings and photographs.

When planning and using visual aids, consider the following points.

(a) Visual aids are **simplified and concrete**: they are easier to grasp than the spoken word, allowing the audience to absorb complex relationships and information.

(b) Visual aids are **stimulating** to the imagination and emotions, and therefore useful in gaining attention and recall.

(c) Visual aids can also be **distracting** for the audience – and for the presenter, who has to draw/write/organise/operate them. They can add complexity and ambiguity to the presentation if not carefully designed for relevance and clarity.

(d) Visual aids impose **practical requirements**.

(i) The medium you choose must be **suitable** for the needs of your **audience**. Demonstrations, or handing round a small number of samples, is not going to work for a large audience. A flipchart will not be visible at the back of a large room; a slide projector can be overwhelming in a small room. A darkened room, to show video or slides, will not allow the audience to take notes.

(ii) **Skill, time and resources** must be available for any pre-preparation of aids that may be required in advance of the presentation.

(iii) **The equipment, materials and facilities** you require must be available in the venue, and you must **know** how to **use** them. (No good turning up with a slide projector if there is no power source, or film when there is no overhead projector, or without proper pens for a particular type of board.)

The following are some **guidelines** for effective use of visual aids.

(a) Ensure that the aid is:

- **Appropriate** to your message, in content and style or mood
- **Easy to see** and understand
- Only used when there is **support** to be gained from it

(b) Ensure that all **equipment** and materials are **available and working** and that you can (and do) operate them efficiently and confidently. This includes having all your slides/acetates/notes with you, in the right order and the right way up.

(c) Ensure that the aid does not become a **distraction**.

(i) Show each image **long enough** to be absorbed and noted, but not so long as to merge with following idea.

(ii) Maintain **voice and eye contact** with your audience, so they know that it is you who are the communicator, not the machine.

(iii) **Introduce** your aids and what they are for, placing the focus on the verbal presentation.

(iv) Hand out **supporting material** either well before the presentation (to allow reading beforehand) or at the relevant point: if you hand it out just before, it will distract or daunt the audience with information they do not yet understand.

(v) **Write or draw**, if you need to do so during the presentation, as quickly and efficiently as possible (given the need for legibility and neatness).

The look of presentation slides (or other visual aids) is very important. Make sure that they are:

- Simple: not too many points
- Visually appealing: use graphics and type styles to create an effect
- Neat: especially if you are preparing them by hand

4.10 Handling questions

FAST FORWARD

Questions are important to help clarify misunderstandings and overcome doubts. It is important that the speaker maintains **credibility**.

Inviting or accepting questions is usually the final part of a presentation.

(a) In informative presentations, questions offer an **opportunity to clarify any misunderstandings**, or gaps that the audience may have perceived.

(b) In persuasive presentations, questions offer an opportunity to address and overcome specific doubts or resistance that the audience may have, which the speaker may not have been able to anticipate.

The manner in which you 'field' questions may be crucial to your **credibility**. Everyone knows you have prepared your presentation carefully: ignorance, bluster or hesitation in the face of a question may cast doubt on your expertise, or sincerity, or both. Moreover, this is usually the last stage of the presentation, and so leaves a lasting impression.

The only way to tackle questions effectively is to **anticipate** them. Put yourself in your audience's shoes, or, more specifically, in the shoes of an ignorant member of the audience and a hostile member of the audience and a member of the audience with a particular axe to grind: what questions might they ask and why? When questions arise, listen to them carefully, assess the questioner's manner, and draw the questioner out if necessary, in order to ascertain exactly what is being asked, and why. People might ask questions:

(a) To **seek additional information** of particular interest to them, or to the group – if you have left it out of your talk

(b) To seek **clarification** of a point that is not clear

(c) To **add information** of their own, which may be relevant, helpful and accurate – or not

(d) To **lead the discussion into another area** (or away from an uncomfortable one)

(e) To display their **own knowledge or cleverness**

(f) To **undermine** the speaker's authority or argument, to 'catch him out'

If you have anticipated questions of the first two kinds (a) and (b) in the planning of your talk, they should not arise: incorporate the answers in your outline.

The important points about **answering questions** are as follows.

(a) You may **seek feedback** throughout your talk, as to whether your message is getting across clearly – and it is common to invite the audience to let you know if anything is unclear – but by and large, you should encourage questions only at the end of your presentation. That way, disruptive, rambling, hostile and attention-seeking questions will not be allowed to disrupt your message to the audience as a whole.

(b) You should **add or clarify** information if required to achieve your purpose. An honest query deserves a co-operative answer.

(c) You need to **maintain your credibility** and authority as the speaker. Strong tactics may be required for you to stay in control, without in any way ridiculing or 'putting down' the questioner.

   (i) If a question is based on a **false premise** or incorrect information, **correct it**. An answer may, or may not, then be required.

   (ii) If a question is **rambling**: interrupt, clarify what the question, or main question (if it is a multiple query) is, and answer that. If it is completely irrelevant, say politely that it is outside the scope of the presentation: you may or may not offer to deal with it informally afterwards.

(iii) If a question is **hostile or argumentative**, you may wish to show understanding of how the questioner has reached his conclusion, or why he feels as he does. However, you then need to reinforce, repeat or explain your own view.

(iv) If a question tries to **pin you down** or 'corner' you on an area in which you do not wish to be specific or to make promises, be straightforward about it.

(v) If a question exposes an area in which you do not know the answer, **admit your limitations** with honesty and dignity, and invite help from members of the audience, if appropriate.

(vi) Try and answer all questions with **points already made** in your speech, or related to them. This reinforces the impression that your speech was in fact complete and correct.

(d) **Repeat** any question that you think might not have been **audible** to everyone in the room.

(e) **Clarify** any question that you think is lengthy, complex, ambiguous or uses jargon not shared by the audience as a whole.

(f) **Answer briefly**, keeping strictly to the point of the question (while relating it, if possible, to what you have already said). If your answer needs to be lengthy, structure it as you would a small talk: introduce what you are going to say, say it, then confirm what you have said!

(g) Keep an eye on the **overall time-limit** for your talk or for the question-and-answer session. Move on if a questioner is taking up too much time, and call a halt, courteously, when required. 'I'll take one more question ... ' or 'I'm afraid that's all we have time for' is standard practice which offends few listeners.

Chapter Roundup

- Whenever you are **communicating** in a **report** or in a **presentation** you should take into account the **audience's thinking sequence**: Respect the client's importance; Consider the client's needs; Demonstrate how your information helps the client; Explain the detail that underpins your information; Remind the client of the key points; Suggest what the client should do now.
- A **research report** typically has the following elements: **Title page**; **list of contents**; **executive summary**; **introduction/problem definition**; **research method** (and limitations); **research findings**; **conclusions**; **appendices**.
- **Tables**, **graphs**, **charts** and **illustrations** of various kinds can **greatly enhance** the **value** of a report because they make it easier to take in information at a glance.
- An **oral presentation** would have the following structure: **Introduction**; **Explanation of research methodology**; **Key findings**; **Conclusions/recommendations**; **Questions**.
- Matters to consider when preparing and delivering presentations include **audience motivation**, **physical factors** in the presentation room, **content**, **clarity**, adding **emphasis and interest**, and **controlling nerves** and **body language**.
- **Visual aids** include slides (acetates and PowerPoint), videos, flipcharts, handouts and props and demonstrations.
- **Questions** are important to help clarify misunderstandings and overcome doubts. It is important that the speaker maintains **credibility**.

Quick Quiz

1 The use of a graph or bar chart illustrates that the writer or presenter is aware of what part of the audience thinking sequence?

2 Which part of a report contains a summary of findings?

3 A graphic aid used to show processes and relationships is a .... chart.

4 If  represents $100m, draw a pictogram for $550m.

5 The following is an example of multiple bar chart. True or false?

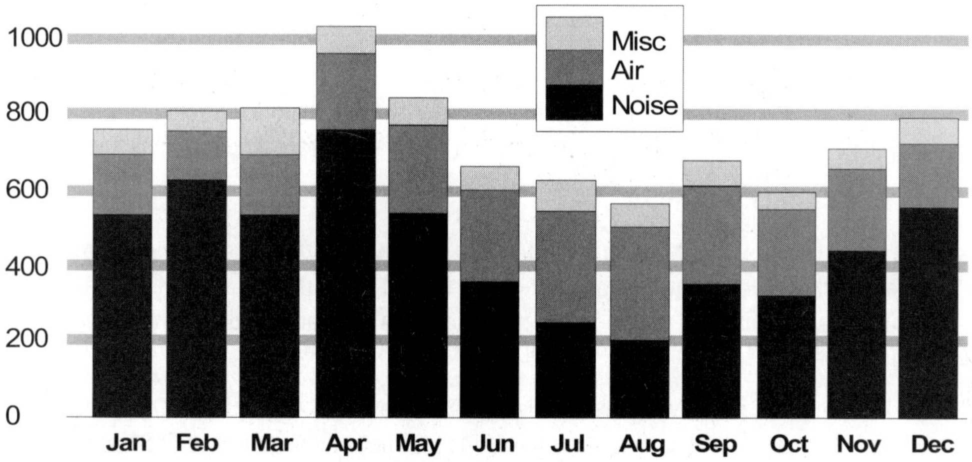

6 List five techniques that can be used to add emphasis.

7 List five reasons why people might ask questions when attending a presentation.

Answers to Quick Quiz

1 The writer or presenter is offering a means of taking in information at a glance therefore he or she is respecting the importance of the audience (not wasting their time).

2 Not the introduction or the conclusion! Remember this in your exam. The summary is contained where you would expect it, in the executive summary.

3 Flow chart

4 

5 False: it is a stacked bar chart.

6 Repetition, rhetorical question, quotation, statistical evidence, exaggeration

7 To seek additional information, to seek clarification, to add information, to lead the discussion into another area, to display their own cleverness, to undermine the speaker.

Action Programme Review

1 **REPORT ON THE WOMEN'S FRAGRANCE MARKET**

For the attention of: Sian Singh
Georgie Brand Manager
Lanroche

Completed by: Wanda Wen
Marketing Assistant

The Brand Tracker Partnership

Date of submission: 10 June 200X

I INTRODUCTION

The Brand Tracker Partnership was commissioned by Sian Singh, Lanroche, to research the women's fragrance market and to investigate reasons for purchasing fragrance products and brand preferences.

II RESEARCH METHODS

The research was conducted during October to December 200X. Secondary data sources were MEAL and Sales/Monitor. These provided industry-wide data and were used to produce advertising expenditure and industry sales figures. In addition women's magazines were analysed for advertising and sales promotion information.

During December primary data was collected by survey from a sample of 300 women aged between 16-55. This is a representative cross-section of the fragrance buying market. From this sample four focus groups were held across the country in order to capture possible regional variations.

III FINDINGS

1. Market size and share

The fragrance market is fragmented (32 fragrances were named). However just 11 brands have 73% of total market share.

Georgie, at fourth place, is one of the leading brands. It has 8.8% market share behind:

Ana – 13%
Eternal – 11%
Possession – 10.5%

The fifth placed brand is Lady with 7.2%.

2. Customer profile

There is no correlation between customers and their socio-economic group. The class profile is flat. ABC1s do not stand out in terms of either buying or receiving premium priced products.

3. Price

Price was only considered important by purchasers of Carlie which, along with Lady and Max Maxa, was at the cheapest end of the market.

64% of fragrances sold were priced at more than £15 per 30ml.

4. Brands and brand recognition

All age groups are attracted to the four leading brands. There is a notable age-based differentiation amongst the others.

16 – 25 years – Charly Klein and Carlie
Thirty-somethings – Cachet
40 – 55 years – Channelle and Esta Lauda

Brand recognition is highest for those brands with the greatest advertising spend (per annum figures).

£1.57m – Possession
£1.2m – Eternal
£1.04m – Ana
£0.955m – Georgie

Note, however, that Esta Lauda with a spend of £0.877m only achieved a 3% spontaneous ad recall.

New entrants to the market may be achieving high recognition figures as a result of point-of-sale and promotional initiatives. Two other forms which these take are: counter samples and scent strips in magazines.

5. Buyer behaviour

The key factors for purchase are as follows (in descending order).

55% – 'tried it in the shop'
53% – 'usual one'
32% – 'something new'
25% – 'saw advertisement'

IV CONCLUSION

Georgie is well established in the market across the complete age range. It is not discriminated against in terms of price and its advertising strategies are effective.

However, Ana with only a slightly larger spend is the most widely recognised brand (22% against 12% for Georgie). This factor warrants further research.

2 Company A specialises in delivering quite large packages quickly
Company B delivers smaller packages fairly slowly
Company C delivers smaller packages quite quickly
Company D delivers fairly small packages slightly more quickly than average
Company E delivers very large packages very slowly
Company F delivers medium to large packages more quickly than average

3 The answer to this depends upon your own experiences.

4 We had in mind a situation when the researcher is conducting qualitative research, particularly focus groups and also when an agency first presents its proposal to a client in a beauty parade.

Now try Questions 15 and 16 at the end of the Study Text

Appendix: Mathematical tables

THE CHI-SQUARED DISTRIBUTION (χ^2)

Degrees of freedom	Percentage p: 99.5	99	97.5	95	90	10	5	2.5	1	0.5	0.1
1	0.0000	0.0002	0.0010	0.0039	0.016	2.71	3.84	5.02	6.63	7.88	10.8
2	0.010	0.020	0.051	0.103	0.211	4.61	5.99	7.38	9.21	10.6	13.8
3	0.072	0.115	0.216	0.352	0.584	6.25	7.81	9.35	11.3	12.8	16.3
4	0.207	0.297	0.484	0.711	1.06	7.78	9.49	11.1	13.3	14.9	18.5
5	0.412	0.554	0.831	1.15	1.61	9.24	11.1	12.8	15.1	16.7	20.5
6	0.676	0.872	1.24	1.64	2.20	10.6	12.6	14.4	16.8	18.5	22.5
7	0.989	1.24	1.69	2.17	2.83	12.0	14.1	16.0	18.5	20.3	24.3
8	1.34	1.65	2.18	2.73	3.49	13.4	15.5	17.5	20.1	22.0	26.1
9	1.73	2.09	2.70	3.33	4.17	14.7	16.9	19.0	21.7	23.6	27.9
10	2.16	2.56	3.25	3.94	4.87	16.0	18.3	20.5	23.2	25.2	29.6
11	2.60	3.05	3.82	4.57	5.58	17.3	19.7	21.9	24.7	26.8	31.3
12	3.07	3.57	4.40	5.23	6.30	18.5	21.0	23.3	26.2	28.3	32.9
13	3.57	4.11	5.01	5.89	7.04	19.8	22.4	24.7	27.7	29.8	34.5
14	4.07	4.66	5.63	6.57	7.79	21.1	23.7	26.1	29.1	31.3	36.1
15	4.60	5.23	6.26	7.26	8.55	22.3	25.0	27.5	30.6	32.8	37.7
16	5.14	5.81	6.91	7.96	9.31	23.5	26.3	28.8	32.0	34.3	39.3
17	5.70	6.41	7.56	8.67	10.1	24.8	27.6	30.2	33.4	35.7	40.8
18	6.26	7.01	8.23	9.39	10.9	26.0	28.9	31.5	34.8	37.2	42.3
19	6.84	7.63	8.91	10.1	11.7	27.2	30.1	32.9	36.2	38.6	43.8
20	7.43	8.26	9.59	10.9	12.4	28.4	31.4	34.2	37.6	40.0	45.3
21	8.03	8.90	10.3	11.6	13.2	29.6	32.7	35.5	38.9	41.4	46.8
22	8.64	9.54	11.0	12.3	14.0	30.8	33.9	36.8	40.3	42.8	48.3
23	9.26	10.2	11.7	13.1	14.8	32.0	35.2	38.1	41.6	44.2	49.7
24	9.89	10.9	12.4	13.8	15.7	33.2	36.4	39.4	43.0	45.6	51.2
25	10.5	11.5	13.1	14.6	16.5	34.4	37.7	40.6	44.3	46.9	52.6
26	11.2	12.2	13.8	15.4	17.3	35.6	38.9	41.9	45.6	48.3	54.1
27	11.8	12.9	14.6	16.2	18.1	36.7	40.1	43.2	47.0	49.6	55.5
28	12.5	13.6	15.3	16.9	18.9	37.9	41.3	44.5	48.3	51.0	56.9
29	13.1	14.3	16.0	17.7	19.8	39.1	42.6	45.7	49.6	52.3	58.3
30	13.8	15.0	16.8	18.5	20.6	40.3	43.8	47.0	50.9	53.7	59.7

STUDENT'S T DISTRIBUTION

1 tail	5%	2.5%	1%	0.5%	0.05%
df 2 tail	10%	5%	2%	1%	0.1%
1	6.31	12.7	31.8	63.7	637
2	2.92	4.30	6.96	9.92	31.6
3	2.35	3.18	4.54	5.84	12.9
4	2.13	2.78	3.75	4.60	8.61
5	2.01	2.57	3.36	4.03	6.87
6	1.94	2.45	3.14	3.71	5.96
7	1.89	2.36	3.00	3.50	5.41
8	1.86	2.31	2.90	3.36	5.04
9	1.83	2.26	2.82	3.25	4.78
10	1.81	2.23	2.76	3.17	4.59
11	1.80	2.20	2.72	3.11	4.44
12	1.78	2.18	2.68	3.05	4.32
13	1.77	2.16	2.65	3.01	4.22
14	1.76	2.14	2.62	2.98	4.14
15	1.75	2.13	2.60	2.95	4.07
16	1.75	2.12	2.58	2.92	4.01
17	1.74	2.11	2.57	2.90	3.96
18	1.73	2.10	2.55	2.88	3.92
19	1.73	2.09	2.54	2.86	3.88
20	1.72	2.09	2.53	2.85	3.85
21	1.72	2.08	2.52	2.83	3.82
22	1.72	2.07	2.51	2.82	3.79
23	1.71	2.07	2.50	2.81	3.77
24	1.71	2.06	2.49	2.80	3.74
25	1.71	2.06	2.48	2.79	3.72
26	1.71	2.06	2.48	2.78	3.71
27	1.70	2.05	2.47	2.77	3.69
28	1.70	2.05	2.47	2.76	3.67
29	1.70	2.05	2.46	2.76	3.66
30	1.70	2.04	2.46	2.75	3.65
40	1.68	2.02	2.42	2.70	3.55
60	1.67	2.00	2.39	2.66	3.46
120	1.66	1.98	2.36	2.62	3.37
∞	1.65	1.96	2.33	2.58	3.29

AREA UNDER THE NORMAL CURVE

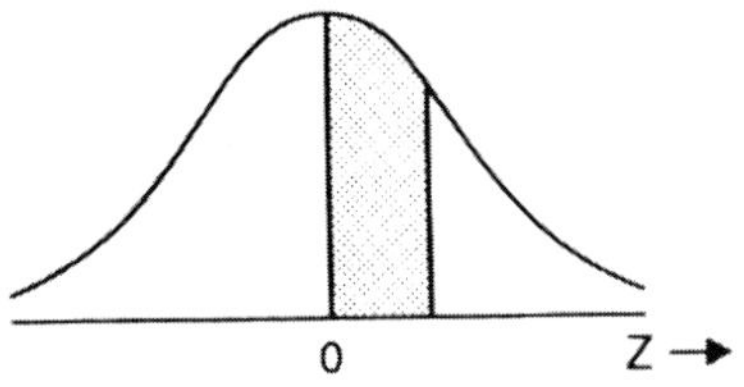

This table gives the area under the normal curve between the mean and the point Z standard deviations above the mean. The corresponding area for deviations below the mean can be found by symmetry.

$Z = \frac{(x-\mu)}{\sigma}$	0.00	0.01	0.02	0.03	0.04	0.05	0.06	0.07	0.08	0.09
0.0	.0000	.0040	.0080	.0120	.0160	.0199	.0239	.0279	.0319	.0359
0.1	.0398	.0438	.0478	.0517	.0557	.0596	.0636	.0675	.0714	.0753
0.2	.0793	.0832	.0871	.0910	.0948	.0987	.1026	.1064	.1103	.1141
0.3	.1179	.1217	.1255	.1293	.1331	.1368	.1406	.1443	.1480	.1517
0.4	.1554	.1591	.1628	.1664	.1700	.1736	.1772	.1808	.1844	.1879
0.5	.1915	.1950	.1985	.2019	.2054	.2088	.2123	.2157	.2190	.2224
0.6	.2257	.2291	.2324	.2357	.2389	.2422	.2454	.2486	.2517	.2549
0.7	.2580	.2611	.2642	.2673	.2704	.2734	.2764	.2794	.2823	.2852
0.8	.2881	.2910	.2939	.2967	.2995	.3023	.3051	.3078	.3106	.3133
0.9	.3159	.3186	.3212	.3238	.3264	.3289	.3315	.3340	.3365	.3389
1.0	.3413	.3438	.3461	.3485	.3508	.3531	.3554	.3577	.3599	.3621
1.1	.3643	.3665	.3686	.3708	.3729	.3749	.3770	.3790	.3810	.3830
1.2	.3849	.3869	.3888	.3907	.3925	.3944	.3962	.3980	.3997	.4015
1.3	.4032	.4049	.4066	.4082	.4099	.4115	.4131	.4147	.4162	.4177
1.4	.4192	.4207	.4222	.4236	.4251	.4265	.4279	.4292	.4306	.4319
1.5	.4332	.4345	.4357	.4370	.4382	.4394	.4406	.4418	.4429	.4441
1.6	.4452	.4463	.4474	.4484	.4495	.4505	.4515	.4525	.4535	.4545
1.7	.4554	.4564	.4573	.4582	.4591	.4599	.4608	.4616	.4625	.4633
1.8	.4641	.4649	.4656	.4664	.4671	.4678	.4686	.4693	.4699	.4706
1.9	.4713	.4719	.4726	.4732	.4738	.4744	.4750	.4756	.4761	.4767
2.0	.4772	.4778	.4783	.4788	.4793	.4798	.4803	.4808	.4812	.4817
2.1	.4821	.4826	.4830	.4834	.4838	.4842	.4846	.4850	.4854	.4857
2.2	.4861	.4864	.4868	.4871	.4875	.4878	.4881	.4884	.4887	.4890
2.3	.4893	.4896	.4898	.4901	.4904	.4906	.4909	.4911	.4913	.4916
2.4	.4918	.4920	.4922	.4925	.4927	.4929	.4931	.4932	.4934	.4936
2.5	.4938	.4940	.4941	.4943	.4945	.4946	.4948	.4949	.4951	.4952
2.6	.4953	.4955	.4956	.4957	.4959	.4960	.4961	.4962	.4963	.4964
2.7	.4965	.4966	.4967	.4968	.4969	.4970	.4971	.4972	.4973	.4974
2.8	.4974	.4975	.4976	.4977	.4977	.4978	.4979	.4979	.4980	.4981
2.9	.4981	.4982	.4982	.4983	.4984	.4984	.4985	.4985	.4986	.4986
3.0	.49865	.4987	.4987	.4988	.4988	.4989	.4989	.4989	.4990	.4990
3.1	.49903	.4991	.4991	.4991	.4992	.4992	.4992	.4992	.4993	.4993
3.2	.49931	.4993	.4994	.4994	.4994	.4994	.4994	.4995	.4995	.4995
3.3	.49952	.4995	.4995	.4996	.4996	.4996	.4996	.4996	.4996	.4997
3.4	.49966	.4997	.4997	.4997	.4997	.4997	.4997	.4997	.4997	.4998
3.5	.49977									

Question and answer bank

1 Data sources

You have recently been appointed as a marketing manager for a marketing consultancy firm, and you have been asked to conduct a review of operations in your firm with a view to attracting new clients. In this context you have been asked to produce a brief report that gives details of:

(a) Possible sources of data that you will refer to in your review of operations. Internal and external sources should be identified. (15 marks)

(b) What types of information each data source will provide. Give specific examples of how the data will be used in the review. (10 marks)

(25 marks)

2 Features of the MkIS

List and describe the features that you would expect to find in any organisation's marketing information system (MkIS). Explain the importance of each feature in providing key information, giving specific examples from your own organisation or any organisation of your choice. **(25 marks)**

3 Integrating internal data sources

Either for your own organisation or an organisation of your choice assume you have just taken on a new role in the marketing department. Your first task is to produce a feasibility report on integrating internal data sources, to begin the process of developing a company-wide marketing management support system. Prepare a brief report that covers:

(a) Internal data sources and their possible application in the new system. (15 marks)
(b) An outline of the hardware required and how it will be used. (5 marks)
(c) An outline of any specific software that you will use to achieve your objectives. (5 marks)

(25 marks)

4 Recent information

For an organisation of your choice, write a report to define and explain some recent developments in information and communication technology (ICT) to present to the Marketing Team. In this context you have been asked to explore how the organisation could make use of ICT to improve the quality of marketing decision making.

The terms that you must define and explain in your written report are:

(a) Intranet and extranet (15 marks)
(b) Data warehousing (5 marks)
(c) Data mining (5 marks)

(25 marks)

5 Database marketing

You are the new marketing manager for a local market gardener who supplies fruit and vegetables to retailers throughout the region, but uses an outdated card system for its database. Write a report to the director outlining the benefits of computerised database marketing.

(25 marks)

6 Marketing research process

Your organisation is concerned to improve customer service through better distribution of its product lines to retail stores. Currently the computer ordering system is linked directly to major retail customers (who represent more than 70% of your total business) through Electronic Data Interchange. Using this technology your firm is able to supply 90% of its product lines in less than three working days and 50% within 24 hours. You have been given the responsibility of conducting marketing research with the aim of identifying areas of possible improvement in the distribution and logistics function. You are asked to provide a report to your Marketing Manager that clearly outlines:

(a) The key stages necessary in conducting such research (15 marks)

(b) What the specific objectives of the marketing research should be and how you propose to conduct the research (10 marks)

(25 marks)

7 Research for product launch

You are newly appointed as a marketing manager in a publishing company and have been given specific responsibility for a new product launch. Your organisation wants to introduce a new magazine aimed at the teenage female market, identified as part of last year's strategic review. You have been given a budget of £30,000 to conduct further market research prior to the launch. Explain how you would plan and conduct this research. You are required to give the specific stages in your research plan and evaluate and justify each of your chosen options.

(25 marks)

8 Secondary sources of data

A well-established Japanese company is thinking of starting up an operation in your country but wishes to assess the commercial potential before committing itself. What are the principal sources of economic and business information, and other secondary sources of data, which may give the company a reliable basis for determining whether or not to proceed? (If you wish, you may specify the business sector in which the Japanese company specialises, eg financial services, pharmaceuticals, fast food, department-store retailing, management consultancy.)

(25 marks)

9 Interviewing methods

Julie Roberts, a member of your marketing department, is about to conduct a number of interviews with users of a particular product that your company supplies. The particular researcher is as yet undecided on the specific research method to be used. Time and cost are obvious considerations and Julie has written you a memo asking for your advice on the suitability of telephone interviews, as opposed to face to face. Julie is also concerned to gather qualitative data as part of the research and thinks it insufficient merely to provide quantitative summaries.

Write a memo to Julie advising her about appropriate research strategies that should be considered in order to gather the qualitative data. Your memo should give clear advice about the relative merits of each approach mentioned.

(25 marks)

10 Research techniques

There are a number of specific marketing research techniques that may be employed to research consumer behaviour. An airline you are advising on marketing research is concerned to find out the following.

(1) What influences a customer's choice of airline?
(2) Which services do customers value highly enough to pay a premium price for?

Write a brief report on the three research techniques below, and explain the appropriateness of the techniques listed to achieve the stated research objectives. You should provide a brief but clear explanation of each technique and discuss how it may be used in this context.

(a) Shopping mall tests
(b) Focus groups
(c) Postal questionnaires **(25 marks)**

11 Data collection using questionnaires

What are the different ways of collecting data using a structured questionnaire? What are the relative advantages and disadvantages of each method?

(25 marks)

12 Sampling

Your organisation is about to conduct some market research into consumer buying habits for the products and/or services that your company has for sale. You have been asked to prepare a presentation for a meeting to be held to discuss the options that are available. Your presentation should cover the following points.

(a) Merits of using an external agency or conducting in-house research (5 marks)
(b) Type of sample to be selected, with reasons for drawing a sample this way (5 marks)
(c) How the sample would be drawn (5 marks)
(d) The purpose of conducting this type of research (10 marks)

(25 marks)

13 Survey report

Surveys are often preferred by marketing research companies when doing consumer research. As the new marketing manager responsible for commissioning and conducting consumer research for your organisation you have been asked to prepare a short report explaining the reasons why this is so. You should explain:

(a) What are meant by survey research methods, illustrating your explanation with an example (10 marks)

(b) Why a survey may be preferred to alternative methods of conducting consumer research (10 marks)

(c) When a survey would be an inappropriate method of eliciting marketing information (5 marks)

(25 marks)

14 Correlation and regression

(a) Give an example of a pair of variables you would expect to be positively correlated and an example of a pair of variables you would expect to be negatively correlated. (5 marks)

(b) An ice-cream supplier has recorded some sales data which he believes show a relationship between temperature and sales. The results shown below are for ten sample days in the summer.

Temperature in degrees Celsius	*Cartons sold*
X	*Y*
13	10
16	11
17	14
19	15
20	16
21	19
23	24
26	25
27	26
28	27

(i) Using the intermediate totals given below, calculate the coefficient of correlation and comment on the value calculated. (5 marks)

$\Sigma x = 210$ $\Sigma y = 187$ $\Sigma x^2 = 4{,}634$

$\Sigma y^2 = 3{,}865$ $\Sigma xy = 4{,}208$

(ii) Plot the data on a scatter diagram. **(5 marks)**

(iii) Draw a free-hand line of best fit and estimate the likely sales when the temperature is 15° and 30°. (5 marks)

(iv) Comment briefly on the two estimates you have made in part (iii). (5 marks)

(25 marks)

15 Market potential

You have been recruited as a consultant by a company in **EITHER** book/magazine publishing **OR** over-the-counter medicines. The company, though international, is not yet active in your region but wishes to evaluate the market potential of the country where you reside. Write a report for your client in which you address the following:

(a) The secondary information sources which should be consulted by the client.

(b) The methods which your client could use in order to establish directly the extent to which its products or services would be successful.

(25 marks)

16 Data collection presentation

You are to give a presentation to marketing students about 'Primary and Secondary Methods of Data Collection in Marketing Research'. Outline the structure of your talk and summarise the main points you would want to get across to your audience in the 60 minutes allotted to you. **(25 marks)**

1 Data sources

Tutorial note. You may have found this question quite tough, because Chapter 1 only scratches the surface of this topic. If so, consider coming back to this question and trying it again when you have read more of the Study Text.

Data required to review marketing consultancy operations

To: The Board of Directors
From: Marketing Manager
Subject: Review of Operations
Date: December 200X

(a) Our department has been asked to conduct a review of all of our consultancy operations with a view to attracting new clients. Please find below an outline of the sources of data that we will be reviewing, and how this data will be essential to our review. The list is split into the two major categories of internal and external data.

Internal data

Internal data is information and records that we hold in-house. Although these data have been produced for other purposes they can be applied to the new client project.

- Sales records
- Customer records
- Purchase records
- Complaints
- Accounts
- Customer tracking data
- Quotation database
- Sales Enquiry Records
- Customer feedback reports
- Corporate strategy

External data

External data is information which has been collected by outside agents together with information published by competitors. These can be in the form of census data or data specifically collected and analysed for market research purposes. This information is often chargeable.

- Competitor information
- Government statistics
- Market reports
- Trade journals

(b) Each of the above **data sources** will provide useful information for our new client review. The table below shows the type of information provided and gives specific examples on how the data will be used in the review.

Internal records

Sales records	Use for the review
Information on past sales and current sales activity. Sales will be split by: • Customer type • Customer size • Service/product type • New customers • Lapsed customers • Month and year	This information can be used to: • Analyse the source of our turnover • Identify any trends and make judgements about potential future activity • Assess which markets we are performing in • Identify poorly performing areas for additional study prior to decisions being made as to whether to drop them from the product portfolio or to develop them into other new markets.
Customer records	**Use for the review**
• Customer type/sector • Size of organisation by employees and turnover • Geographic location • Historical data on individual customers • Project scoping documentation • Inventory on work carried out • Duration of project • Purchase patterns • Lapsed customers	• To identify the characteristics of a 'good' customer • Reveal market specific needs • To identify the most appropriate service/products to be offered to different segments • To reveal seasonal trends to contribute to promotional/marketing campaign planning • Identify areas of poor performance which are losing customers
Accounts	**Use for the review**
Profitability • Split by customer type • Split by product/service **Expenditure** • Allocation to each product/ service type • Allocation to each customer type • Debtor days • Bad debts	• To identify our most profitable services/products • Identify most profitable customer types • Highlight poor performing or non-profitable services
Customer tracking data	**Use for the review**
How many phone calls, mailshots, personal visits and presentations did it take to convert the sale?	• Determines the cost of making a sale in different markets and different customer types • Determines the cost of making a sale for different service types

Quotation database	Use for the review
Project outline, client type and whether won or lost	• Indication of price sensitivity amongst markets • Use to highlight poor performance for further investigation
Sales enquiry records	**Use for the review**
Who enquired, where did they get our information from, type of enquiry, services requested, contact information and outcome	• Highlight areas for new service development • Identify whether enquiries are being followed up • Monitoring advertising effectiveness • Monitoring promotional effectiveness
Customer feedback reports	**Use for the review**
What we do well, areas where we need to improve, how we compare to our competitors.	• Highlight areas for improvement • Provide examples of unique selling propositions for marketing

External data

Competitors	Use for the review
Numbers, size, structure, market position, product portfolio, client portfolio. Pricing, future intentions and likely reaction to pro-active marketing from our organisation. Gap analysis could be performed to find a competitive advantage.	• This will give information for how we compare to the competition • Market share • Use for the development of USPs
Government statistics	**Use for the review**
Performance of particular sectors of the markets and economy	Background information to aid selection of new market sectors
Trade journals	**Use for the review**
Wealth of information on markets, competitors, forthcoming legislation and events	• Use for background information on the market • Reveal threats and opportunities for the consultancy • Identify potential new customers • Background information on customers • Information on competitors
Market reports	**Use for the review**
Industry specific reports with information on market size, structure, growth, spend on consultancy by market sector, trends and developments	Background information to highlight the best opportunities for new market development or product/service development

We have a large amount of **in-house information** which will allow us to review our current operations. Using this we will be able to gauge which products/markets are profitable and worth developing and which ones we need to review. This kind of information also contributes to decision making on which products/services to target to which new markets.

It is likely that we do not have all of the information which we require in a format which we can use, in which case additional recommendations may be made to review our internal records systems.

The external data can give clues to external influences on our company, together with valuable ideas for new product developments or new markets to target. Collecting this kind of data should become an ongoing process and all sources should be documented and referenced to facilitate future operational and strategic reviews.

2 Features of the MkIS

Applied Marketing Information System (MkIS)

Marketing Information Systems (MkIS) are used to help marketing managers make better decisions. As many business environments are undergoing change at an ever increasing pace, the making of swift and well judged decisions is essential to all businesses. An efficient MkIS system will provide timely and accurate information and will also prevent managers from being overloaded with redundant information.

A Marketing Information System consists of four major components (Kotler, 1988).

Internal Reporting System

This part of the MkIS utilises internal records of the company. Although these records have been generated for some other purpose, they provide an insight into the current activity and performance of the company. Data such as sales records, invoices, production records and accounts are used in a system of this type. Many of these records are now stored on computerised databases and therefore storage, retrieval and analysis of such records is relatively quick and easy.

These records prove invaluable in an MkIS system as the current operations of a business can be analysed and understood. It is good marketing practice to build any strategy or plan from an understanding of 'where we are now' and this system provides that understanding.

In our organisation, for example, these records have been used to provide an understanding of size and growth of customer segments, buying patterns, product profitabilities and many other areas.

Marketing Intelligence System

This system collects and stores everyday information about the external environment, such as industry reports, competitor marketing materials and competitor quotes. Information collected here allows a company to build a more accurate profile of the external environment.

Taking our company as an example, it allows us to calculate market sizes and growth patterns and competitor positioning and pricing strategy. This information has assisted us in decision making in many areas such as gap analysis, segmentation and targeting, market development and pricing strategy.

Marketing Research System

This system uses primary marketing research techniques to gather, evaluate and report findings in order to minimise guesswork in business decisions. The system is used to fill essential information gaps which are not covered by the other components of the MkIS system.

We have used marketing research in the past to provide detailed information on new product concepts, attitudes to marketing communication messages, advertising effectiveness and customer perceptions of our service delivery.

Analytical Marketing System

This system provides the tools to undertake complex analysis of the information gained in other parts of the MkIS system.

In our organisation the analytical marketing system is still under development. However, we have developed a price sensitivity analysis tool which provides a good example of this type of system. This computerised tool uses internal data from our sales records, together with market share and pricing information on competitors to calculate the price sensitivity on our best selling products.

Each of the components of the MkIS system is important in providing key information for business decision making. By using information of this type, decisions can be based on more detailed and accurate information and therefore the risk associated with decision making is minimised.

3 Integrating internal data sources

To: Managing Director
From: Marketing Manager
Subject: Integrating internal data sources
Date: 8 December 20XX

The following report examines the feasibility of integrating internal sources of data in order to develop a company-wide marketing management support system.

Within our industry, availability of information has grown rapidly since the introduction of IT into our pubs and bars. Information availability has been further enhanced by the computerisation of our head office with its centrally located functional departments.

As almost all sales, stock, ordering and invoicing systems are now computerised, the possibilities for storing, retrieving and analysing information has been made easier and quicker.

(a) **Internal data sources and possible system applications**

As we already have a wealth of computerised internal information, it is appropriate for us to begin the process of development with an internal reporting system. Information to be used in this system would be as follows.

(i) **From bars and pubs**

Overall and by product sales, stocking and ordering information from the individual outlets

(ii) **From head office**

Outlet accounting information such as variable and fixed costs, product profitability, personnel and staffing records

This information could be analysed in order to assist decision making in different areas such as product and outlet life cycle analysis, price sensitivity analysis, product promotions effectiveness, supplier performance analysis and even non marketing related areas such as management incentive schemes and staff appraisal.

(b) **Hardware requirement**

Most of the hardware requirement for setting up an internal records system is already in place. At the outlets we already use EPOS (Electronic point of sale) technology to gather sales information. Information gathered by the system is very comprehensive and we do not use it to its fullest extent. As each operator has to swipe their personal swipe card to enter the tills, we gather information on product sales, price, time sold and staff member serving. All this information is stored on site on a PC and is used to run the stocking and ordering systems for the outlet.

In order to take full advantage of the information we must collect and analyse it centrally at Head Office. To do this we must incorporate communications technology within the outlet PCs. Using communications and networking hardware, we could send the information to a PC at Head Office.

(c) **Specific software**

Major software to be used on such a system would be database, spreadsheet and communications software. Even though we are dealing with large amounts of data it would be possible to use Windows based packages such as an MS Access database, Excel spreadsheets and networking software to transfer information between the PCs.

Currently the EPOS systems are storing data on a bespoke software package designed specifically for stocking and ordering purposes. I am informed by IT, that the information can be easily transferred to a proprietary database such as Access. Having it in this format is recommended, as this package is far more flexible in manipulating and analysing the data. The data can also easily be transferred to a spreadsheet for analysis and graphing purposes.

4 Recent information

(Chosen organisation – a franchised motor car dealer)

REPORT

To: S Moss, Head of the Marketing Team
From: A Pass
Date: 13 June 20XX
Subject: New communication technologies

Further to your request for an explanation of recent developments in Information and Communication Technology (ICT) and its use improving the quality of marketing decisions, please find below the definition of terms and a discussion of their use.

Definition of terms

(a) **Intranet:** a network based on Internet technology belonging to an organisation, usually a corporation, accessible only by the organisation's members, employees, or others with authorisation. An intranet's web pages look and act just like any other web pages, but the firewall surrounding an intranet fends off unauthorised access. Like the Internet itself, intranets are used to share information. Secure intranets are now the fastest-growing segment of the Internet because they are much less expensive to build and manage than private networks based on proprietary protocols.

This can be used to circulate information around the firm: an example may be forthcoming promotions, or details of local events such as the plan for a local motor show. It can also be used to access internal databases on items such as the availability of spare parts or servicing dates and times. This would enable staff to add value to their information services.

An **extranet** is an intranet that is partially accessible to authorised outsiders. Whereas an intranet resides behind a firewall and is accessible only to people who are members of the same company or organisation, an extranet provides various levels of accessibility to outsiders. You can access an extranet only if you have a valid username and password, and your identity determines which parts of the extranet you can view. Extranets are becoming a very popular means for business partners to exchange information.

This can enable dealers to become part of the information system of the supplier (Ford has long had electronic data interchange (EDI) links with its business partners). If the dealer has customers who have fleets of cars, they too can become part of the secure web. Banks are a case in point.

Account holding customers can now access the relevant secure part of the banks' network with the appropriate access codes.

(b) A **data warehouse** is a centrally stored source of data that has been extracted from various organisational databases and standardised and integrated for use throughout an organisation. Data warehouses contain a wide variety of data that present a coherent picture of business conditions at a single point in time.

This could enable the sales and service departments to pool their respective databases to give them improved customer profiles, eg the service records could be used by the sales department to identify customers with high mileage vehicles, who may be an ideal target market for appropriate products.

(c) **Data mining** is a class of database applications that look for hidden patterns in a group of data. For example, data mining software can help retail companies find customers with common interests. The term is commonly misused to describe software that presents data in new ways. True data mining software doesn't just change the presentation, but actually discovers previously unknown relationships among the data.

Data mining could, for example, be used to match associated traits in buyer behaviour. Motorists who book in for accident repairs more than once in two years, and have also revealed low mileage between annual services, could be targeted to inform them of courses in advanced driving techniques run by the garage.

5 Database marketing

To: A. Director
From: A. Marketing Manager
Date: June 20XX
Subject: **Benefits of computerised database marketing**

The objective of this report is to outline the contribution that a **marketing database** could make to the development and support of our business.

A marketing database is a collection of all available information of past, present and prospective customers, structured so as to make it highly analysable. The real value of a marketing database lies in its ability to be an invaluable aid in **decision making** and **communications strategy** development. The database can be used repeatedly, so reinforcing the point that it is four times more expensive to gain a new customer than it is to retain an existing one.

Database marketing is a customer-orientated approach to marketing, and its special power lies in the techniques used to harness the capabilities of computer and telecommunications technology. Building accurate and up-to-date profiles of existing customers would enable the company to increase its market share by:

(a) Increased customer retention, by staying close to the target audience through better targeting and contact

(b) Better use of resources, and cost reduction, due to less duplication of information

(c) Better decision making through quality management information.

The database may be used to meet a variety of objectives with numerous advantages over traditional marketing methods.

- Focusing on prime prospects
- Evaluating new prospects
- Cross-selling related products

- Launching new products to potential prospects
- Identifying new distribution channels
- Building customer loyalty
- Converting occasional users to regular users
- Generating enquiries and follow-up sales
- Targeting niche markets

An effective database can provide the following **management information**.

(a) **Usage patterns** eg reasons for account closures/loyal repeat customers/seasonal or local purchase patterns/demographic purchase patterns and purchase patterns in response to promotional campaigns

(b) **Evaluation of marketing activities** eg response rates

(c) **Segmentation analysis** to ensure accurate targeting

(d) **Account analysis** eg value or product type

A database can only be as effective as the information which is input. This means that **accurate data is essential** and this will require investment of time and effort to ensure that both data capture and data entry are accurate. **Variables** which could be considered for inclusion are name, address, telephone number, gender, age occupation, services used, frequency of use, time of day of visit etc.

The **customer database** could be maintained through our new **EPOS system**. Other sources of data would include **transaction documents** such as order forms, invoices and customer account records, any customer care **feedback** questionnaires which are now distributed to all our customers and the new customers who visit our stalls at the shows and exhibitions we attend.

In conclusion, the development of a marketing database would take **time and money**. Consideration needs to be given as to whether we develop our own database or whether we purchase an **off-the-shelf package** and then set about tailoring it to our specific requirements. Overall, a marketing database has the potential to provide us with invaluable data regarding a wide range of marketing and consumer issues, as well as providing us with a tool for **competitive advantage**.

I look forward to discussing the contents of this report next week at our scheduled meeting.

6 Marketing research process

REPORT

To: Marketing Manager
From: Jill Riley
Date: 21 January 20XX
Subject: Identifying areas of improvement in the distribution and logistics function

This report outlines the marketing research process, giving the key stages in undertaking research and the specific research objectives and methodology to be followed.

(a) **Marketing research process – key stages**

(i) Define the research problem
(ii) Set the objectives of the research
(iii) Construct the research proposal
(iv) Specify data collection method(s)
(v) Specify technique(s) of measurement
(vi) Select the sample
(vii) Collect the data

(viii) Analyse the result
(ix) Present the final report

The following points relating to each key stage should be borne in mind.

(i) Some exploratory research may be necessary to clarify problem areas and further understand customer requirements.

(ii) Research objectives need to be SMART – Specific, Measurable, Actionable, Reasonable and Timescaled.

(iii) Proposals need to be submitted for the category of research to be undertaken and must be agreed by all parties.

(iv) Data can be primary (field research) or secondary (desk research). Collection methods will vary according to the type of research.

(v) At the measurement stage, all the factors under investigation will need to be converted into quantitative data to allow for analysis.

(vi) Sample size will be dependent on time and resources but must be sufficient to be statistically significant.

(vii) Decisions as to who will undertake the research and how will it be carried out must be made.

(viii) Statistical analysis may involve using manual techniques, computer techniques or a combination of both.

(ix) Findings will need to be presented and a formal report submitted.

(b) **Specific research objectives and method of conducting research**

(i) **Research objectives**

Separate objectives are needed for the two groups of customers, those using Electronic Data Interchange (EDI) and those not using it.

(1) **Customers using EDI**

- To establish how they rate current distributive and logistics processes
- To identify areas where improvements can be made
- To establish to what extent perceived customer service levels can be improved by better distributive and logistics processes

(2) **Customers not using EDI**

- To establish reasons for non-use of EDI
- To identify incentives to encourage non-users to invest in EDI technology
- To quantify the likely benefit in improved customer service

(ii) **Conducting the research**

The most cost-effective way to undertake the research is likely to be a combination of in-house and external agency resource. My proposal is as follows.

(1) Draw up a research brief internally

(2) Short list and then commission a specialist marketing research agency

(3) Ask the agency to compile questionnaires (one for EDI customers, one for non-EDI users)

(4) Use the company's sales representatives to collect questionnaire data

(5) Await questionnaire analysis and presentation of findings by the agency

The questionnaire format should be such that the sales team can conduct semi-structured interviews. This would facilitate the collection of quantitative data (tick box, pre-coded choices) and qualitative data (views and opinions recorded from open-ended questions). Probing questions, such as 'What other factors are there?' can also be used to clarify responses or gather additional information. They are also useful for triggering further responses. More skill is required in conducting semi-structured interviews, but these should be within the capabilities of the sales team, provided that they are given an adequate brief.

7 Research for product launch

The following report outlines the market research plan to be conducted prior to the launch of our new magazine aimed at teenage females.

Research conducted last year revealed the UK female teenage market as a viable new market for our magazine publications. The secondary research carried out at this time has defined a demographic and psychographic profile of our target market.

The following plan has been developed for **pre-launch research** into the market to define the most successful product characteristics, pricing and advertising support. As a wealth of secondary research has already been gathered, this plan will focus entirely on primary sources of information.

The plan is structured to cover each stage in the standard research process. Sections therefore cover the following areas.

- Define the research objectives
- Ascertain the best methods for obtaining the information
- Collect the data
- Process the data
- Make recommendations
- Implement the recommendations

Research objectives

Research objectives must be devised to be specific, measurable, actionable, reasonable and timescaled (ie SMART). Suggested objectives for the research are as follows.

- To investigate attitudes to magazine content and layout styles amongst the target group, to discover the most appropriate product mix
- To investigate attitudes to advertising message and content amongst the target group to discover the most appropriate advertising mix
- To quantify media consumption of the target group
- To investigate attitudes to magazine pricing amongst the target group

Methods for obtaining information

There are a two appropriate primary research methods which could be used to obtain qualitative data of this type. These methods are discussed in the sections below.

Focus groups

This is a research method which should be given consideration. In this method, a group of six to ten respondents from the target group is engaged in a group discussion with a moderator. Typically, the sessions are recorded or videoed through a two way mirror for later analysis. This format of research allows props to be used, such as advertising visuals and magazine layouts.

Hall tests

The usual format of this method is to recruit respondents from the target group on the street and to invite then to a nearby research room to view material and test their reactions. This could also be combined with a short interview. This method would allow props to be used and appropriate qualitative data could be obtained.

The recommendation is to use focus groups for this research for the following reasons.

- It is a more cost-effective way of gathering respondent data, leading to larger number of respondents being involved within the budget
- The recording of focus groups allows more in depth analysis of the discussion
- The target group is more likely to 'open up' in a group
- There are potential legal and/or moral implications surrounding street recruitment of this target group

Collect the data

The first issue to consider is that of sampling. Although we have defined demographic and psychographic profiles of the target group, it is recommended that we address geographic considerations for the sample. Previous research projects have used specific city locations in the North, Midlands and South East of the UK to mirror the UK population. It is suggested that this research uses the same locations.

Respondents will be recruited through snowballing techniques which could be achieved through schools and colleges within the target areas. We must also consider the legal and moral implications of respondent recruitment. We will need to gain parental permission and possibly parental accompaniment for the respondents.

Process the data

Discussions will be captured on video. Transcripts of discussions will be produced and qualitative analysis techniques applied to the results.

Recommendations

The results will be written into a report format and a presentation given to company directors and marketing management.

Resource/Costs/Timing issues

We do not have the in-house expertise to conduct a research project of this type. A research brief will be written and submitted to two external marketing research companies. Previous experience would suggest that the budget of £30,000 will finance recruitment, data collection, analysis and reporting of 15 focus groups. The likely timescale for this project is two months from the awarding of the contract.

8 Secondary sources of data

Tutorial note. Obviously it is best to choose a business sector that you know something about yourself; you are likely to be familiar with the data that is available.

Introduction

This answer will focus on a Japanese financial services organisation looking to retail investment products to the UK.

Marketing research

This is the systematic and objective collection of information to be used in the decision making process. It does not exist on its own, but will be used in conjunction with other management information (financial, operations etc) to develop the organisation's strategic plans.

There are different types of research – primary and secondary, field and desk, qualitative and quantitative. In this scenario we are focused on secondary research which consists of analysing existing data, reports and research. (Primary research, in contrast, is concerned with first-hand commissioned surveys, questionnaires and interviews and is much more time consuming and expensive.)

Sources of secondary data

The prime source of secondary data for the financial services sector is that produced by the government.

Government statistics

Relevant information would include the following.

(a) Trade cycle statistics. Is the economy in recession or boom? Where are we in the trade cycle? Which phase are we likely to be moving into? Ideally it could be most advantageous to time the entry into the market to coincide with the recovery phase.

(b) Interest rate levels (historical and current so that predictions may be made)

(c) Inflation rates

(d) Employment levels (significant for predicting disposable income)

(e) Population data via census statistics

Other sources

Numerous other sources exist, including the following.

(a) The Personal Investment Authority, which regulates companies offering investment products

(b) The Association of British Insurers, who can provide information on the numbers of different investment products available, market share, sales figures, and other significant and relevant information concerning this specific market

(c) Reuters, the international information service, or Bloomberg

(d) Extel, which provides information on specific companies (ie the potential competition)

(e) The Stock Exchange TOPIC facility can provide information on stock markets, exchange rates and levels of investment activity

(f) Trade and specialist journals such as:

- Financial Adviser
- Money Marketing
- Money Management
- What Investment?
- Investors Chronicle
- Economist

(g) Quality newspapers, particularly the *Financial Times*, will also give economic and business commentaries as well as current unit prices of investment products. They may also be a potent source of information on significant political trends (the stability of the government, dates of general elections, reports on political opinion polls, possible policy shifts).

Conclusion

The sources of secondary data listed will need to be considered in the light of the relevance and reliability of the information.

Such material may be very volatile, and so particular attention will have to be paid to when the data was collected. Adjustments may then need to be made. The basis of calculations may have to be examined – for instance there has been some criticism of the way in which government employment figures have been calculated (and also the numerous changes in the methods of calculation) which could be misleading and disguise the true levels of unemployment.

The different sources will provide different qualities of data, which will be of significance at different stages of the decision making process.

Thus the Japanese company might be well advised to start with a basic appraisal of the UK economy and the trade cycle before moving on to consider the political framework. Next an analysis of the financial and investment services market would be appropriate, before an examination of the competition, market opportunities and specific competitive advantages which might exist.

One other option which might be considered is to commission a reputable business school or market analyst to gather the specialised secondary data on behalf of the company.

9 Interviewing methods

Tutorial note. The context of the question made it clear that telephone and face-to-face interviewing were to be evaluated, not every conceivable research technique.

MEMORANDUM

To: Julie Roberts
From: Amanda Green
Date: December 2 20XX
Subject: Appropriate research strategies and their respective merits

There are three suitable research strategies available to you. All three can provide qualitative data to a greater or lesser extent.

(a) Face-to-face interviews (either semi-structured, unstructured or depth)
(b) Group discussions/focus groups
(c) Telephone questionnaires

(a) **Face-to-face interviews**

(i) **Semi-structured**

Such interviews consist of both open and closed questions. The former give respondents a free choice of response and hence facilitate the gathering of qualitative data. 'Which factors do you consider to be most important in selecting this product?' is an example of such a question. Closed questions have a choice of a number of pre-determined answers. With open questions, further probing questions can be asked to glean more information relating to attitudes and behaviour. For example you could ask 'Why do you consider cost to be the most important factor in selecting a product?'

Probing techniques can be used to gain very specific information from respondents but they require considerable technical interviewing skills.

(ii) **Unstructured**

Unstructured interviews are not constrained by a formal questionnaire structure but instead interviewers work from a checklist of areas to be covered. The interviewer controls the interview but uses the checklist to ensure that the areas covered are consistent from interview to interview. The technique is highly qualitative and gives respondents the chance to discuss particular issues in some depth. Unstructured interviews are useful both in helping to formulate semi-structured interview formats and in gaining additional qualitative data in areas in which probing questions from semi-structured interviews yielded promising data.

(iii) **Depth**

These interviews allow deeper levels of thought to be explored. They can uncover deep-seated motives and explain behaviour patterns which semi-structured and unstructured interview techniques cannot reveal.

Their principal merit is that they allow personal material to be discussed to uncover the true motives and attitudes of individuals. There are, however, a number of disadvantages to such interviews. Depth interviews are time consuming; it is seldom possible to conduct more than three or four per day. They are also more costly than group discussions (which will be covered later in this memo).

Generally, face-to-face interviews benefit from allowing two-way communication. Skilled interviewers can observe and evaluate non-verbal communication as well as verbal responses. The interview location can be chosen such that respondents feel relaxed and at ease.

(b) **Group discussions** (including focus groups)

Group discussions generally comprise 8-10 respondents with a skilled interviewer (often a trained psychologist) taking the role of group moderator. The moderator ensures that all key issues are discussed without meandering too far from the point. He or she also encourages respondents and regulates any dominant personalities. The sessions can be videoed or taped for later analysis. Group discussions are not expensive to conduct and a number can be conducted over a short period of time. They provide an excellent source of qualitative data which is particularly useful at an early stage of the research since it can assist the design of the programme. They are useful in identifying important variables which need to be explored in greater detail. There are a number of other advantages to group discussion.

(i) They establish a non-intimidating environment conducive to obtaining quality responses.

(ii) Group discussions stimulate ideas on the part of other participants and hence a range of attitudes can be studied.

(iii) Social and cultural influences can be evaluated.

A skilled interviewer is essential to moderate proceedings.

(c) **Telephone questionnaires**

Telephone research is a faster and more cost-effective means of gathering data compared to face-to-face interviews or group discussions. It is most suited to the collection of relatively small amounts of information. Opportunities for qualitative input are therefore limited. The technique has proved particularly useful in industrial research.

The key advantages of telephone questionnaires are as follows.

(i) High probability of locating respondent
(ii) Reasonable co-operation levels
(iii) A wide spectrum of respondents can be contacted

(iv) Open-ended questions are possible
(v) Respondents can be screened for research suitability
(vi) Relatively fast, allowing a considerable number of interviews to be carried out

In summary, all the techniques considered will produce qualitative data. The final choice will depend on the exact nature of the views being sought and the depth of research required. It could, of course, be beneficial to use a combination of the techniques discussed above.

10 Research techniques

Tutorial note. It is assumed in the context of this question that shopping mall tests refer to mall intercept surveys and not hall tests.

REPORT

To: Marketing Director
From: Consultant
Date: December 6 200X
Subject: Alternative marketing research techniques

Three alternative marketing research techniques and their appropriateness to achieving the stated objectives will be briefly discussed, but firstly we need to identify respondents.

Respondents will need to be drawn from two segments – business users and holiday travellers. These can be further sub-divided into existing or non-users of the airline. If tour operators need to be canvassed, some form of depth interviews would need to be conducted.

(a) **Shopping mall tests**

Shopping mall tests or intercept surveys are carried out in shopping centres or malls in busy town centre areas. They are a form of face-to-face interview. The interviewer takes up a suitable position and makes approaches to potential respondents. Interviews are normally fairly brief, lasting no more than ten minutes.

There are a number of benefits of this type of face-to-face interviewing.

(i) Response rates are relatively high.
(ii) Initial questions can be asked in order to check the suitability of the respondent.
(iii) Use of a structured questionnaire will ensure that questions are asked in the correct order.
(iv) Targets can be set (percentage split between male and female respondents, for example).
(v) The interviewer can check that questions have been understood.
(vi) Respondents can be prompted to answer question fully.

Clearly shopping mall tests would be inappropriate to target business users. They would also seem not entirely appropriate for holiday makers since most people select a package holiday from a tour operator and book through a travel agent. Few travellers purchase 'flight only' tickets, enabling them to fly with a preferred airline. Also, the short questionnaire format of intercept surveys does not lend itself to obtaining the qualitative data (views and opinions) which are being sought.

(b) **Focus groups**

These are groups of individuals (normally 6-10) who are selected to discuss a particular topic in some depth. The members are chosen using strict criteria so as to be representative of the target market. Focus groups are conducted at a suitable location (often a local hotel). A trained moderator guides the discussion and controls any dominant personalities. Focus groups sessions are often recorded for later analysis.

Focus groups are suitable for obtaining qualitative data, particularly at an early stage of the research. Benefits include the following.

(i) Group interaction stimulates discussions and views.
(ii) Differences between consumers and their influences are highlighted.
(iii) A cheaper and fuller analysis is obtained than with depth interviews.

Focus groups would seem to be very appropriate for carrying out the airline research. The key target groups of business users and holiday makers can be selected and group sessions can comprise customers, non-customers or a pre-determined mix. The in-depth discussion generated should provide the necessary qualitative data.

There are a number of disadvantages to focus groups, however.

(i) The sample size will necessarily be limited, which may lead to managers forming premature conclusions.

(ii) The quality of discussion will depend to a large extent on the skill of the moderator.

(iii) Recruiting representative samples of people may be problematical; in the case of business users, these need to be the decision makers who book or influence the choice of airline reservation.

(iv) Analysis and interpretation can be difficult.

(c) **Postal questionnaires**

These are questionnaires which are sent to respondents for self-completion. They are often pre-coded to facilitate subsequent analysis. Postal questionnaires are often of a 'tick-box' format for ease of completion. For this reason they lend themselves to quantitative research (obtaining facts and figures). However, some qualitative information can be sought. Postal questionnaires have a low response rate (10% would be considered a good rate of return) and therefore costs can be high if a large sample is needed. However, response rates can be increased by good, clear questionnaire design, the inclusion of a well-composed covering letter, and, in some cases, by pre-testing. Benefits include speed of response and suitability for computer processing.

This technique is worthy of consideration but may not generate the qualitative data sought. Also, some form of incentive, such as a prize draw for a free flight might be necessary to boost the level of response. Questionnaires sent by fax might generate a higher response amongst business users. Holidaymakers would need to be accessed via a suitable commercial database. Other questionnaire distribution techniques could be considered (such as asking passengers to complete questionnaires during the flight).

11 Data collection using questionnaires

Once it has been decided that quantitative data will be collected using a structured questionnaire, there are various ways in which the questionnaire can be administered.

(a) Face to face in the person's home or office
(b) Face to face in the street or shopping mall
(c) Over the telephone (with the interviewers either working from home or from a central location)
(d) By post or fax
(e) Other self-administered (eg in a restaurant, in a hotel room or in a magazine)
(f) Via the Internet (e-mail)

Each of these methods will be looked at in the table below which shows the relative positive and negative points.

Method	Advantages	Disadvantages
(a)	Respondent at ease; body language visible; home/office can be observed; interviewer can explain/probe; long interview possible (up to 1 hr); visual aids can be used; CAPI* can be used.	Growing resistance to letting strangers into one's home; expensive; difficult to monitor interviews; may be many interruptions.
(b)	Interviewer can show, probe and explain.	People often in a hurry; many potential interruptions; can be uncomfortable (weather, nowhere to sit etc); sample=people who shop in that locality at that time of day.
(c)	Sample can be chosen randomly; interviewer can probe and explain; CATI* can be used; supervisors can listen in (central location of interviewers)	Difficult to use visual aids unless sent in advance; long interviews not possible; supervisor cannot listen in (if interview from home); respondent may be distracted.
(d)	Similar to postal. May be treated as more urgent (until junk faxes start to annoy)	Similar to postal. Confidentiality could be a problem; only owners of fax machines would be sampled.
(e)	Similar to (d); specialist magazines and journals are good way or researching certain segments.	Sample self selecting and only users; otherwise similar to (d)
(f)	Fast and easy to use; delivery is certain; reasonable cost; flexibility in response (e-mail or fax); less paper wasted.	Only reach e-mail subscribers; size of questionnaire may be limited (form configuration); fear of computers.

***CAPI/CATI** = Computer Assisted Personal/Telephone Interviewing

As has been shown above, each method has its own strengths and weaknesses and these should be borne in mind when choosing the most appropriate method to use in a survey.

12 Sampling

Tutorial note. Your answer should not just be a regurgitation of rote-learned material. It should demonstrate that you understand the material. As the question relates to a presentation, your answer may well consist of bullet points with a concise but knowledgeable explanation of each point.

(a) **Merits of an external market research agency**

(i) **In-house expertise in market research techniques**

The agency should have necessary expertise in marketing research techniques, allowing them to develop a cost effective research programme on a tighter time-scale.

(ii) **Skills in data monitoring and interpretation**

They should possess skills in monitoring and interpreting data which will allow the programme to be reviewed and modified as required.

(iii) **Minimises disruption of marketing department human resources**

Disruption to the normal working of the marketing department from extra demands on existing staff will be minimised.

(iv) **External agency can be more objective in its input**

The agency can give the input more objectively without the bias which may exist when using in-house resources.

(v) **Controllable costs**

The costs can be agreed with an external agency on a contractual basis from the outset, thus avoiding the possibility of cost overruns which may occur when using in house marketing resources.

(vi) **Assured confidentiality**

The agency will have a duty of client confidentiality when dealing with such research, which may well be more problematical when using in-house resources.

Merits of in-house research

(i) **The project can be costed on a marginal costs basis**

Assuming that the marketing department overheads are budgeted for without the project in question, only those marginal costs relating to the project need be accounted for.

(ii) **Broadens the experience of the marketing department**

The department will learn from each new experience it encounters (by outsourcing the research, the department will not learn from the experience).

(iii) **Project may benefit from the in house *esprit de corps***

The marketing department may benefit from a building of team spirit, which can be adapted into a results oriented motivation and approach.

(b) The sampling can broadly be designed in the following ways.

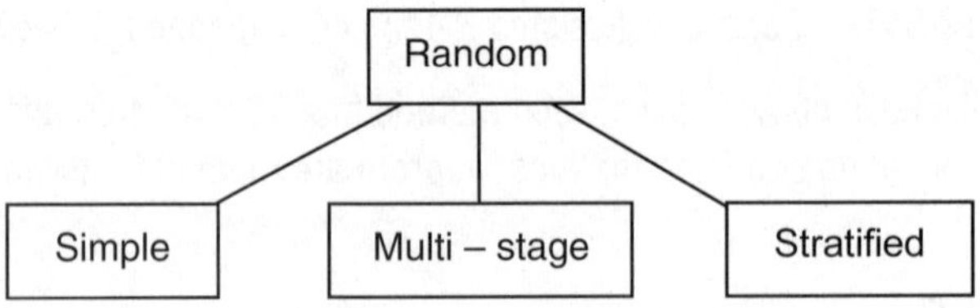

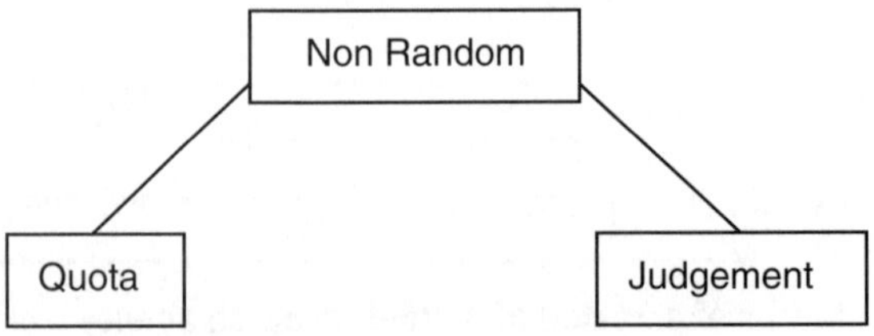

Notes for presentation

Random sampling

This means that each member of the relevant population has an equal chance of being selected for the sample. The larger the sample group, the more likely it will tend towards being representative of the whole population.

- **Simple random sampling**

  This is used as a crude and basic measure, by taking members at random from the entire population under consideration.

- **Stratified sampling**

  This is used to increase the representativeness and precision of the findings where populations contain different, identifiable and mutually exclusive characteristics which are of interest, for example age, gender, regions (consider its use in market segmentation exercises).

- **Multi-stage sampling**

  This involves dividing the area concerned into logical areas such as counties or TV regions, which are further divided and sub-divided to obtain a manageable amount of target interviewees. Used to reduce the costs involved in gathering data over wider geographical areas.

Non random sampling

In many surveys sampling frames do not exist (eg 'Housewives') so quota sampling is used in this type of situation. Initially, important characteristics of the group are identified (as in stratified sampling) and the sample is divided into these groups as far as possible. It is then left to the individual field workers.

- **Quota sampling**

  This is used to avoid the time and expense necessary to search for individuals chosen by a random sample, and involves the field workers interviewing the local target population in proportion to the wider characteristics defined above.

- **Judgement sampling**

  This is used where the researcher uses a mixture of hunch, prior knowledge and judgement to select his / her sample with no attempt at stratification. Any such non random procedure may invalidate subsequent analysis. This method would be used where a 'quick and dirty' data frame is required.

(c) (i) A sample unit needs to be defined that gives everyone in the target population an equal or known chance of being sampled.

(ii) The sample size must be determined using statistically based (normal distribution) models.

(iii) The probability sample of the population should be drawn which would allow the calculation of the confidence limits for sampling error.

(iv) In drawing a sample, the researcher needs to ensure that:

- The sample is representative of the population as a whole and is not biased
- It adequately covers the population to be surveyed
- It is up to date and accurate
- There is no repetition of data
- The data is readily accessible and conveniently arranged

(d) **Purposes of conducting this type of research**

The objective of sampling is to investigate the population to find data, and ultimately information about the intended target market, prior to a marketing initiative. The reasons for choosing samples rather than entire populations are:

(i) **Practicality**. The population is likely to be very large and thus it would be impractical or impossible to sample the whole population.

(ii) **Time**. It would be too time consuming to cover the entire population

(iii) **Cost**. The cost of taking data from the entire population is likely to be too high

(iv) **Errors**. The chance of error increases with large sample frames.

Market research should permit managers to manage their product or service offering based on the facts of their existing and potential markets, in the most cost effective way possible, using statistical and other techniques.

Market research helps to reduce uncertainty by obtaining a flow of information covering markets, customers and consumers, competitor activities, environmental variables and the results of marketing activities.

13 Survey report

REPORT

To: Mark Hodd
From: Ruth Bolton

Reasons for using survey research methods

(a) What is meant by survey research methods?

Research would be either:

(i) **Primary** – original data collected in the field (this could be by experimentation, survey (census or sample) or by observation), or

(ii) **Secondary** – the investigation of pre-existing data held on the firm's own records or as commercially available, eg Experian.

The data can be **qualitative** (eg how much do you like a product or service?), or **quantitative** (eg how much will a consumer buy at a series of given prices?)

Surveys are conducted on a population in which the organisation has an interest. For example we may be interested in the views of potential buyers of a new sports utility vehicle (SUV). As the population interested in buying a new SUV is likely to be in the tens of thousands, to survey this population would entail considerable expense. A survey would take a representative sample of those who have the characteristics of SUV buyers, eg (say) people between 18 and 50 years, income bracket of between (say) £20k and £50k and JICNAR classifications B to D.

We could either undertake original quantitative and qualitative market research designed to support marketing decisions, or it may be more cost effective to purchase such information in the form of secondary market research from an organisation such as MORI.

(b) A survey involves asking questions of the target market or population. By collecting the data by valid survey methods, the sample frame can be considerably smaller than the population size as a whole. The theory of central tendency that underpins the normal distribution indicates that once a correctly structured and representative sample reaches a certain size, the results closely resemble those of the whole population under consideration. This offers a more cost effective method of data collection, with only a small sacrifice of information accuracy.

(c) A survey would be inappropriate when the nature of the market research requires interaction between the researcher and the respondent, such as discovering reactions to a range of tastes. It would also be inappropriate where group responses are required or in other situations where a controlled environment is required to provide a useful response.

14 Correlation and regression

(a) Variables expected to be positively correlated are those which either depend one on the other, or which both depend on some third factor, where low values of one variable are associated with low values of the other, and high values of one variable are associated with high values of the other.

An example would be the cost of fixed assets in the balance sheet and the depreciation charge in the profit and loss account. Another would be the value of sales and the value of cost of sales in the profit and loss account.

(b) (i) Correlation coefficient $= \dfrac{n\sum xy - \sum x \sum y}{\sqrt{[n\sum x^2 - (\sum x)^2][n\sum y^2 - (\sum y)^2]}}$

$$= \frac{10 \times 4{,}208 - 210 \times 187}{\sqrt{[10 \times 4{,}634 - 210^2][10 \times 3{,}865 - 187^2]}}$$

$$= \frac{2{,}810}{\sqrt{2{,}240 \times 3{,}681}}$$

$$= \frac{2{,}810}{2{,}871.49} = 0.98$$

The correlation is positive which means that sales increase as the temperature increases and the value of 0.98 means that the correlation between the level of sales and temperature is extremely strong.

(ii)

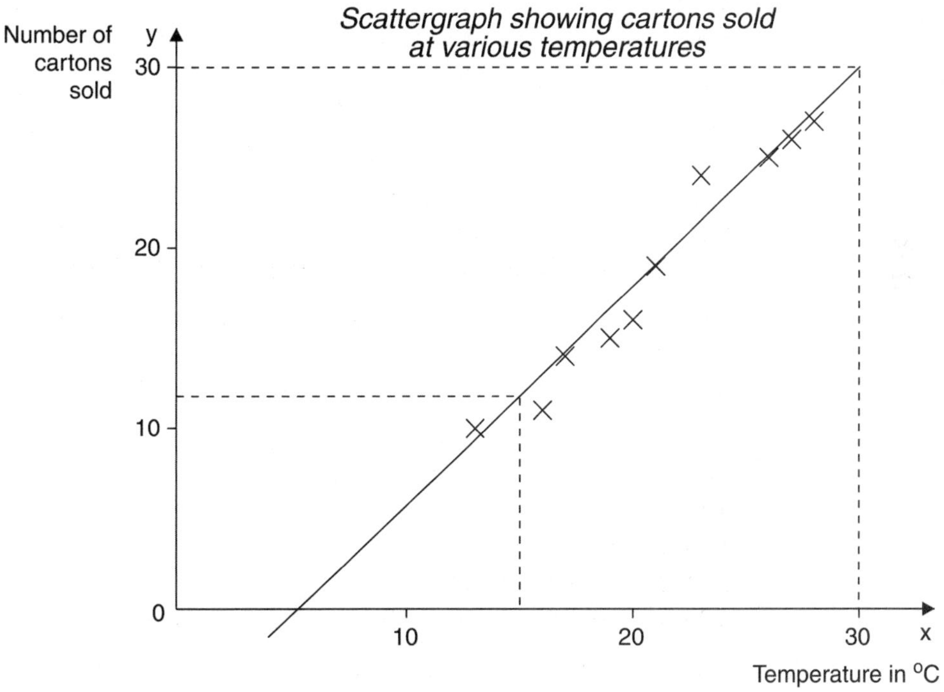

(iii) From the diagram it can be seen that when the temperature is 15°C, 11 or 12 cartons are likely to be sold.

When the temperature is 30°C, the corresponding level of sales is likely to be 30 cartons.

(iv) Correlation is extremely high and so the estimates should be reliable, although it would be better if the sample were larger. 15°C is within the range of the data used and so the estimate at that temperature will be rather more reliable than that at 30°C, which is slightly outside the range of the original data.

15 Market potential

To: Managing Director, Taurus Publishing
From: Marketing Executive
Date: 4 December 200X
Subject: UK Market Potential

Introduction

Taurus Publishing are considering entering the UK magazine market and so wish to evaluate the market potential. This report will firstly outline the secondary information resources which could be consulted, and will then move on to consider the primary research methods which could be employed in order to directly establish the extent to which its products could be successful.

Secondary information sources

A wide range of relevant secondary data sources exist, but the challenge for the researcher is to determine which are likely to be the most valid and reliable. Any research needs to be scrutinised to ensure that there is no biased information, and this can be determined by identifying the source and the research instrument. For example the contents of a questionnaire can be examined to ensure that questions were posed in such a way as to allow the respondent free choice.

Relevant secondary research sources

Sources	Comment
ABC circulation statistics	These show how other companies' magazines are performing over a period of time
ACORN	A Classification of Residential Neighbourhoods – this provides consumption indices by class of neighbourhood
Commercial reports	Research organisations such as Mintel, Keynote and Euromonitor produce substantial market based reports
Environmental scanning	Newspapers, trade magazines, exhibitions and published accounts from competitors could all provide information about the marketplace and the competitive environment
Social Trends	This is an annual, government publication which would help to identify relevant demographic trends

Research methods

Once it has been established that the UK has market potential, it will be necessary to undertake primary research to determine the precise extent and nature of product demand. There are a wide variety of research methods available but in this context questionnaires and interviews are recommended.

Research measure	Comment
Questionnaire	For gathering demographics, attitudes and opinions – relatively cheap and quick. A thorough pilot would need to be undertaken to ensure that all options are provided and the sampling process needs to be carefully monitored to ensure that it is representative of the target market.
Focus groups	To provide the qualitative element – this would involve groups of 10 respondents and would focus on behaviour, motivation, needs and perceptions. This could involve comparisons of competitive products. One needs to ensure that a trained moderator facilitates these and the same rigorous sampling procedure is applied, as discussed above.

Conclusion

It is imperative that Taurus Publishing undertake a thorough and extensive secondary research review before considering the commissioning of any primary research. This will ensure that decisions are made on an informed basis with careful use of time and money. I look forward to discussing the contents of this report at our next meeting.

16 Data collection presentation

If I am preparing a lecture for marketing students I shall assume that they have a basic knowledge of the subject and its terminology. I shall prepare overheads and handouts to avoid tedious note taking and shall attempt to lighten the lecture with anecdotes, an occasional joke and a brief exercise.

The overall plan of the session would be as follows.

(a) Introduction
(b) Secondary methods of data collection: definitions and sources
(c) Primary methods of data collection: definitions and sources
(d) Examples of secondary methods: group to identify advantages and disadvantages
(e) Examples of primary methods: group to identify advantages and disadvantages
(f) Exercise
(g) Review and conclusions

In more detail, key points would include the following.

Introduction

Marketing intelligence is the cornerstone of successful marketing activities. It involves the collection of relevant data to allow sound decision making by marketing managers, and is the basis for well-informed and sensible managerial decisions. Commonly a distinction is drawn between primary and secondary research (data collection methods), although both have sub-sets and both contribute to the necessary database for sound decision making. This could be illustrated diagrammatically as follows.

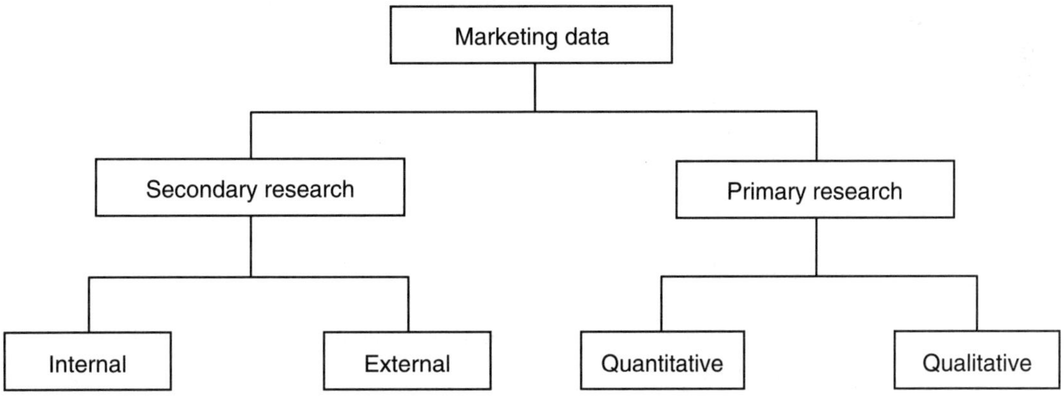

Secondary research

(a) Often known as 'desk research' and involves the collection and analysis of already existing data.

(b) Usually (always?) done **before** primary research is undertaken.

(c) Internal sources

(i) Sales reports
(ii) Production reports
(iii) Past company accounts
(iv) Previous market research reports

- (v) Research & development reports
- (vi) Sales force reports

(d) External sources

- (i) Census
- (ii) DTI
- (iii) Libraries
- (iv) Professional journals
- (v) Trade reports
- (vi) Embassies
- (vii) Credit agencies
- (viii) Commercial databases
- (ix) The Internet

(e) **Advantages**

- (i) Can help identify useful areas for primary research
- (ii) May help develop ideas for product/service innovation
- (iii) Gives essential background information on the area and a knowledge of previously-conducted research
- (iv) Relatively cheap

(f) **Disadvantages**

- (i) Could be biased
- (ii) May have been conducted/commissioned for a particular purpose which is not obvious and which could lead to manipulation
- (iii) May be out of date

Primary research

(a) Is tailor-made/designed to meet a specific marketing need.

(b) Observational methods

- (i) Personal
- (ii) Mechanical
- (iii) Electronic (eg EPOS)

(c) Survey methods

- (i) Questionnaires (often interviewed)
- (ii) Structured interviews
- (iii) Telephone surveys (now commonly computer aided)
- (iv) Postal surveys

(d) Distinction between quantitative (numerical, factual, 'hard' data) and qualitative (attitudinal, values, emotional data) research.

(e) Focus groups are a specific and growing source of qualitative data which operate on a small sample, but which offer much greater 'depth' of information.

(f) **Advantages**

- (i) Specifically designed to generate the required data
- (ii) Can reach a large audience and hence produce a more representative sample
- (iii) Up-to-date

(g) **Disadvantages**

(i) Needs specialist expertise to design and interpret
(ii) Can be time consuming to design, conduct and analyse
(iii) Expensive

Exercises

This will be a simple group discussion along the following lines.

'You are thinking of opening a restaurant in your locality. Identify the secondary and primary research which you might conduct to help your key decision making.'

I would allow only ten minutes for the discussion, with ten minutes for playback using a flipchart to summarise the key suggestions.

Conclusion

Revisit summary overhead, emphasising key points.

Any questions.

Thanks.

Pilot paper and answer plans

CIM Professional Series
Stage 2

Marketing Research and Information – Specimen Paper

PART A

Donaldson Builders Merchants

Donaldson Builders Merchants is a small chain of builders merchants located in the central belt of Scotland. The company has four outlets located around the edge of the major conurbations of Edinburgh and Glasgow. These supply small builders, plumbers, roofers, and similar tradesmen, as well as some members of the public (i.e. those more skilled in major do-it-yourself renovations and house improvements). Customers may collect items direct from the trade counter at the warehouse or can have the items delivered direct to the building site or house by the company's fleet of 14 lorries. The lorries are equipped with hoists for handling the larger items.

Donaldson supplies:

- Timber and Timber Products.
- Bricks and Paving.
- Sand and Aggregates.
- Roofing Materials.
- Plumbing and Heating Supplies.
- A small range of Hand Tools.

The company provides credit to the majority of its trade customers. As a result it has a computerised database with details on most of its trade customers relating to name, trading address, telephone number, type of business and purchasing patterns. There are approximately 1,100 customers on the database, which probably represent around 85% of the company's customers. For the other 15% of customers (the public and trade customers who don't have a credit account), the database holds no record, with the exception of a delivery address if delivery is required.

The market in which Donaldson operates is becoming more competitive, with the company losing share to national chains such as Jewson and a number of recently opened B&Q trade depots. Tom Donaldson, the Managing Director, feels that the company's personal service and flexibility is far superior to these competitors, and is therefore keen to build on this and find ways in which to compete other than on price. The company has never undertaken research before but is keen to find out more from its customers about:

- Their existing and future purchasing behaviour.
- Their attitudes towards Donaldson Builders Merchants (such as product range, service, flexibility of delivery, etc.).
- Their suggestions about improvements required in Donaldson's offering.

They are willing to spend up to £50,000 on the research project.

PART A

Question 1.

You are a Director of a market research agency and have been asked to:

a. Identify any further information that you would require from Tom Donaldson prior to writing a proposal.

(10 marks)

b. Having made reasonable assumptions regarding the answers to the information required in Question 1a., produce a short 3-5 page proposal to address the needs of Tom Donaldson. (For the purpose of this question, your proposal should exclude the sections relating to Personal CVs, Related Experience and References and Contract Details).

(40 marks)
(50 marks in total)

PART B – Answer TWO Questions Only

Question 2.

Tom Donaldson in Question 1. is keen to make more use of his company's database and turn it into a customer database for marketing intelligence and customer relationship purposes. He has asked you as a newly qualified Marketing Executive within the firm to produce a report which sets out:

a. The benefits and weaknesses of database information to a company such as Donaldson Builders Merchants.

(7 marks)

b. The manner in which data should be stored and processed for it to be of most use in the provision of marketing intelligence and customer relationship activity.

(9 marks)

c. The need for the distinction between marketing research and the creation of databases for direct marketing purposes.

(9 marks)
(25 marks in total)

Question 3.

Design a questionnaire to meet the research objectives of the project set out in Question 1. At this stage the layout of the questionnaire is not important, but the questionnaire should clearly demonstrate your knowledge of sequencing, question wording and question/response format.

(25 marks)

Question 4.

As Mr Donaldson in Question 1. has never undertaken research before, he needs guidance in his selection of an agency to undertake the research. He has received proposals from three agencies and he has asked you as an old friend who has used agencies in the past to provide a report on:

a. The selection criteria to use in determining the successful agency.

(15 marks)

b. The elements of the professional codes of marketing and social research practice that relate to the relationships between researchers and clients.

(10 marks)
(25 marks in total)

Question 5.

As one of the Director's in the agency that has been awarded the contract for doing the research for Donaldson Builders Merchants in Question 1., you are writing a memorandum to your staff to prepare them for the presentation and evaluation of information at the end of any project. The memorandum should include the following:

a. An explanation of two approaches that can be used to analyse transcripts from a series of group discussions.

(10 marks)

b. An explanation of the importance of an understanding of the audience's thinking sequence to the preparation of the final report.

(15 marks)
(25 marks in total)

A plan of attack

If this were the actual exam paper in front of you right now, how would you react? Having read all the questions, would you be panicking, or feeling relieved because a favourite topic had come up? Would you be dreading all the work ahead of you over the next three hours?

What you should really do is spend a good **5 minutes looking through the paper**, working out which questions to do and the order in which to attempt them.

Part A

Question 1

Question 1 must be attempted if you are going to pass this paper. Take a calm look at it, understand your role and break down the requirements. You are to answer from the point of view of a Director of a market research agency. There are two components and they are related.

Part (a) asks you to identify **any further information** that you would require from Tom Donaldson prior to writing a proposal. This should give you a hint that you are going to be asked to write a proposal, so check part (b) immediately. This tells you that you can omit some the last few elements of a proposal, but you are going to have to write sections on the, so what information will you need?

Background	Is there any significant difference between the outlets in terms of type of customers? Why does Tom Donaldson feels that his company' personal service and flexibility is superior to competitors – specific examples would help. What are the company's strategic plans: for instance does it wish to take advantage of the huge interest in DIY amongst the general public thanks to programs like *Changing Rooms* and expand its sales to the general public?
Objectives	As in the case study
Approach and method	Precisely what data does the database contain about existing purchasing patterns? Are records of complaints kept? Should customers of other chains such as Jewson be approached too?
Reporting and presentation	No instructions or requirements are given in the scenario. Does Mr Donaldson have any particular requirements
Timing	What is the deadline is given for the research
Fees	You have an indication of how much they are willing to pay (£50,000) so that takes care of the fees part (though they'd probably appreciate paying less!)

Part (b)

Background

Summarise the key points in the case study. Don't copy it out: summarise it!

Objectives

To investigate the customers of Donaldson Builders Merchants in terms of:

- Their existing and future purchasing behaviour
- Their attitudes towards Donaldson Builders Merchants product range
- Their attitudes towards Donaldson Builders Merchants level of personal service
- Their attitudes towards Donaldson Builders Merchants flexibility
- Their suggestions about improvements required in Donaldson's offering

Approach and method

This is your opportunity to show off knowledge from all relevant parts of the syllabus. For instance you can analyse the existing customer database to find out about existing purchasing behaviour and use various statistical techniques to extrapolate information about likely future behaviour. There is likely to be a good deal of secondary research on this market. You can talk about various techniques for finding out about customer attitudes: focus groups for in-depth knowledge, especially about suggestions for improvements; questionnaires for intended future purchasing behaviour and attitudes towards the current offering.

Reporting and presentation

You'll most likely be producing written reports with lots of table and charts about existing and future purchasing behaviour. Your oral presentations could include video footage from the focus groups. Recommendations might include a loyalty card scheme.

Timing

It should not take too long to complete the research since there are only about 1300 customers. If you don't want to commit yourself in terms of days and weeks you can still indicate the phases of the research, eg Phase 1: extract and analyse data from the database and complaints system; conduct secondary research. Phase 2: Design and test questionnaire. Phase 3 … and so on.

Fees

You have an indication of how much they are willing to pay (£50,000, though they'd probably appreciate paying less!) You could allocate this amount amongst the phases you have identified, eg Data collection: £2,500 (the approximate cost of printing and sending out questionnaires with an SAE).

Part B

Question 2

Question 2 is about customer databases: benefits and weaknesses; storing and processing data (don't forget about data cleansing; mention the various ways in which databases can analyse and extract data); and keeping direct marketing and market research distinct. Chapter 3 in this text covers all of these issues in detail: with a thorough knowledge of that you should have no difficulty with this question.

Benefits and Weaknesses

The main weakness in this case is that the information is incomplete (it only covers 85% of customers).

Benefits include:

(a) Operational support

(b) Analytical uses

(c) Enhanced lead follow-up

(d) Cross-selling

(e) Better targeting (eg by overlaying geodemographic profile information)

(f) Better use of resources (targeting, less duplication of information handling)

(g) CRM: helping the formation of relationships that will lead to more customer satisfaction and increased sales through repeat purchasing

Data storage and processing

Storage in tables consisting of records divided into fields. A relational database allows the greatest flexibility and storage efficiency by splitting the data up into a number of tables, which are linked and can be integrated as necessary.

Consistent layout for each record is essential.

In order to extract meaningful information the data must be cleansed, before, during or after input or import (properly formatted, validated, and deduplicated).

The distinction between marketing research and direct marketing

Marketing research should not be used subsequently to create marketing databases that are used for direct marketing. This is considered unethical because the data was not supplied with that purpose in mind. It is also contrary to data protection legislation.

It is only acceptable to enrich a customer database with marketing research information so long as personal data is represented in an anonymous form and is partly aggregated.

Question 3

Question 3 is the inevitable questionnaire design question, and you are expected to follow the methodical approach mentioned in Chapter 8: develop question topics, select question and response formats, choose wording carefully, then think about the sequence of the questions. It is worth spending some time doing an answer plan for this question.

Classification: What type of customer – trade or general public?

Sequencing is important: for existing purchasing behaviour details should be available from the database for credit customers, but for non-credit customers there should be a section of questions similar to those below relating to customers' past behaviour.

Future purchasing behaviour: How often customers expect to buy, eg, sand and aggregates and in what quantity? Whether they would use the delivery service or make their own arrangements? Would non-credit customers like to open an account?

Attitudes towards Donaldson's: 'Donaldson's stock every item that a builder could possibly require: Strongly agree etc.' (If customer disagrees direct them to a list of other available products or brands: sequencing again). 'I use Donaldson's because I know my purchases will be delivered on time: Strongly Agree, etc.'. 'Jewson's standard of customer service compared with Donaldson's is: Higher/Lower/About the same'

Suggested improvements: This is covered to some extent by the attitudes part. There could be a blank space for additional comments. The responses will be more difficult to analyse, but there are relatively few customers.

Use a variety of styles of question showing your full knowledge of what is possible, but be careful to avoid the pitfalls such as ambiguity and so on.

Question 4

Question 4 is probably the most straightforward question in the entire paper and can be answered directly from book knowledge.

Selection criteria

How well the agency appears to understand the research brief and the market of the organisation

How well you get on with the agency staff

How well they communicate

The quality of the proposal: is it just a standard solution or has it been designed specifically for your research problem, in line with the research brief

The proposed fee and timescale for the research

Past experience in this type of research

Capabilities and resources (eg field research, telephone research, data analysis skills)

Location

Reputation

Financial stability

References from other clients

Elements of the ICC/ESOMAR code of practice relating to the relationships between researchers and clients

The Researcher must inform the Client if the work will be combined or syndicated with work for other Clients

The Researcher must inform the Client If any part of the work sub-contracted outside the agency

The Client does not have the right to exclusive use of the Researcher's services, but the Researcher must try to avoid clashes of interest.

Marketing research briefs and the research findings are the property of the Client and should not be disclosed by the Researcher to others. This does not apply if it is agreed and clearly understood that the results will be syndicated.

Marketing research proposals and cost quotations are the property of the Researcher and should not be disclosed by the Client to others

The Researcher must not disclose the identity of the Client to any third party without the Client's permission

The Researcher must allow the Client to check on the quality of fieldwork and data preparation

The Researcher must provide the Client with all appropriate technical details of any research project carried out for that Client.

The Researcher must make a clear distinction between the findings as such, the Researcher's interpretation of these and any recommendations based on them

If the findings of a research project are published by the Client, the Client must ensure that this is not done in a misleading way

Question 5

Question 5 is in two unrelated parts. The first part is about Content analysis of qualitative data, and part (b) on the audiences thinking sequence

Analysing transcripts

Techniques include:

- The tabular method
- Spider-diagrams
- Annotation
- Computerised methods.

The audience's thinking sequence

- Respect the client's importance: in other words don't waste their time with irrelevant, badly structured or presented, over-long information.
- Consider the client's needs: the client needs to make a marketing decision.
- Demonstrate how your information helps the client: relate the research findings to the original objectives
- Explain the detail that underpins your information: why should your findings be believed? Because you have evidence that 'Nine out of ten dogs prefer ...' or whatever. This is the place for tables and charts, apt quotes from respondents and so on.
- Remind the client of the key points
- Suggest what the client should do now: there will usually be a variety of options. It is the client's decision, but it is usual to give recommendations.

List of key concepts and Index

BPP LEARNING MEDIA

REVIEW FORM & FREE PRIZE DRAW

All original review forms from the entire BPP range, completed with genuine comments, will be entered into one of two draws on 31 January 2008 and 31 July 2008. The names on the first four forms picked out on each occasion will be sent a cheque for £50.

Name: ______________________ **Address:** ______________________

____

____

How have you used this Text?
(Tick one box only)

☐ Self study (book only)

☐ On a course: college ______________

☐ With BPP Home Study package

☐ Other ______________

Why did you decide to purchase this Text?
(Tick one box only)

☐ Have used companion Kit

☐ Have used BPP Texts in the past

☐ Recommendation by friend/colleague

☐ Recommendation by a lecturer at college

☐ Saw advertising in journals

☐ Saw website

☐ Other ______________

During the past six months do you recall seeing/receiving any of the following?
(Tick as many boxes as are relevant)

☐ Our advertisement in *Marketing Success*

☐ Our advertisement in *Marketing Business*

☐ Our brochure with a letter through the post

☐ Our brochure with *Marketing Business*

☐ Saw website

Which (if any) aspects of our advertising do you find useful?
(Tick as many boxes as are relevant)

☐ Prices and publication dates of new editions

☐ Information on product content

☐ Facility to order books off-the-page

☐ None of the above

Have you used the companion Practice & Revision Kit for this subject? ☐ Yes ☐ No

Your ratings, comments and suggestions would be appreciated on the following areas.

	Very useful	*Useful*	*Not useful*
Introductory section (How to use this text, study checklist, etc)	☐	☐	☐
Introduction	☐	☐	☐
Syllabus coverage	☐	☐	☐
Action Programmes and Marketing at Work examples	☐	☐	☐
Chapter roundups	☐	☐	☐
Quick quizzes	☐	☐	☐
Illustrative questions	☐	☐	☐
Content of suggested answers	☐	☐	☐
Index	☐	☐	☐
Structure and presentation	☐	☐	☐

	Excellent	*Good*	*Adequate*	*Poor*
Overall opinion of this Text	☐	☐	☐	☐

Do you intend to continue using BPP Study Texts/Kits/Passcards? ☐ Yes ☐ No

Please note any further comments and suggestions/errors on the reverse of this page.

Please return to: Jaitinder Gill, BPP Learning Media, FREEPOST, London, W12 8BR

REVIEW FORM & FREE PRIZE DRAW (continued)

Please note any further comments and suggestions/errors below.

FREE PRIZE DRAW RULES

1 Closing date for 31 January 2008 draw is 31 December 2007. Closing date for 31 July 2008 draw is 30 June 2008.

2 Restricted to entries with UK and Eire addresses only. BPP employees, their families and business associates are excluded.

3 No purchase necessary. Entry forms are available upon request from BPP Learning Media. No more than one entry per title, per person. Draw restricted to persons aged 16 and over.

4 Winners will be notified by post and receive their cheques not later than 6 weeks after the relevant draw date. List of winners will be supplied on request.

5 The decision of the promoter in all matters is final and binding. No correspondence will be entered into.